Howard Clifford

Alaska/Yukon Railroads:
An Illustrated History

PUBLISHED BY
Oso Publishing Company
31328 N. Brooks Creek Road
Arlington, WA 98223

Library of Congress Cataloging-in-Publication Data

Clifford, Howard.
    Alaska and Yukon railroads: an illustrated history/Howard
  Clifford.
       p. cm.
  Includes bibliographical references.
  ISBN 0-9647521-4-X
    1. Railroads--Alaska--History. 2. Railroads--Yukon Territory--History. I. Title.
  HE2771.A4C538 1999
  385'.09798--dc21   99-26904
                                                                                   CIP

Printed and bound in the United States of America.

Originally published in 1982 as *Rails North* by Superior Publishing Company, Seattle, Washington.

First Printing.

Copyright 1999 Oso Publishing Company, Incorporated.

All rights reserved. No part of this book may be reproduced or transmitted by any mechanical or electronic means, including photocopy, scanning, or digitizing, or any other means, without written permission from the publisher, except for purposes of critical review.

Manuscript editor: Teri Kieffer
Proofreader: Teri Kieffer
Historical editor: Steve Hauff
Design and production: James D. Kramer design services, Everett, WA 98208

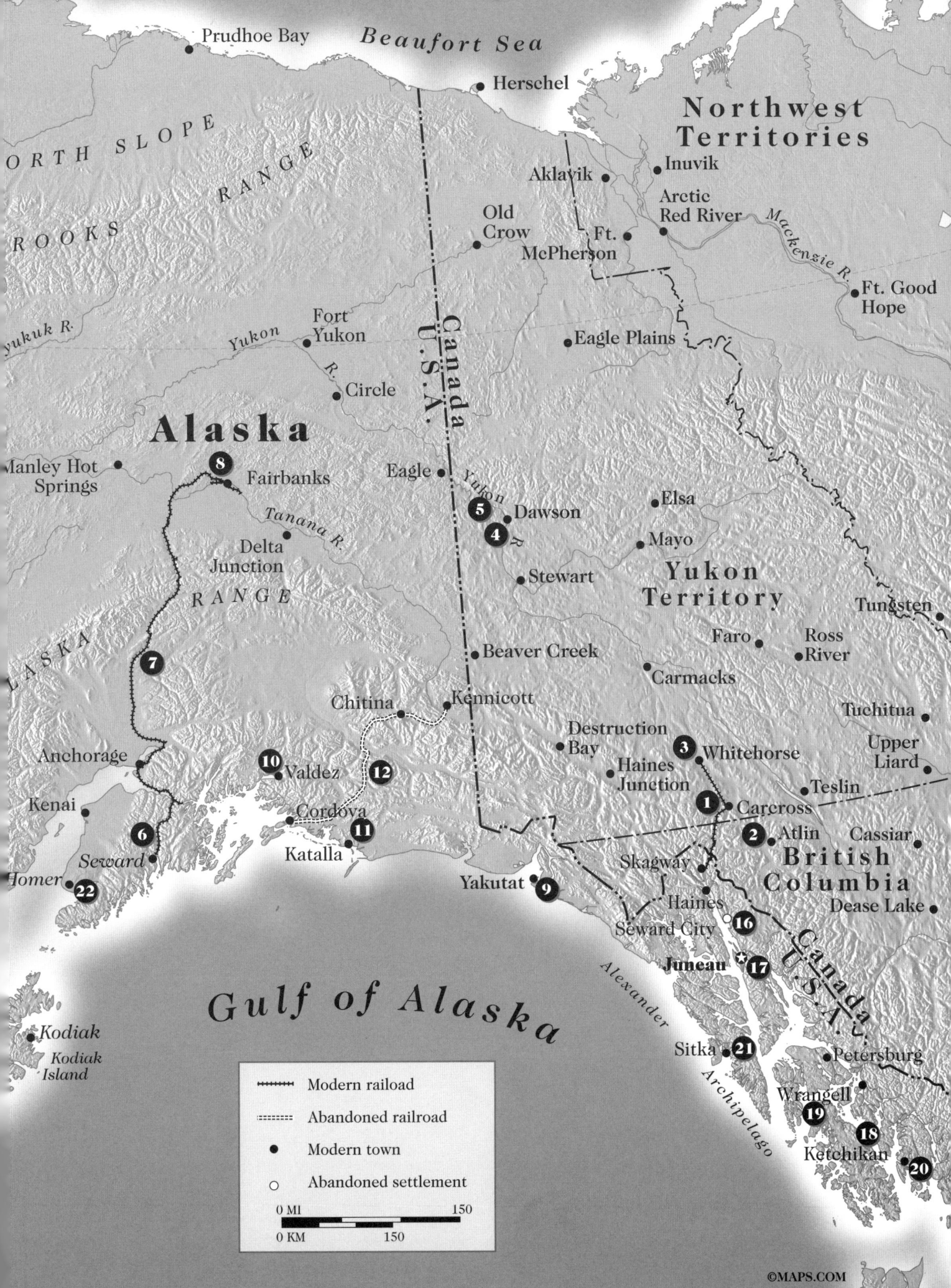

Table of Contents

Foreword .... *vi*
Historical Notes .... *vii*

Chapter 1
White Pass & Yukon Route   1

    White Pass & Yukon Route
        Steam Locomotive Roster 37
        Points of Interest 42
        USA Engines 44

Chapter 2
Taku Tram   57

    Taku Tram
        Steam Locomotive Roster 60
        Gas Locomotive Roster 60

Chapter 3
Whitehorse Tramways   61

Chapter 4
Klondike Mines Railway   63

    Klondike Mines Railway
        Locomotive Roster 68

Chapter 5
Klondike Short Lines   69

    Coal Creek Coal Company
        Locomotive Roster 73
    Detroit Yukon Mining Company
        Locomotive Roster 73
    Northern Light, Power & Coal Company
        Locomotive Roster 74

Chapter 6
Alaska Central Railway   75

    Alaska Central Railway
        Locomotive Roster 82

Chapter 7
Alaska Northern Railway   83

    Alaska Northern Railway
        Locomotive Roster 86

Chapter 8

The Alaska Railroad Commission and the Birth of the AEC   87

    Alaskan Engineering Commission
        Narrow-Gauge Locomotive Roster 91

Chapter 9

Alaska Railroad   93

    Alaska Railroad
        Steam Locomotive Roster 115
        Diesel Locomotives 124
        Evans Jones Coal Company 142
        Battery Locomotives 142
        Alaska Railroad Railcars 142

Chapter 10

Tanana Mines Railway, Tanana Valley Railroad   145

    Alaskan Engineering Commission (Nenana–Chatanika) 145
    Tanana Mines Railway/Tanana Valley Railroad
        Locomotive Roster 153

Chapter 11

Yakutat & Southern Railroad   155

    Yakutat and Southern Railroad
        Locomotive Roster 158

Chapter 12

Valdez and the Keystone Canyon Caper   159

Chapter 13

Katalla, Where the Rails Meet the Sails   171

Chapter 14   179

Copper River & Northwestern Railway   179

    Copper River & Northwestern Railroad
        Steam Locomotive Roster 199

Chapter 15

Wild Goose, Geese, or Gooses?   203

    Wild Goose Railroad
        Steam Locomotive Roster 210
    Wild Goose Railroad (Golofin Bay Railway) 210
    Nome Arctic Railroad
        Steam Locomotive Roster 210

Chapter 16

Council City & Solomon River Railroad   211

    Council City & Solomon River Railroad
        Steam Locomotive Roster 216

Chapter 17

Seward Peninsula   217

    Seward Peninsula(r) Railroad
        Steam Locomotive Roster 221

Chapter 18

Minor Railroads in Alaska and the Yukon   223

    Atlin Consolidated Mining Company 223
    Berners Bay Gold Manufacturing Company 224
    Alaska-Juneau Gold Mine Railroad 224
    Alaska-Gastineau Mining Company Railroad 224
    Salmon Creek Dam Railroad 225
    Treadwell Mine Railroad 225
    Rush and Brown Copper Mine Railroad 225
    Alaska Marble Company Tramway 226
    Ketchikan Pulp Company 226
    Ketchikan and Northern Terminal Company 226
    Alaska Lumber and Pulp Company 226
    Cook Inlet Coal Field Company Railroad 227
    Apollo Consolidated Mining Company 227
    Crooked Creek and Whiskey Island Railroad 227
    Minor Lines 227
Alaska-Gastineau Mining Company
    36"-Gauge Electric Locomotives 228
Alaska-Juneau Mining Company
    Electric Locomotives 228
Salmon Creek Dam Railroad
    Locomotive Roster 228
Rush and Brown Copper Mine
    Locomotive Roster 229
Apollo Consolidated Mining Company
    30"-Gauge, Steam Locomotive Roster 229
Cook Inlet Coal Fields Company
    42"-Gauge Locomotive Roster 229
Alaska Lumber & Pulp Company
    Diesel Locomotives 229
Ketchikan Pulp Company
    Diesel Locomotives 230
    Abbreviations: 231

Chapter 19

On the Drawing Board   233

    The Russian Connection 233
    Ties to the South 48 235
    Connections Within Alaska 237

Index   241

Foreword

Over the years, countless tales about Alaska and the Yukon have related the discovery of gold and other valued minerals, the development of the territory and state, and the struggle with the elements, a never-ending battle in the north. However, little has been written about the railroads of this vast and wild territory—or of the people who risked their lives and fortunes to build them. Few know the harrowing and exciting tale of how these pioneering lines were built; about the battle with the elements, not just during the winter but during all 12 months of the year; or about the great rivalry between the various railroad companies—the battle for the "one and only route." The story is one of intrigue, politics, and even warfare and murder. This is the account of the railroads of Alaska and the Yukon, which has intrigued me for the two decades I have spent conducting research throughout the north, collecting tidbits of information, and gradually piecing it together to write this book.

The research and writing of this book was accomplished with the help of many knowledgeable and informative people who donated their time and effort. There are hundreds of folks who lent me a hand in one way or another. To list them all would be impossible, but my sincere thanks go to each and every one. They made this book possible.

There are some who went well beyond the call of duty, spending hours and going out of their way to supply valuable materials and information. Thanks go to Bob Monroe and his staff at the University of Washington Library, Northwest Collection, Seattle, WA; to Paul McCarthy and his staff at the University of Alaska, Rasmussen Library, Fairbanks, AK; to Diane Johnston, archivist, Yukon Archives, Whitehorse, AK; to Phyllis Nottingham, State of Alaska Historical Library, Juneau, AK; M. Diane Brenner, Museum Archivist, Anchorage Historical and Fine Arts Museum; to Mrs. Dorothy Clifton, Valdez, Clifton private collection of Alaskana; to H. L. Berry of Homer, AK, and Sequim, WA, who dug into his own collection to find valuable information and photographs; to Louise Bremmer, assistant to the general manager of the Alaska Railroad, Anchorage, AK, who provided access to railroad archives and collections of photographs; to Cornelius W. Hauck, Cincinatti, OH, railroad historian, editor, and one of the founding fathers of the Colorado Railroad Museum; to Omar LaValle, author and historian, Montreal, Quebec; to the staff of the Canadian Pacific Railroad archives; to Lone Janson, Anchorage, AK, railroad historian and author; to Frank Downey, White Pass & Yukon Route, Seattle, WA; to Bruce LeRoy, director, and Frank Green, librarian, Washington State Historical Society, Tacoma, WA; and to Bruce Campbell, former commissioner of highways, state of Alaska, Juneau, AK.

Howard Clifford

Historical Notes

In the nearly two decades since this book was originally published, a significant amount of new research material has come to light regarding the railroads of Alaska and the Yukon Territory. Wherever possible, we have incorporated this new material, and used it to clarify the original text. Time and space constraints precluded answering all questions that remained—even with all the new data that was available. The process of updating a book is constant, and the publisher would welcome corrections, clarifications, and suggested additions to the book.

Republishing a work, particularly when it involves factual re-editing, can be a Herculean task. A modest group of Alaska and Yukon rail historians stepped forward—willing and able—to assist in the project. Don Marenzi poured over literally dozens of rosters to make sure we kept track of the locomotives correctly. Eric Johnson became our Yukon authority and cleaned up the facts on all the railroads in the territory. John Henderson, Bob Barrett, and Curt Fortenberry added much information to the diesel rosters. Dave Brann supplied the history of one of the more obscure lines. Ed Hauff searched his library to sort out where locomotives came from, or went to.

Constructed during the height of the 1898–99 winter storms, the tunnel at Tunnel Mountain was one of many difficult tasks for White Pass & Yukon Railway construction workers. A trestle at the mouth of the tunnel had to be built so that workers and equipment could reach the site. A work train with locomotive No. 5 is seen entering the tunnel. (University of Washington Historical Library, Northwest Collection)

Many others helped—often with just a single e-mail or letter—with suggestions on where to look to answer a question or solve a riddle. Certainly not the least among those who helped was my wife Mary, who assisted with the typing (a talent that seems to have passed me by), proofreading, and with her patient listening while I verbally attempted to sort out railroad esoterica—some of which may not have been of paramount interest to her.

To everyone who helped with this effort, my heartfelt thanks.

Steve Hauff, historical editor
Port Angeles, Washington
1999

The Alaska Juneau Gold Mine in all its glory. The mine was one of the most productive in Southeast Alaska and was a mainstay of the Juneau economy for many years. Most of the mine buildings (upper right) have been torn down since the facility was closed shortly after World War II. Miles of track ran through the many tunnels, and battery-powered locomotives and trolleys pulled the ore trains. The mine docks on the waterfront are still used for commercial purposes. (H. Clifford)

Chapter 1

White Pass & Yukon Route

The White Pass & Yukon Route was once known as "the road that couldn't be built." It started as the dream of Captain William (Billy) Moore, a sailor who had engaged in close to a dozen gold rushes from California to the Bering Sea over a 50-year period. Captain Moore was a pioneer among pioneers, a colorful old gentleman who had made and lost three fortunes and had hopes of making a fourth in the declining years of his extraordinary life.

In the summer of 1887, a Canadian government survey party, headed by William Ogilvie, hired Moore to assist them in packing over wilderness trails and in building and navigating a barge loaded with supplies down the Yukon River. This was a rather formidable assignment for a 65-year-old man, but the Canadians needed Moore's expertise to carry it off.

At that time, entry into the Upper Yukon Valley was gained via Chilkoot Pass, a precipitous and rugged route. Captain Moore, having visited and traveled in the area over a period of years, had heard about another route from sea level to the Upper Yukon, some 600 feet lower than the Chilkoot, which could be reached from the placid waters of Skagway Bay[1]. Moore was determined to attempt the new route, so while the main Ogilvie party took the old trail, he started up the Skagway River, accompanied by an old Indian friend, Skookum Jim (Mason). Skookum Jim was destined to be one of the discoverers of the Klondike gold fields, which would eventually fulfill Captain Moore's dream of wealth.

It took Moore and Skookum Jim many days to make the perilous trip over the 45-mile pass. They traveled without a trail of any kind over precipitous switchbacks, hillsides, and canyons. When they reached Lake Bennett, one of the headwaters of the Yukon, the main Ogilvie party had been waiting for them for several days.

Despite the hardships of the trip, Captain Moore was enthusiastic about the new route. Accepting Moore's report that the route was passable and showed promise of easing the trek to the Upper Yukon, Ogilvie named the pass after Thomas White, Canadian minister of the interior. As Ogilvie recalled years later, the old man's imagination was inspired. "Every night during the two months he remained with us, he would picture tons of yellow dust yet to be found in the Yukon Valley," Ogilvie

Long before anyone discovered gold in the Klondike, Captain William (Billy) Moore had visions of a railroad over White Pass to the rich mineral fields of the Yukon. Moore built the first dock at Skagway and the foundation of some White Pass facilities. He also explored the route that eventually became the White Pass & Yukon and lived to see his dream fulfilled—trains making their way over the pass. (Clifford Collection)

---

[1] For many years "Skagway" was also spelled "Skaguay." By the 1920s the "w" spelling seems to have won universal acceptance.

Skagway as it looked in 1897–98 when work on the wagon road to the summit of White Pass was started by George Brackett. During the gold rush Skagway became a booming town of 15,000. (Clifford Collection)

said. "He decided then and there that Skagway Bay would be the entry point to the golden fields and that White Pass would reverberate with the rumble of railway trains, carrying supplies in and the precious gold out." That dream would be fulfilled in the next decade.

Captain Moore was so enthusiastic about his new route that on October 20, 1887, he settled at the present site of Skagway, pitching his tent on a small knoll along a creek and staking a claim to 160 acres. Before winter, he and his son Ben

The infamous Chilkoot Pass, "the other way to the summit," was shorter but more hazardous than the White Pass Route later developed by the White Pass & Yukon. Stampeders landed at Dyea, about 4 miles from Skagway, to take the Chilkoot route. (Clifford Collection)

Beginning in 1897, workers cleared the right-of-way for the Brackett Wagon Road to the White Pass summit using sledgehammers and crowbars, the tools of the day. Notice how relaxed the worker holding the drill steel appears as the other worker is about to strike it with a sledgehammer. (National Archives)

had constructed a small dock on the tide flats along the high cliff, which they used to land supplies and equipment to assist in their task. Of their settlement Moore said to his son, "I fully expect before many years to see a pack trail through the pass, followed by a wagon road, and I would not be at all surprised to see a railroad through to the lakes."

Less than 10 years later, the Klondike discovery triggered the greatest stampede in history, a gold rush in

George Brackett, kneeling center, developer of the Brackett Wagon Road to the summit of White Pass, goes over plans with some of his construction crewmembers on one of the log bridges that crossed the many streams in the area. The cabin in the background was constructed to house work crews along the route. (National Archives)

One of the rivals of the White Pass Trail for traffic to the Klondike gold fields was the aerial tramway system that helped stampeders haul goods over the Chilkoot Pass route. Some of the towers that supported the four tramways are still standing in the Chilkoot Pass area. (University of Washington Library, Northwest Collection)

which more than 50,000 people battled their way over White Pass and to a lesser extent nearby Chilkoot Pass, the original route to the interior.

The first prospectors to arrive via White Pass were seven young men from California who had traveled on the steamer Rustler. They started their trek with seven tons of freight on February 2, 1895. These men were the first to make use of 2 miles of Moore's trail over the ridge to avoid the falls at the junction of the upper and lower canyons.

For many years, Captain Moore tried with-

The financial success of the Brackett Wagon Road to the White Pass summit depended on tolls. This is a toll bridge over one of the branches of the Skagway River en route to the summit. Teamsters rebelled against paying tolls and often destroyed the toll gates, resulting in the calling out of army troops to restore order at one location. (National Archives)

out success to win financial support from the Victoria, B.C. business community for his Skagway venture. Perhaps too many recalled his sorry financial history. He seemed like a poor risk. Early in 1896, however, before the Klondike discovery, Captain Moore approached E. E. Billinghurst of the British Columbia Development Company, who was an agent for the British capitalist and promoter C. H. Wilkinson. Captain Moore was so persuasive about the future prospects of Skagway Bay as a gateway for a wagon trail and railway to the Yukon Territory that Wilkinson arranged to advance the old sea captain $1,800 for supplies, two horses, a couple of cows, 6,000 board feet of rough lumber, and other materials in return for a lien on Moore's preemption at Skagway. From this humble beginning came the British capital that would finance the construction of the White Pass & Yukon Railway.

Moore's supplies arrived in Skagway in June 1896, and since Billinghurst guaranteed the payment of wages for five men that season, Captain Moore's son, Ben, was able to improve the wharf, which is the foundation of the wharf used by passenger boats and the White Pass & Yukon trains. The workers also began construction of a trail over the pass. Later 15 men were employed to build a pack trail along the bank of the Skagway River and bridges over the canyons.

Advertising a through route for both summer and winter, the Brackett Wagon Road, which was the predecessor to the White Pass & Yukon Railway, was a favorite and practical way to reach the lakes at the White Pass summit. (Clifford Collection.)

The following gold rush created the town of Skagway almost overnight, and Captain Moore transferred 60 acres of his original preemption to the British Yukon Company. The company immediately laid out a town site and promised the Canadian minister of the interior to build a wagon road through White Pass—a distance of 50 miles at a cost of $2,000 per mile.

Before any real improvements were made on the route between Skagway and the lakes, many companies had put in bids to provide transportation. As early as 1887, the U.S. secretary of the interior received bids from promoters for the construction of trails across the Alaska panhandle from tidewater to the headwaters of the Yukon.

Edward Bean had written to the Secretary asking for a charter to construct a pack trail from the head of Lynn Canal to the trail from Lake Bennett, for which a charter had been granted by the government of British Columbia. Secretary L. Q. C. Lamar denied the request on the basis that such a franchise could be secured only through congressional action. The next year, David Flannery and Samuel O. Wheeler, having learned of Captain Moore's trip over White Pass, attempted to "steal his thunder" by proposing to build a trail using his route. Their charter was turned down by Interior Secretary William F. Vilas.

Tons of equipment have been discarded along the Brackett Wagon Road 3.5 miles below the White Pass summit. Many Klondikers gave up during the climb and tossed their equipment aside as the going got rough. Today the White Pass & Yukon Route carries tourists over much the same path north of Skagway. (Clifford Collection)

By the time Captain Moore had built his wharf and cabin, he had applied to Alaska Governor A. P. Swineford for a similar concession. The governor replied that he was powerless to grant it and referred him to the secretary of the interior. It was not until three years later, in 1891, that Captain Moore finally got around to making his formal application. In April of that year, he proposed to open a pack trail from Skagway Bay through White Pass to Summit Lake. This trail, to be blasted, or cribbed, from the mountainside, would be 5 feet wide and graded. All unfordable streams would be bridged. As considerable expense would be involved in construction, Moore applied for a franchise to levy a toll. He requested a right-of-way of 1 mile on either side of the trail. He received the same reply as the other applicants.

Within six months the interior secretary received a request from Miner W. Bruce and Charles W. Young of Juneau for a "charter to construct a toll road up the Chilkat." Secretary John W. Noble, like the others, denied the request.

Despite earlier discouragements to obtain permits, Captain Moore had been able to get financial backing from the Alaskan and Northwestern Territories Trading Company, and because of the urgency and excitement, proceeded to rough out a trail without taking the pains to secure the right-of-way and the privilege of charging tolls until a trail had been opened.

Twelve days after the first stampeders landed at Skagway, Noble Rowan of the Alaskan and Northwestern Company wrote Secretary of the Interior Cornelius N. Bliss, informing him that the company had completed "a trail from Skagway Bay . . . over the White Pass entirely at its own cost." Rowan requested the right "to levy a small toll of one cent per pound on the goods going over the trail." This request was denied, with the warning to Rowan that "no person or persons could lawfully take possession of the White Pass Trail and charge tolls until authorized by Congress."

As it became apparent that the trail couldn't accommodate the volume of travelers landing at Skagway, Rowan applied to the secretary to build a wagon road from Skagway Bay through White Pass to Lake Bennett. His company was prepared to begin

The Brackett Wagon Road was used during the summer and winter months. When there was too much snow for wagons to operate, horses pulled sleds that could be loaded with up to 1,400 pounds of supplies over the route. There was no natural food supply for horses en route, and during the winter there was no water. Pack animals were horribly mistreated in the rush to get supplies over the pass. If their duty was completed or they were unable to continue, they were simply abandoned. This is how the route became known as Dead Horse Trail. (Hegg photo from Clifford Collection)

work immediately and complete the road, if it was allowed to charge a reasonable toll. Before the secretary could reply, he received a telegram from John Campbell, dated August 6, 1897. The telegram stated that thousands would have to take other routes to the Klondike unless improvements were made on the trail, which would result in great suffering and even death from privation and exposure since winter was approaching. He also applied for permission to build a road in the interest of the Yukon Miners Association. Both requests were denied because the secretary lacked the authority to make such concessions.

At the same time, Secretary Bliss was being pressured by interests in the nearby town of Dyea that were opposed to the opening of a competing route across White Pass. Sam Herron, manager of Healy & Wilson's Trading Post at Dyea, stated that if Canadian interests were permitted to open the trail they would soon begin operating a line of steamers from Victoria that would "deprive the Territory of Alaska of the Yukon trade." Land rights at Skagway, he pointed out, were held by Bernard Moore, Captain Moore's son and a naturalized citizen.

Railroads were proposed too, the first ones by residents of Sitka and Juneau who were planning a line through Chilkoot Pass as early as 1885, five years after the first prospectors reached the headwaters of the Yukon. Major M. P. Berry, Frank Myers, Abraham Cohen, W. R. Mills, and George Nowell petitioned Congress for a charter for

Packers with horses and dogs make their way through the wooded area on the lower reaches of the White Pass Trail. The narrow trail caused problems as those hauling loads to the summit tried to pass the oncoming traffic traveling back down the pass. (Clifford Collection)

the Chilkoot Pass and Summit Railroad Company. The company wanted construction bonds in the amount of $1 million and a title to 1 mile of land on each side of the future road. The undertaking failed, partly because of a lack of sufficient funds but also because no law allowed the construction of such a road.

Following the discovery of gold in the Yukon and the gold rush of 1897, Congress passed a bill permitting the use of resources for building railroads and providing for right-of-way, terminals, and stations. One of the first routes proposed under the new law was the Stikine route, which was to extend from Taku Arm to the Atlintoo River and the headwaters of the Yukon, thus connecting the upper Stikine with the Yukon.

In 1897, an order-in-council of the Canadian government authorized MacKenzie & Mann of Toronto to build a 150-mile-long railroad from Telegraph Creek, the head of navigation on the Stikine River in British Columbia, to the head of Teslin Lake. The lake, about 85 miles long, stretches through British Columbia into the Yukon. Four hundred men were transported to Telegraph Creek to start this project, but the life of this route was a short and merry one, ending abruptly when the Canadian Parliament refused to ratify the agreement. Contractors cleared right-of-way and built corduroy roads on the Teslin Trail at a cost of $280,000. Many MacKenzie & Mann employees migrated to Skagway and eventually worked on the construction of the White Pass & Yukon Route. Another rail route was projected from Chilkat Inlet on the line of the Dalton Trail to the Yukon River by way of the Yukon to Dawson City.

In August 1897, George W. Garside, engineer for the British-American Transportation Company, surveyed a 62-mile route for a railroad. The route extended from Skagway Bay over White Pass to Lake Tagish and then through Three Mile River to Lake Atlin, headquarters of the Hootalinqua. From Lake Atlin, passengers would be transferred to steamers operated by the company and carried to Dawson and Forty Mile. In the same month, the Sitka syndicate headed by P. L. Packard and William A. Pratt, surveyed a route from Taku Inlet on the Alaska coast to Tesline (Teslin) Lake and then into the Yukon Territory.

In September 1897, the Chilkoot Railroad and Transportation Company of Washington State proposed to build a route from Dyea to Camp Linderman, a distance of 15.9 miles. In December the Chilkoot Pass Transportation Company of West Virginia filed to build from Dyea over Chilkoot Pass to Lake Linderman. Then came the deluge. In May 1898, five companies filed to construct railroads that they hoped would reach the riches of the Klondike one way or another, as shown in this list:

- The Yukon Railway Company of New Jersey filed to build a 39.3-mile route from Skagway to Lake Bennett.
- The Yukon Mining, Trading, and Transportation Company of West Virginia proposed building along the Taku Inlet and the Taku River to the international boundary, a distance of 20 miles.

It was in the bar of the St. James Hotel in Skagway that Sir Thomas Tancrede and Michael Heney met and planned the building of the White Pass & Yukon Railway (WP&Y). The hotel was moved to its present location on Fourth near Broadway from its original Fourth and State location following the gold rush. (Western Airlines)

Building the White Pass & Yukon Railway was a real challenge for turn-of-the-century workers. There was no modern equipment—only picks, shovels, and blasting powder. Workers prepared for the blasting, and then after the blast they moved down to the wagon road below to remove the debris so that the wagons could continue to travel over the pass. Below the wagon road is the old Moore Trail. (University of Washington Historical Library, Northwest Collection)

- The Alaska and Northwestern Railway Company, incorporated under the laws of West Virginia, filed to build a 36-mile route from Portage Cove on Lynn Canal to the international boundary.
- The American and Canadian Transportation Company of Washington State proposed building from Skagway to White Pass and onward.
- The Chilkat and Yukon Railway Company of New Jersey planned a route from Haines Mission to the head of the Klehane River.

The Pacific and Arctic Railway and Navigation Company of West Virginia filed its proposal as well, and it ultimately became the U.S. section of the White Pass and Yukon Railway. Other filings included the Chilkat Inlet Railway and Navigation Company of Washington State, which planned to build from Pyramid Harbor to Chilkat River and to the boundary at the crossing of the Chilkat River. The company filed its routing in November 1902. This was followed by the Haines Mission and Boundary Railroad Company of Washington State, which filed in January 1907 to build a 41.35-mile route from Haines Mission on Lynn Canal to Pleasant Camp. Another was the

Lynn Canal and Short Line Railroad, which bought out the old Shellcross-Richards Telephone Line connecting Dyea and Skagway to obtain the right-of-way from the Dyea Post Office to the Kelly Dry Goods Store in Skagway.

Meanwhile, the struggle for supremacy between Skagway and Dyea as to the favored route to the Yukon continued. By mid-August 1897, Dyea was favored as conditions over the White Pass Trail worsened. As it became more difficult to get a horse to the summit of White Pass, Indian packers were being paid from $12 to $40 per hundredweight to pack goods over the Chilkoot.

As things got worse, it was estimated that there were more than 3,000 stampeders trying to get over the White Pass Trail out of Skagway, while the Chilkoot was relatively clear, with perhaps 50 or so rushers in town awaiting transportation of their goods over the route. By September, packers could no longer get over White Pass, which became known as Dead Horse Trail. Of about an estimated 5,000 attempting the route, only 10 percent were successful, with many backtracking and going over the Chilkoot.

Many aerial tramways had been constructed along the Chilkoot route: the Chilkoot Railroad and Transport Company, headed by Hugh C. Wallace of Tacoma, Washington, had built one. There was also the Dyea-Klondike Transportation Company bucket tramway, Burns's Hoist, and the Alaska Railway and Transportation Company's bucket tramway. This company was owned outright by the Pacific Coast Company, which hedged its Klondike bets by also purchasing the Alaska Southern Wharf Company in Skagway. The Pacific Coast Company also owned the Columbia and Puget Sound Railroad, a supplier of much of the early White Pass motive power. All of these companies eventually joined in an agreement that gave the Chilkoot a big edge.

This is Broadway, the main street in Skagway, with the White Pass & Yukon Railway tracks down the center of the street. The railroad tracks remained here until World War II when a bypass was constructed to accommodate the heavy military traffic. Most of the buildings shown here are still standing. (Clifford Collection)

The White Pass & Yukon Railway was in reality three railroads: one incorporated in the United States, another in British Columbia, and the third in the Yukon. This building, photographed in June 1898, housed the headquarters for the U.S.-chartered Pacific and Arctic Railway & Navigation Company. S. H. Graves was president of the P&AR&N as well as of the White Pass & Yukon Route. (Yukon Archives)

To many, Jefferson Randolph (Soapy) Smith was a notorious character in Skagway, but builders of the railroad credit him with assisting the project. During a construction worker strike, radical leaders threatened to destroy much of the work that had been completed. Soapy and some of his followers arrived on the scene and restored order after other means had failed. Smith was later killed in a shoot-out on the Skagway waterfront. (Denver Public Library, Western History Department)

As winter came, however, and the bogs and rivers froze, the White Pass Trail gained a considerable edge since packhorses were able to travel the entire distance with full loads. Pack trains were able to make it to the lakes in four days with 250 pounds per horse. The White Pass Trail gained additional favor when a disastrous slide at Sheep Camp on April 3, 1898, took lives on the Chilkoot route.

In the meantime, Captain Charles E. Peabody of the Washington & Alaska Steamship Company urged George A. Brackett, former mayor of Minneapolis and an engineer who had helped drive the Northern Pacific Railroad across the Dakotas, to seek development of better transportation over one of the passes.

Heading north aboard ship in mid-September 1897, Brackett met J. A. Acklen, a Tennessee lawyer and former Congressman. They discussed transportation over the passes and visited both Dyea and Skagway. Brackett decided that Chilkoot had the most potential. Acklen invited Norman Smith, who had made a survey over White Pass, to join forces with him in a proposed wagon road from Skagway. Fourteen potential charter members held a meeting in Charles Kelly's store in Skagway. The group agreed to organize a company with capital stock of $300,000, of which $150,000 would go to the charter members for their efforts.

On their way back to Washington D.C. to incorporate, Acklen and Smith met with Brackett and convinced him to join their company. On October 13, 1897, the group incorporated the Skagway & Yukon Transportation and Improvement Company. C. A. Bullen of the Bullen Bridge Company was asked to join the group of promoters because he owned a 250-foot steel bridge that was believed suitable to span the East Fork of the Skagway River.

Meanwhile, Acklen was unable to raise funds in the East and did not get support from Congress as promised. He was soon ousted from the group, along with Smith and Treasurer David Samson. Brackett took charge of the entire operation.

Even without the additional funds, Brackett and his crews completed 4 miles of roadway out of Skagway, which they opened to traffic on November 23, 1897. By mid-December, 8 miles had been completed. Bullen's bridge arrived and was found useless. By December 20, 1897, Brackett was broke. He returned to Seattle and tried to raise money from Captain Peabody and others, but without success he continued on to Minneapolis. Starting with a small nest egg from the Great Northern, Brackett was able to raise additional cash from the Canadian Pacific and others.

He returned to Skagway in mid-January and increased his labor force, but construction was cut short by outlaws who had taken over part of the trail right-of-way, claiming they had located minerals under the roadway. Brackett summoned his old friend Jefferson Randolph (Soapy) Smith and his followers, who frightened the outlaws into making a hasty retreat. Smith apparently realized the importance of minimizing competition. Work on the roadway continued.

Despite the fact that the road had not been completed to the summit and there was no bridge over the East Fork, Brackett started charging tolls of 2¢ per pound for freight; $1 each for pedestrians; $1 for a horse, mule, or ox; 25¢ for sheep; and $10 for a wagon using the completed part of the road. Hard-boiled freighters and packers refused to pay and destroyed Brackett's toll gates. Brackett wired a friend in the War Department, who explained to higher-ups that a "roudy (sic) element had seized the wagon road and had placed the country in a state of terror." This brought troops from Dyea, and order was restored.

By mid-April, the bridge over the East Fork was completed and the toll road was bringing in a modest $1,000 to $1,500 a day, not as much as Brackett had hoped for. Despite additional financial assistance from the backers in the States and passage of the amended Lacey Bill, extending the Homestead Act to Alaska and providing for the construction of wagon roads, trails, and railroads in the territory, Brackett was still strapped for money and faced a continuing and losing battle with packers and freighters who refused to pay tolls.

Meanwhile, three Victoria businessmen, who had known Captain Moore and were familiar with his idea of a railroad over White Pass, became interested in the venture and applied for a charter to build a railroad over the Canadian part of the route to the gold fields. They obtained financing from the British firm Close Brothers to get the project started, but they were unable to start work within the time allotted by their charter. The English capitalists took over the franchise and decided to build the railroad

Prior to the completion of the White Pass & Yukon Route, one of the ways to travel between Whitehorse or Dawson City and Skagway was by dog team. This is a team from Dawson City that arrived in Skagway on Christmas Day 1898. The St. James Hotel, where Sir Thomas Tancrede and Michael Heney met and formulated plans for the construction of the White Pass & Yukon Route, is in the background. The hotel still stands in Skagway, although it has been moved from Fourth and State Street to a location just off Broadway. (Clifford Collection)

themselves without looking over the area or ensuring that the proper construction experts were available for the job.

Close Brothers sent Sir Thomas Tancrede to Skagway, along with Samuel H. Graves of Chicago and Erastus C. Hawkins, a Seattle engineer, to determine whether construction was possible. Upon looking over the terrain, Sir Thomas determined that the mountains were too massive, the walls of the cliffs too sheer, and the grades too steep to build a railroad, which he communicated to his backers.

Workers with picks and shovels, along with a little blasting powder, make a cut through the mountains on the White Pass right-of-way. This photo was taken during the height of construction in August 1898. (Yukon Archives)

Following his report, Sir Thomas met Michael J. Heney, a Canadian railroad contractor who had gained fame in the construction of the Canadian Pacific Railroad and who had just completed his own survey of the White Pass route. Heney was not deterred in his plan to build a railroad over the pass, provided financing was available, and after an evening of discussion (actually, well into the early hours of the next morning) in the bar at Skagway's St. James Hotel, he convinced Sir Thomas that the project was feasible. As dawn broke they drank a toast to the success of the operation.

Workers literally hung on by "the skin of their teeth" as they worked on the sides of cliffs while building the White Pass & Yukon Railway. This photo was taken at Fisk's Cut on Tunnel Mountain in 1898. (Yukon Archives)

Key personnel involved in the building of the White Pass & Yukon Railway pose in front of the foreman's tent at Construction Camp No. 3. Left to right are the camp foreman, Mr. Foy; Dr. F. B. Whiting, railroad surgeon who also participated in the construction of the Copper River & Northwestern; Mike Heney, builder of the White Pass and the Copper River & Northwestern; E. C. Hawkins, an engineer who was also with Heney on the Copper River; Samuel H. Graves, president of the White Pass and representative of the money interests in the project; and John Hislop, chief surveyor—one of the three H's (Heney, Hawkins, and Hislop) instrumental in the building of the WP&Y. (British Columbia Provincial Archives)

The Pacific & Arctic Railway and Navigation Company, with Samuel H. Graves as president, was incorporated in the state of West Virginia to obtain the rights for the U.S. section of the route. Previously, the British Columbia Yukon Railway Company had been chartered by the legislature of British Columbia for the construction of the portion through that province; the British Yukon Railway Company chartered for the portion through the Yukon Territory by an act of Parliament of the Dominion of Canada.

The White Pass & Yukon Railway Company, Ltd., an English corporation, registered on July 30, 1898, to carry out the charter rights and concession of the three companies for the construction of a 325-mile railway from Skagway Harbor to Fort Selkirk on the Yukon. By 1902, the company would be referred to as the White Pass & Yukon Route, reflecting its steamship, sled, and wagon operations, as well as its railway. Over the years, the company popularly became known as the White Pass.

Graves negotiated an agreement with Brackett whereby his firm would receive $50,000 compensation for any damages or losses suffered in the construction of the railroad. The firm would also receive an option to purchase his "toll road and all its franchises, appurtenances and rights, etc., at any time before July 1, 1899, upon payment of an additional $50,000." At the time, Brackett had already invested $185,000 in construction, but his project had come to a halt because of all the government red tape of the two nations involved.

Following the purchase of the right-of-way, the railroad engineers surveyed five routes over the summit. They decided that the best one was that originally discovered and explored by Captain Billy Moore. In a cost-saving move, the railroad company decided to construct a narrow-gauge line with rails 3 feet apart instead of the more common standard gauge of 4 feet 8-½ inches. This resulted in a 10-foot roadbed instead of the standard 15-foot roadbed.

Nearly all of the work between Skagway and the summit was in rock. Workers used immense quantities of dynamite and blasting powder to clear the way. In one case a rock cliff 120 feet high, 70 feet wide, and 20 feet thick was blasted away. Sometimes the mountainsides were so steep that men had to be suspended by ropes to keep from falling while they cut the grade. A short distance from the summit, a deep V-shaped canyon was spanned by a steel cantilever bridge 215 feet high, the northernmost bridge of its type and height in the world.

There were many adversities inherent in construction, one of which the builders at Tunnel Mountain had to cope with—the weather. Construction began in late November at the height of storm season with temperatures at 30 degrees below zero and gusting winds. Workers were usually exposed to the weather, and many days were too stormy and cold to work. Or the builders would spend a day clearing snow from the area only to have it drift back during the night.

Building the trestle at the mouth of the proposed tunnel was just as difficult. Workers became numb from the cold, and drifting snow hampered visibility. Often they could not see across the 40-foot gap, and the loudest shout could not be heard. The men would have a post swung up and almost ready to drop into place, and a gust of wind would sway it out of line and out of their reach. By sheer perseverance, they finally succeeded and the trestle was built.

Track was laid over the summit on February 16, 1899, and the first passenger train with a load of excursionists traveled from Skagway to White Pass on February 20, 1899. The first major hurdle was overcome less than a year after the start of work on the railroad.

In the construction of the White Pass & Yukon Route, Mike Heney had to overcome the problem of crossing the international boundary into Canada, despite the fact that the money to finance the railroad was British. At that time, the summit of White Pass was considered the boundary between the United States and Canada. When Heney's spike drivers and track layers reached the summit, they were courteously

Construction work on the White Pass & Yukon Railway continued through the winter months despite severe storms in the mountains. Here a bridge crew works through a blizzard on the timber trestle at Tunnel Mountain. (University of Washington Historical Library, Northwest Collection)

informed by the Royal Northwest Mounted Police that their so-called wildcat railroad could go no farther. The "Irish Prince," as Heney was known, sent his trusted friend and coworker Stikine Bill Robinson as an informal ambassador to the summit with instructions to proceed in the spirit of diplomacy and untie the red tape.

The story goes that Bill's only baggage on the trip was a bottle of scotch in each pocket of his mackinaw and a box of cigars under each arm. He found a guard pacing the boundary line. Two days later the guard woke up from a long and heavy sleep, and the

This steep section of track, located at Heney, Alaska, was part of the construction facility for the White Pass & Yukon Railway. In September 1898, it was used as a feeder track to haul supplies for the construction crews. (Yukon Archives)

first thing he saw was Heney's construction gang working like beavers, laying track well over the international line and already a mile or so down the shore of Summit Lake.

Shortly thereafter, a worker strike halted construction, and it was not until June that trackage was laid much beyond the summit. During the months between the completion of the railroad to the summit and the continuation of the project to Lake Bennett, the White Pass sponsored the operation of the Red Line Transportation

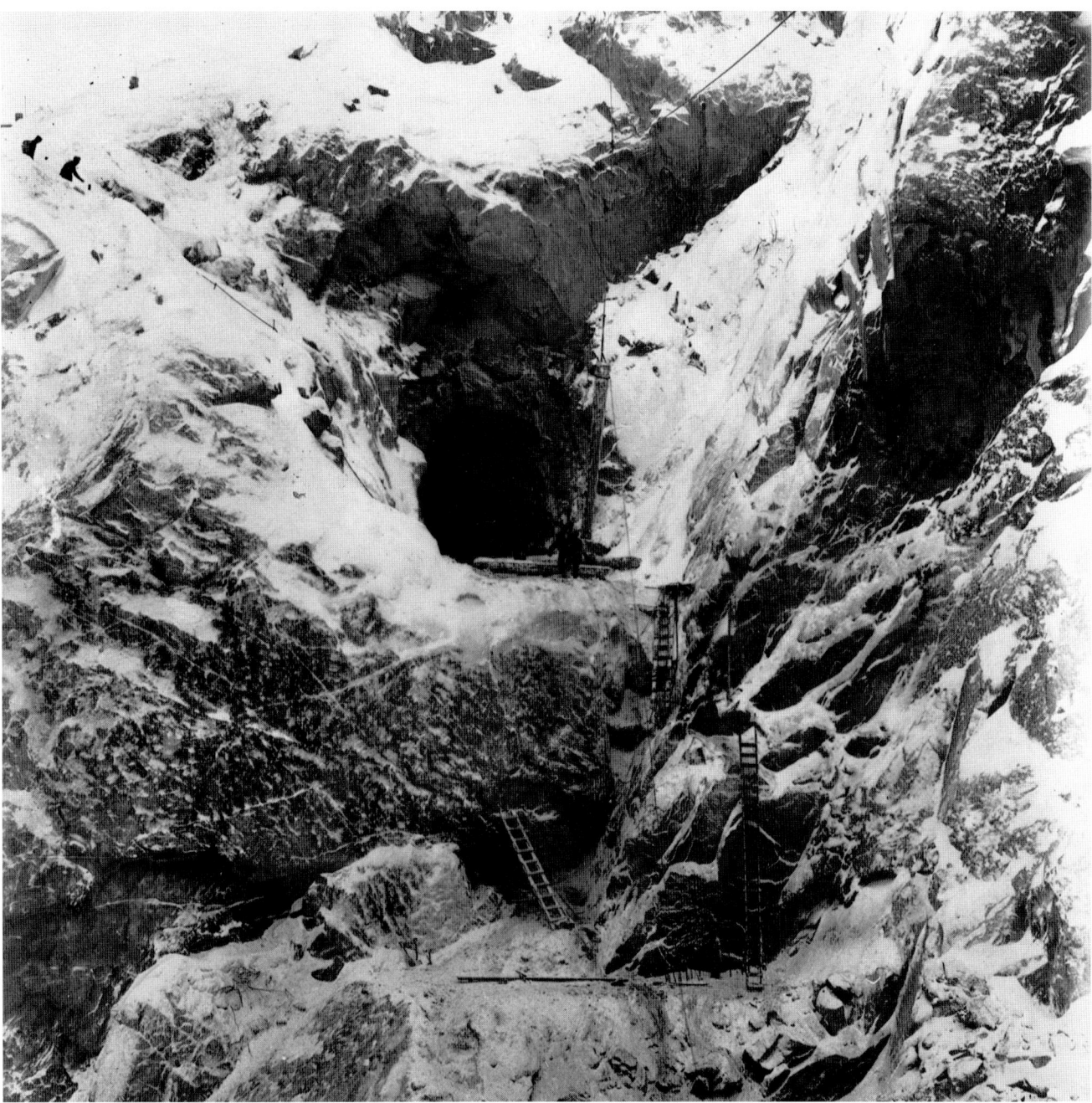

Tunnel building during the construction of the White Pass & Yukon was difficult work in 1898. Crews cut through the rock of Tunnel Mountain with picks, shovels, and blasting powder. There was no power equipment in those days. This photo was taken during the cold winter months when work was almost at a standstill. (University of Washington Historical Library, Northwest Collection)

The first passenger train traveled over the White Pass & Yukon to the summit of White Pass on February 20, 1899. The train in this photo, pulled by locomotive No. 3, crosses the East Fork of the Skagway River on one of the many trestles built to carry the rails through the mountains and over streams and rivers. (University of Washington Historical Library, Northwest Collection)

Company, locally known as the Red Ball Express, which carried passengers and cargo to and from Dawson City and other points on the Yukon.

The Red Line Transportation Company project involved assembling all of the teamsters who had operated over the White Pass Trail and forming them into a scheduled operation that met all trains and Lake Bennett stern-wheelers. The project, led by Stikine Bill Robinson, operated successfully between the completion of the railroad to the summit and its continuation to Lake Bennett. More than 300 horses, with a corresponding number of wagons, teamsters, and the like were involved. Work on the railroad resumed on June 20, 1899, and from that date on the track layers put down 3 miles of track per day, with two shifts each working 12 hours a day.

Early on the morning of July 6, 1899, a steamer carrying 200 passengers came up the Yukon and landed at Bennett. When they disembarked, the passengers saw a sign across the front of a tent that read, "White Pass & Yukon R.R. Ticket Office." Though there was no railroad there nor a rail or tie to be seen, many rushed in to buy tickets.

When construction of the White Pass & Yukon Railway reached the summit of White Pass, transportation became necessary between the summit and the steamer terminus at Lake Bennett. To accommodate this need, all of the teamsters from the Skagway area joined under the leadership of Stikine Bill Robinson to form the Red Line Transportation Company, locally known as the Red Ball Express. Red Line met the trains at Summit Station and the steamers at Bennett. Here horses and wagons are lined up at the rail terminus awaiting the next train. (Yukon Archives)

"We'll take care of you," the ticket agent blandly told them. "The train leaves at 2 p.m. sharp."

"Whereabouts does it start from?" asked a man in a broad white hat.

"It will leave from this depot at 2 p.m.," was the reply.

With that, the agent refused to provide any more information. He gave his attention to the stamping of tickets, the counting of money, and the weighing of gold dust.

When all the passengers had bought tickets, they sat and listened to the ceaseless ring of the steel spike-mauls on the spikes. Many went to see the men at work. The end of the track had been 2 miles away when they landed; it was nearer now.

Hundreds of workers had been clearing the track near the summit of White Pass when a winter storm hit. This photo shows the track completely buried by the storm, which passed through on March 20, 1899. (University of Washington Historical Library, Northwest Collection)

Having battled its way through the snow and ice over White Pass, the WP&Y's first rotary snowplow and its crew take a welcome break in the winter battle against the elements. (University of Washington Historical Library, Northwest Collection)

Some of the prospective passengers were so eager to continue their journey that they wanted to help the workers; they had gold dust that was spoiling to be spent. Others longed to reach Seattle.

Finally, amidst wild enthusiasm, the last spike was driven and the first through-passenger train pulled out of the depot on schedule. On July 20, 1897, the first pack train had crossed the range from the head of Lynn Canal. A year later, on July 20, 1898, the first locomotive ran on the White Pass and Yukon line. On February 20, 1899, the first through-passenger train climbed to the summit of White Pass. On July 8, 1899, only a little over a year after the road construction began, the first through-passenger train traveled to Bennett.

When it became obvious that the road would be completed, those who had predicted its failure began to prophesy that it would never earn even operating expenses. As a matter of fact, the 20 miles from Skagway to the top of the hill earned enough to pay for the expensive extension to Bennett and more. The first $130,000 earned after the line was completed to Bennett showed a net profit of $100,000. It cost about $25,000 to run the railroad during the month of August, the first full month after completion of that portion of the line. The gross earnings that month were about $200,000, not a bad month for a 40-mile railroad.

When the rails reached the head of Lake Bennett, an immense quantity of rails, ties, stores, construction plants, and rolling stock had to be transported down Lake Bennett to Carcross

The tallest and northernmost steel bridge of the time was this structure over Dead Horse Gulch on the White Pass & Yukon Railway over White Pass. This bridge was in daily service on the railroad until 1969 when a shorter bridge and tunnel were constructed, making the structure unnecessary. It served its purpose well for almost seven decades. (Yukon Archives)

Snow, sometimes 10 to 20 feet deep in the passes, presented a winter problem for the White Pass & Yukon trains. Locomotive No. 7, a Baldwin 2-8-0 built in 1899 that was later used on the Klondike Mines Railway as No. 3, makes its way through drifts higher than the engine stack. This photo was taken near Glacier in December 1899. (Yukon Archives)

(Caribou Crossing). For this purpose, a barge with a capacity of about 150 tons of freight was designed. All cargo was carried on its deck for convenience in loading and unloading. The barge was a flat oblong box, with sloping ends that projected over the shore landings and facilitated freight handling. Bill Robinson was put in charge of this important project.

When the barge was finished, Bill walked around it and inspected both ends carefully. Finally he said, "I think we'll make this end the stern," whereupon the word "stern" was chalked in large letters on that end.

The next move was to install upright boilers with the engine attached to three propellers. On a short trial trip, the craft traveled so fast that it was named the Torpedo Catcher. Finally Bill's flagship was ready and loaded for its maiden voyage down Lake Bennett. Stikine Bill was in the pilot house. He blew his starboard whistle, jingled the engine-room bells, and backed out from the Bennett wharf. With all three propellers working, Bill wanted to show the crowd assembled on the bank how he could turn the TC within its own length. He did, but it kept turning and turning until the watchers on the bank struck up a popular tune of the day, "Waltz Me Around Again, Willie." Bill finally got his steamship straightened out and chugged down the lake to Carcross.

The pace of work increased, with construction at both the Carcross and Whitehorse locations heading toward one another. On August 8, 1899, and on the days that followed, however, 1,500 employees grabbed their picks and shovels (valued at $16 each) and started off pell-mell on a gold stampede to the fields at Atlin B.C. Only a few hundred men were left on the job, and more had to be hired to fill vacancies. These new workers also had to be trained, and a new supply of picks and shovels had to be ordered.

Construction on the railroad between Caribou Crossing and Whitehorse was completed on June 8, 1900, and the Bennett to Caribou Crossing section on July 29, 1900, joining the chain of steel from Skagway to Whitehorse. Dignitaries of the period, both American and Canadian, took part in the Golden Spike Ceremonies. An experienced trackman started the spike upright and gleaming beside the rail. The officials on hand, by this time feeling the effects of the Yukon hospitality that typically marked such an auspicious occasion, struck with vigor at the spike with heavy sledgehammers, but to

The White Pass & Yukon's first locomotive is assembled on Broadway, the main street in Skagway, on July 20, 1898, prior to being put into service. Numbered No. 2 and later No. 52, the little Brooks, built in 1881, is now on display in Skagway. (University of Washington Historical Library, Northwest Collection)

no avail. The spike remained battered but undriven. Deeming it a most successful affair, the dignitaries, led by the company's president, retired to partake of better things. The track superintendent remained behind, removed the battered spike, replaced it with one less noble, and drove it home, thus completing the rail link.

The building of the railroad was one of the most difficult ever engineered. There was no heavy equipment available, and most of the work through the solid rock along the route was done by hand drills and blasting powder. Mike Heney and his able assistants Stikine Bill, E. C. Hawkins, Dr. F. B. Whiting, and others were later involved in the building of another northern railroad under similar difficult conditions—the Copper River & Northwestern—from Eyak (which Heney later named Cordova) to the rich copper fields of the Interior.

All told, there were 35,000 men at work on the White Pass & Yukon from June 1, 1898, to October 1, 1900, and of this number there were only 35 deaths from sickness and accidents. The railroad employed a very intelligent class of worker. On one occasion, the company surgeon, having an operation to perform, sent out among the workers for assistance. A skilled physician was found among the graders. He came in, assisted in the operation, and then took up his pick again. Many of the workers were anxious to reach the gold fields but were awaiting water transportation. Others had worked throughout the summer, exhausted their funds, and wanted to

Impressive ceremonies were held on July 6, 1899, at Lake Bennett when the "last spike" was driven, marking the completion of the White Pass & Yukon Railway from Skagway to Lake Bennett. Government and business leaders of the day took part. Lake steamers stood by to take gold rushers on to Whitehorse and Dawson City. (University of Washington Historical Library, Northwest Collection)

Local residents of Skagway took advantage of the completion of the White Pass & Yukon to the summit of White Pass to ride the winter excursion train to the top on February 20, 1899. Notice the winter clothing of the day and the many tourists with their cameras. (University of Washington Historical Library)

replenish them so that they could continue prospecting. No Asian laborers were employed on the project.

From sea level at Skagway, the WP&Y climbs to the summit of White Pass (2,885 feet) in 21 miles. The average grade to the summit is 2.6 percent, with the steepest grade at about 4 percent. The line, from terminal to terminal, is 110.7 miles, of which 20.4 miles is in Alaska, 42.2 miles in British Columbia, and 58.1 miles in the Yukon. Cost of construction at the time the railroad was built was about $10,000,000.

In 1901, the White Pass expanded its transportation services mainly because river service was irregular and unreliable. The organization bought the John Irving Navigation Company, which served the Atlin-Bennett region, and the Canadian Development Company, which operated ships and a winter stage line from Whitehorse to Dawson City. Included in the purchase were several stern-wheelers, and the WP&Y formed a river division, the British Yukon Navigation Company (B.Y.N.), to operate them. The firm built three new vessels, the 779-ton Dawson, the 777-ton Selkirk, and the 1120-ton Whitehorse, along with several others, including the colorful Yukoner.

At the same time river services became available, the White Pass also took over the contracts for the winter hauling of both American and Canadian mail and the many sled dog teams involved in the project. The American contract covered the route between Juneau and St. Michael, via Whitehorse, with a branch to Nome and several other points off the Yukon River. The Canadian contract called for the transport of Canadian mail between Skagway and Dawson City, with a branch to Atlin, B.C.

The WP&Y did not particularly want the winter routes nor the 500 dogs involved, but it had to take them over to continue with the summer routes, which paid a good portion of the operating costs of the stern-wheelers on the river.

After one summer of maintaining 500 dogs, transferred with keepers, facilities, and the like to a large island in Lake LaBarge[2], the company

On July 6, 1899, the first White Pass & Yukon train made its way to Lake Bennett. En route back to Skagway, the train carried more than $500,000 in gold from the Klondike. (University of Washington Library)

gradually began using horse-drawn sleds, which could also carry passengers. Thus it was able to maintain the lucrative summer haul of the mail and even make a little on the winter haul thanks to the passenger service. The horse-drawn vehicles remained in service until 1921.

---

[2] LaBarge became known as Dog Island.

While the river remained open, the White Pass & Yukon built roadhouses at intervals along the trail and stored supplies for people and horses. When snow and ice hit, the roadhouses—small log hotels heated by roaring fires—provided comfortable beds and good meals. Meals were $1.50, with beds at $1 per night. Baggage up to 25 pounds per passenger was carried free, with fares costing $125 one way, plus roadhouse expenses between Whitehorse and Dawson City. In later years, service was canceled if the temperature fell under 40 degrees below zero.

By 1905, the era of pick and shovel miners was ending in the Yukon, and machinery was beginning to be used. The Guggenheim syndicate moved in from New York and acquired control of the Eldorado, Bonanza, and other creeks. In 1906, the firm began construction on a $3 million, 70-mile-long ditch to bring in water for hydraulic mining. Additional millions went into the construction of a fleet of seven dredges to rip up the gravel, providing much-needed traffic for the WP&Y riverboats.

Stern-wheelers continued to be the main means of transportation, but many were already ashore and abandoned. Others came to more tragic ends. On September 25,

An early day White Pass & Yukon locomotive on the turntable at the railroad shops in Skagway in 1899. Skagway has remained the major maintenance terminal for the White Pass & Yukon Route. (Yukon Archives)

One of the many sights along the White Pass & Yukon Route is Hanging Rocks at Clifton. Steam locomotives passed this way half a century ago, just as the diesels do today. The locomotive pictured is No. 7, a Vauclain compound, one of the few of this type seen in the north. The engine is now on display at Minto Park in Dawson City. (Dedman photo from the Clifford Collection)

Jitneys line up at the right to whisk WP&Y passengers to Skagway hotels and nearby outgoing steamers when trains arrive from Whitehorse. This train is on Broadway, Skagway's main street, with Pioneer Hall in the near background. The tracks have been removed from Broadway, but Pioneer Hall remains in the same location today. (Yukon Archives)

1906, the Columbia was bound for Dawson on her last trip of the season. A crewmember decided to shoot ducks from the vessel's deck but unfortunately stumbled and fired into 3 tons of blasting powder on the bow.

Because of dwindling traffic, the Columbia was not replaced for five years.

In 1911, the B.Y.N. launched the Casca, a 1,079-ton stern-wheeler, which became the flagship of the fleet. Next was the Nasutlin and in 1913 the Yukon. By then, the B.Y.N. was engaged in a rate war with Northern Transportation, the major U.S. firm still on the river. Fares between Whitehorse and Dawson dropped from $26 to $5, a rate that officials of both companies knew would eventually bankrupt them. Consequently, they reached an agreement. In April 1914, the White Pass & Yukon bought Northern Transportation.

In 1923, new competition for the B.Y.N. arrived, and there was no answer. This time there could be no buy out. The competition would be a rival railroad—one with the backing of the American federal government. The Alaska Railroad was completed on Alaska's southern coast from Seward, 460 miles to Fairbanks. Additional stern-wheelers joined those already decaying along the river and at St. Michael. The B.Y.N. operated 11 vessels on the Canadian section of the river, but these gradually dwindled in number. The Dawson was wrecked in Rink Rapids in 1926, the Selkirk in the fall of 1930, and in 1936 Thirty-Mile River claimed both the Klondike and the Casca.

In 1937, a flurry of activity began along the river. A new 1,363-ton Klondike and a 1,300-ton Casca came from the shipyards at Whitehorse. In addition, the Keno was built and the Nasutlin was thoroughly overhauled. This was to be the last major building of stern-wheelers in North America. World War II gave the vessels another life, but completion of the Alaska Highway and roads originating from it once again reduced the need for transportation by water.

In 1951, a road linked the mining community of Mayo to Whitehorse, and ore from the mine went by WP&Y trucks. In 1953, the road was completed to Dawson City, and the remaining stern-wheelers were hauled onto the ways at Whitehorse, their working days over.

The Klondike was given a short reprieve following World War II when the White Pass, in conjunction with Canadian Pacific Airlines, spent $100,000 refurbishing her to stimulate the summer tourist trade. She was fitted with a dance floor, a lounge, a full bar, and even a $1,000 record player. The experiment failed, and in 1955 she too was hauled ashore at Whitehorse. Today, after a disastrous fire that destroyed the Whitehorse and the Casca, only the Keno at Dawson City and the Klondike at Whitehorse remain of the more than 200 stern-wheelers that at one time were the key to transportation in the Yukon.

As far as the railroad itself was concerned, there were good years and bad, but by the 1920s gold production had started to fall off and the drop continued through the 1930s. The Yukon's population declined precipitously. Some silver, lead, and zinc mining operations were developed in the Mayo district. The ore was carried to tidewater by the White Pass river and rail divisions, and the Yukon communities maintained a reasonable level of business during the summer months; but business dropped to an extremely low level during the winter.

Over the years, the railroad ran deeper and deeper into the red and at times was barely able to pay its bond interest. To keep solvent, the firm went into the wholesale petroleum business with a pipeline long before the introduction of tank cars to the railroad. Despite all this, during the winter months all senior officers of the company worked without salary.

June 1934 marked the inauguration of an aviation division by the White Pass & Yukon Route when President Herbert Wheeler hired Vernon Bookwalter, a veteran northern pilot who

During the summer of 1899, the White Pass & Yukon Railway terminated its run at Lake Bennett. Here trains turned around without the benefit of a turntable before heading back down the track to Skagway. Lake Bennett was a popular luncheon stop for travelers en route between Skagway and Whitehorse. (University of Washington Historical Library, Northwest Collection)

During the winter months, travel between Whitehorse, the terminus of the White Pass & Yukon Railway, and Dawson City, the territorial capital, was done by sledges. Passengers, well bundled in furs, stopped en route at various roadhouses between the two cities for meals, overnight accommodations, and an occasional warmup. No matter what the weather, it was a chilly way to travel. This sledge was operated by the White Pass & Yukon Route. (Yukon Archives)

was flying for Clyde Wann's Skagway Airlines, to operate the new division.

The White Pass's first aircraft was a Loening Keystone Commuter, a strange-looking flying boat that was soon nicknamed "The Duck." Bookwalter first brought the aircraft to Whitehorse, where company officials lost little time in taking advantage of its time-saving ability to line up wood along the Yukon River for the hungry boilers of the stern-wheelers that plied the waters between Whitehorse and Dawson. Normally, such a journey took weeks. Wood-buyer Wheeler was able to make the trip in a matter of hours, saving days of valuable time. The WP&Y was now in the aviation business.

Soon a 10-passenger Ford Tri-Motor, the largest such craft in the Yukon, was added for the route between Skagway, Whitehorse, Mayo, and Dawson City. In July 1935, Ed Wasson, a partner in Northern Air-

The White Pass & Yukon stern-wheeler Whitehorse makes its way along the Yukon between Whitehorse and Dawson City, pushing an empty barge back to Whitehorse. The stern-wheelers and barges were generally loaded to the gunwales on downstream trips to the Klondike. (Yukon Archives)

ways, was named chief pilot of the aviation division, and a Fairchild 82 was added to the fleet as headquarters was moved from Skagway to Whitehorse.

Other aircraft were added, the facilities at Whitehorse were improved, and airstrips were built at Carmacks, Minto, and Selkirk. As competition over the various routes increased—at times there were four or more aviation companies operating out of Whitehorse—the White Pass added a still larger plane to its fleet, a Curtis Condor, which carried 18 passengers. The Condor featured two 750-horsepower Wright Whirlwind engines, turning three-bladed control-pitch propellers, and cruised at 170 miles an hour.

In October 1937, the White Pass and Yukon gained a government contract to carry mail by air

This 18-passenger Curtis Condor was added to the White Pass & Yukon fleet as competition increased and fares dropped to as low as $5 per person between Whitehorse and Dawson City. A short time later, the WP&Y got out of the airline business, selling out to Grant McConachie, who later became president of Canadian Pacific Air. (Yukon Archives)

Whitehorse was the northern terminus of the White Pass & Yukon Railway and the jumping-off point for the Klondike. River steamers carried gold rushers down the Yukon to Dawson City during the summer months and then were stored ashore during the winter since ice closed the river to all navigation. This photo was taken in 1901. (Yukon Archives)

These three modes of transportation show the way people traveled in the days of the Klondike gold rush and for many years thereafter. At Carcross along the White Pass & Yukon Route are the following: an old White Pass & Yukon stage that was used to carry passengers between the railroad and the riverboats and to interior towns in the Yukon; the stern-wheeler Tutshi, later destroyed by fire, which plied the nearby waters of Nares and Tagish Lakes; and the historic little locomotive Duchess, which toiled for the Taku Tram, a WP&Y subsidiary before being retired and put on display. (Yukon Travel and Information)

The White Pass & Yukon Route entered the air age with this Loening Keystone Commuter amphibian aircraft in the mid-1930s. Nicknamed "The Duck," this plane was the first of several operated by the railroad in competition with other airlines in the Yukon. The plane flew between Whitehorse and Dawson City. (Yukon Archives)

between Dawson City, Mayo, and Whitehorse, where it was turned over to the United Air Transport. The United Air Transport was headed by Grant McConachie who would later become president of Canadian Pacific Air while still in his 30s. Another competitor in the area that flew from Juneau to Fairbanks via Whitehorse was Pacific Alaska Airways, a subsidiary of Pan American World Airways.

By 1939, more equipment was added, and just as with the boats, competition beat the price on the Dawson-Whitehorse Route down to $5, including luggage. No company could survive at this rate, and the various operators soon got together and established a tariff of $50 for a one-way ticket. More planes came and went, as did the pilots, but bad luck and bad weather plagued the aviation division, and late in 1939 President Herbert Wheeler sold the aviation division lock, stock, and barrel to McConachie and his Yukon Southern, as United Air Transport had become known.

A dramatic and sudden change came over the WP&Y with the impact of World War II. The system went to war and, despite being a Canadian corporation, donned the uniform of the U.S. Army. Its rail line and river system were strained to their limits carrying the military equipment and construction machinery that arrived at the docks at Skagway and was carried inland to help build the Alaska Highway (Alcan) and the Canol pipeline system. The company was leased to the Army on October 1, 1942, and the soldiers landed in the north country at the beginning of one of the coldest winters on record. Temperatures at Whitehorse dipped to 75 degrees below zero and stayed under 40 below for weeks at a time. Lt. Colonel William P. Wilson, who had been superintendent of the Burlington's frosty route across the Rockies in Colorado, was the commanding officer of the battalion.

One of the last survivors of the hundreds of Yukon River stern-wheelers, which provided river transportation during the early 20th century, is the Keno, now on display at Dawson City, Y.T. The Keno, along with the Klondike at Whitehorse, is all that remains of this once proud fleet of stern-wheelers owned by the White Pass and Yukon Route. (Clifford Collection)

The story of the first winter is one of hardship, privation, and enduring cold that cut more sharply than a razor. The workers in the 770th Railway Operating Battalion came from such railroads as the Southern Pacific, Texas Pacific, and Santa Fe, but they had never seen snow before, let alone the most frigid weather on the continent. An unending effort filled with hairbreadth escapes and daring rescues pulled them through, and they have not been forgotten in a country where such exploits are common. On one occasion, a train was buried under huge snowdrifts at Fraser Loop, about 30 miles from Skagway, and an avalanche occurred a few miles behind, cutting off all communication in either direction. The engine ran out of water, and crews were forced to draw the fires to keep from destroying the boiler. Coal for the stoves in the passenger cars ran out, and the few aboard chopped

The White Pass & Yukon played an important role in the construction of the Alcan Highway during the early days of World War II. Military construction equipment landed at Skagway and was transported to the Yukon via the WP&Y. A trainload is seen in front of the depot, heading north on Broadway. The dome of the Golden North Hotel is visible in the upper left-hand corner. (Clifford Collection)

up the interior appointments to keep from freezing in the 30-degree-below-zero temperatures. The food was soon exhausted.

After seven days in this precarious situation, a tractor traveling 40 miles from Carcross over the Lake Bennett ice and pulling three heavy sleds of supplies reached the trapped train. Everyone was rescued safely. Meanwhile, rotary plows working from both directions finally broke through the snow and restored traffic over the line.

As spring approached, the military received help in the form of narrow-gauge locomotives diverted from foreign delivery, which the soldiers called Gypsy Rose Lees since they were stripped for action. The army purchased additional locomotives from Colorado narrow-gauge lines, and freight cars, built for services elsewhere, were hurriedly diverted north for use by the WP&Y.

This brought about a complete change. Trains were highballed over the pass every few hours. On one occasion, the battalion put 34 trains through the Log Cabin station

An early day White Pass & Yukon train crosses one of the many trestles and bridges encountered en route to the Lake Bennett area. (University of Washington Historical Library, Northwest Collection)

in a single day. August 1943 was the record month, with 45,000 tons hauled an average of 1,500 tons a day.

The line was returned to civilian management on May 1, 1946, and it appeared that the end was near. Equipment was worn out, business was at a low ebb, and all that remained was old and inefficient. Even the employees were long past their prime but remained on the payroll because there was no retirement plan. The company became unpopular in both Skagway and Whitehorse. Damage claims on shipments ran high. Delayed shipments were blamed on the railroad whether it was responsible or not. The White Pass & Yukon became the scapegoat for just about everything that went wrong.

Container trucks were another means of transporting materials on the White Pass & Yukon. Containers could also be carried on trains, barges, and ships. (White Pass & Yukon Route)

In 1947, the last steam locomotives purchased by the WP&Y, No. 72 and No. 73, were put into service. These Baldwins were also the last steamers to operate over the line; they were retired from service on June 30, 1964. In 1951 a new Canadian company, the White Pass & Yukon Corporation, was formed. The next years were ones of growth and modernization. The White Pass & Yukon Corporation trains remain quaint, with old-fashioned coaches for the tourist trade, but its locomotives are modern, diesel units. Even more important, the line became a real pioneer in containerization. It made the big move in the early 1950s. Although not yet booming, prospecting and exploration were on the upswing and had produced a slight increase in transportation costs and a secure relationship to the future of the rail line and the territory.

The White Pass & Yukon Corporation entered into containerization with the Clifford J. Rogers, the world's first ship designed specifically to handle containers and containerized freight. The 4,000-ton Rogers was named after the longtime president and general manager of the railroad, who had worked his way up through the ranks from an assistant in the freight office at Dawson City in 1904 to chief executive officer of the company. The Rogers made more than 500 trips between Vancouver and Skagway in 10 years of service before it gave way to the new White Pass container ships of advanced design, the Frank H. Brown and the Klondike. Both are 6,000-ton vessels, with the Brown (named for the president of the White Pass & Yukon Corporation) launched in April 1965 and the Klondike a few months later. Both have since been converted to barges and are towed between Vancouver and Skagway by ocean-going tugs.

The White Pass & Yukon Corporation used other means of transportation, as well as the railroad and oil pipeline, over the mountain passes. Ore was trucked from mines in the interior of the Yukon to the railroad in specially designed cargo units. The complete unit was placed aboard the White Pass & Yukon freight cars and moved to the docks at Skagway for shipment to other parts of the world. (White Pass & Yukon Route)

On October 15, 1969, a fire that started in a caboose under repair destroyed six buildings in the White Pass & Yukon roundhouse and shop complex, including the roundhouse, blacksmith shop, boiler room, oil room, and the worker's wash and lunchroom building. Also lost in the blaze were two of the new diesel locomotives, Nos. 102 and 105; a switcher, No. 3; an old steam engine, No. 72; one caboose, one parlor car, and a flatcar. The loss was estimated in the millions of dollars. Earlier, in December 1943, a fire in the roundhouse at Whitehorse had damaged two locomotives, Nos. 10 and 14, which were later returned to Seattle and scrapped in December 1945.

Federal Industries Ltd., a Winnipeg-based firm, acquired the White Pass & Yukon Corporation, Ltd., in June 1973, including the shares of the major stockholder, Angelo American Corporation of Canada, Ltd.[3] A reorganization program was put into effect.

A slacking off in the mining industry in the Yukon and the opening of the Skagway-Carcross highway cut into traffic and revenues. The company headquarters was eventually moved to Whitehorse.

In 1982, the end arrived for the WP&Y--or so it seemed. Mine closures in the Yukon sapped the revenue base of the railroad, and without freight traffic there was not enough financial justification for the line to continue. After the summer season, the railroad shut down. Ironically, 1982 was the year that Mikado No. 73 had been returned to service as an attraction to the increasing numbers of tourists that wanted to ride the White Pass. All dressed up, but with no place to go, its fires were again banked.

Two container car trains pass one another at Lake Bennett between Skagway and Whitehorse on the White Pass & Yukon Route. One of the trains also has a series of passenger coaches and one or two cars for carrying automobiles. Cargo traffic was a crucial part of the White Pass & Yukon operation. Lake Bennett was the point from which the sourdoughs of '98 built their boats and rafts for the trip down the lake and the Yukon River to the Klondike gold fields. (White Pass & Yukon Route)

---

[3] Federal Industries is also owner of the Neptune Terminals Ltd., a Vancouver-area mineral terminal.

Over the next few years, some equipment was sold--the Montreal diesels and container cars headed to South America and the undelivered Bombardier units finding a new home at U.S. Gypsum's Plaster City, California railroad.

Mike Heney's Klondike dream, however, was not quite ready to die, and in 1988 the railroad re-opened as tourist line initially hauling passengers to White Pass and return. The success of the line has grown with each operating season and the length of line gradually increased--first to Fraser, then Lake Bennett, and during the 1998 season, all the way to Carcross. New passenger equipment has been added and the venerable GE shovel-noses haul more than 75,000 passengers each season over the railroad built by gold fever. The railroad will celebrate its 100th anniversary back on sound financial footing with a bright future. It appears that the slim-gauge iron-ponies of the White Pass will be retracing the Trail of 98 for many years into the future.

White Pass & Yukon Route

Steam Locomotive Roster

Road No.	Wheel Arr.	Builder	C/N	Year	Cylinders	Drivers	Notes
Duchess							Probably never operated as WP&Y. See Taku Tram.
1	2-6-0	Brooks	Note 1	1881	14-½ x18	42"	New boiler and cylinders, 1900; built for Utah & Northern, sold November 1889; to Columbia & Puget Sound 2nd No. 3, sold 1897; to WP&Y, renumbered 51, Taku Tram 1919–1931, retired 1941, on display in Whitehorse, Y.T.
2	2-6-0	Brooks	Note 1	1881	14-½ x18	42"	New boiler and cylinders, 1900; built for Utah & Northern, sold 1890; to Columbia & Puget Sound 2nd No. 4, sold 1898; to WP&Y, renumbered 52, Taku Tram 1931–1937, on display in Skagway, AK.
3	2-8-0	Grant		August 1882	15-½ x20	36"	Built for Toledo Cincinnati & St. Louis No. 63, returned; to Grant Locomotive Works, sold 1887; to Columbia & Puget Sound No. 9, sold 1898; to WP&Y, renumbered 53, scrapped 1918, Seattle, WA.

(Following page) One of the White Pass & Yukon Corporation container ships, the *Frank F. Brown,* was converted to a barge for towing by ocean-going tugs. The vessel is pictured here as it plies the waters of Lynn Canal between Skagway and Vancouver, B.C., under its own power. The vessels carried rich minerals from the Yukon to markets in western Canada. (White Pass & Yukon Route)

The White Pass & Yukon Route highway division headquarters at Whitehorse. The WP&Y used trains, trucks, barges, and a pipeline to transport materials in the far north. (White Pass & Yukon Route)

Steam Locomotive Roster (continued)

Road No.	Wheel Arr.	Builder	C/N	Year	Cylinders	Drivers	Notes
4 (first)	4-4-0	Baldwin	4294	March 1878	12x16	42"	Built for Olympia & Chehalis Valley No. 1 "E.H. Quimette," sold May 1891 to Columbia & Puget Sound No. 10, sold 1898; to WP&Y, renumbered 54, sold 1905; to Tanana Mines Railway No. 50, sold in January 1907 to Tanana Valley Railroad No. 50, sold 1917; to AEC No. 50, transferred in 1923 to Alaska RR No. 50, retired before 1924, scrapped 1930.
4 (second)	2-6-2	Baldwin	37564	March 1912	15x20	37"	Built for Klondike Mines Railway No. 4, sold July 1942; to WP&Y, retired 1952, sold 1955; to Oak Creek Central, transferred 1960; to Peppermint & Northwestern RR, sold 1964; to Petticoat Junction RR, sold 1972; to Gold Nugget Junction RR, sold September 1984; to Midwest Central RR, sold October 1984; to Steve Wild, stored. Note 2.
5	2-8-0	Baldwin	7597	May 1885	15x18	36-½"	Built for Columbia & Puget Sound No. 8, sold 1897; to WP&Y, renumbered 55, sold 1905; to Klondike Mines Railway No. 2, on display Dawson City Y.T., 1961. Note 2.
6	2-8-0	Baldwin	16455	January 1899	11-½ & 19x20	38"	Renumbered 56, scrapped 1938.
7	2-8-0	Baldwin	16456	January 1899	11-½ & 19x20	38"	Renumbered 57, sold 1906; to Klondike Mines Railway No. 3, on display Dawson City, Y.T., 1961. Note 2.
8	3-truck	Climax	167	December 1897	14x14	32"	The first 3-truck Climax, only narrow-gauge 3-truck Climax; built for Colorado & Northwestern No. 2, sold 1898; to Pacific Contract Co. No. 8, sold 1900; to WP&Y No. 8; to White Star Lumber Co., sold 1903 (standard gauge); to Maytown Lumber Co. (standard gauge).
51	2-6-0	Brooks		1881			See No. 1.
52	2-6-0	Brooks		1881			See No. 2.
53	2-8-0	Grant		August 1882			See No. 3.
54	4-4-0	Baldwin	4294	March 1878			See No. 4 (first).
55	2-8-0	Baldwin	7597	May 1885			See No. 5.
56	2-8-0	Baldwin	16455	January 1899			See No. 6.
57	2-8-0	Baldwin	16456	January 1899			See No. 7.
58	3-truck	Climax	167	December 1897	14x14	32"	See No. 8.
59	4-6-0	Baldwin	17749	May 1900	17x20	42'	Scrapped 1941.
60	4-6-0	Baldwin	17750	May 1900	17x20	42"	Retired 1942, used as rip rap, 1949, removed from river about 1988.
61	2-8-0	Baldwin	17814	June 1900	17x20	38"	Retired 1944, used as rip rap, 1949, removed from river about 1988.
62	4-6-0	Baldwin	17895	June 1900	17x22	44"	Retired 1945, used as rip rap, 1949.

Steam Locomotive Roster (continued)

Road No.	Wheel Arr.	Builder	C/N	Year	Cylinders	Drivers	Notes
63	2-6-0	Brooks	522	1881	14x18	41"	Built for Kansas Central Railway No. 7 (UP No. 102, 1885) "Sidney Dillon," sold 1890; to Trail Creek Tramway, sold 1896; to Columbia & Western Railway, sold 1899; to Canadian Pacific Railway, sold 1900; to WP&Y, sold 1902; to Klondike Mines Railway No. 1, on display Dawson City Y.T., 1961. Note 2.
64	2-6-0	Hinkley	1878				Trail Creek Tramway No. 2, sold 1896; to Columbia & Western Railway No. 2, sold 1899; to Canadian Pacific Railway, sold 1900; to WP&Y, scrapped 1918.

The White Pass & Yukon roundhouse and shop facilities at Skagway as they appeared prior to the fire of October 15, 1969, which destroyed six buildings, two new diesel locomotives, and other equipment. (Dedman Photo Shop)

Steam Locomotive Roster *(continued)*

Road No.	Wheel Arr.	Builder	C/N	Year	Cylinders	Drivers	Notes
65	2-6-0	Brooks	578	1881	14x18	42"	Built for Kansas Central Railway No. 8 (UP No. 103, 1885), sold 1890; to Trail Creek Tramway No. 3, sold April 1896; to Columbia & Western Railway No. 3, sold 1898; to Canadian Pacific Railway, sold August 1900; to WP&Y, sold September 1906; to Tanana Mines Railway No. 51, sold in January 1907 to Tanana Valley Railroad No. 51, sold in December 1917 to AEC No. 51, transferred in 1923 to Alaska Railroad No. 51, retired before 1924, scrapped, 1930.

Little remained of the roundhouse after the fire of October 15, 1969, destroyed the WP&Y facility at Skagway. These are the remains of two new diesel locomotives and a switcher that were totally destroyed. The little No. 52 steam locomotive at the far end was out of reach of the flames. Six buildings were destroyed in the blaze, and the damage was estimated to be in the millions of dollars. (Anchorage Historical and Fine Arts Museum)

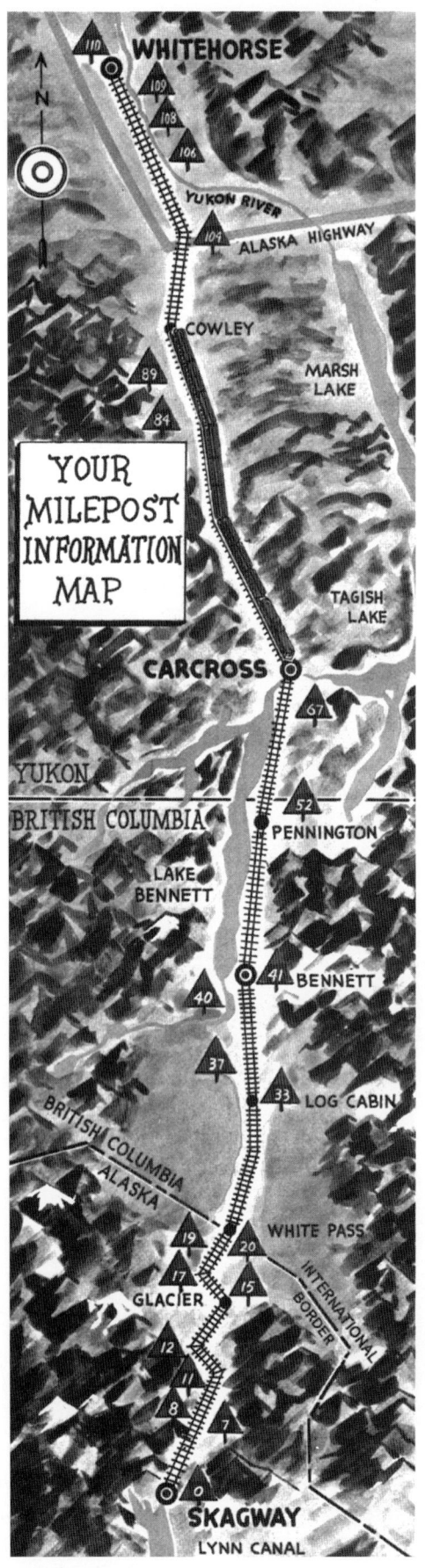

Points of Interest

(Numbers represent miles from Skagway)

67	**Carcross**	Famous old Yukon town on the Trail of '98.
41	**Lake Bennett**	Old sourdough stopping place where boats were built to float down the Yukon to the Klondike. Famous "homestyle" meals served.
40	**Lake Linderman**	Head of navigation during the gold rush.
37	**Beaver Lake**	Home of many beaver.
33	**Log Cabin**	Start of the Fan Tan Gold Tail trail to Atlin. Once a gold rush town.
20	**White Pass Summit**	Elevation 2,900 feet. International Boundary.
19	**Dead Horse Gulch**	Named for 3,000 pack animals that died here during the gold rush of '98.
17	**Inspiration Point**	"Camera Stop" Magnificent scenery—historical spot.
15	**Tunnel Mountain**	White Pass Railway tunnel 1,000 feet above the floor of the gulch. Magnificent view.
12	**Bridal Veil Falls**	As many as twenty-two cataracts have been seen tumbling down the gorge.
11	**Black Cross Rock**	1,000-ton granite block buried two men during blasting in 1898. The Black Cross marks their resting place.
8	**Clifton**	See huge over-hanging rock.
7	**Rocky Point**	Magnificent view. Railway crosses trail of '98.
0	**Skagway**	The Gateway to the Yukon. Once a city of 15,000 during the gold rush. Headquarters for the White Pass & Yukon Railway.

A map of the White Pass & Yukon Route from Mile 0 in Skagway to Mile 110 in Whitehorse. Most of the map and explanations pertain to the sections between Skagway and Carcross, probably some of the most interesting and historic trackage in North America. (Clifford Collection)

Steam Locomotive Roster *(continued)*

Road No.	Wheel Arr.	Builder	C/N	Year	Cylinders	Drivers	Notes
66	4-6-0	Baldwin	18964	May 1901	17x20	42"	Retired 1953, used as rip rap, October, 1967.
67	4-6-0	Baldwin	18965	May 1901	17x20	42"	Retired 1941, used as rip rap, 1951.
68	2-8-0	Baldwin	30998	June 1907	19x22	40"	Destroyed in rock slide, August 1917.
69	2-8-0	Baldwin	32962	June 1908	21x22	44"	Damaged in roundhouse fire February 12, 1932, rebuilt to oil-burner, 1951, cab from No. 66; to Black Hills Central, May 1956; to Nebraska Midland, 1973, "Klondike Casey," operating.
70	2-8-2	Baldwin	62234	May 1938	17x22	44"	To Dollywood Park, 190-class tender, operating.
71	2-8-2	Baldwin	62257	January 1939	17x22	44"	To Dollywood Park "Cinderella," 190-class tender, operating.
72	2-8-2	Baldwin	73351	May 1947	17x22	44"	Destroyed in roundhouse fire 1969; to Dollywood Park as spare parts.
73	2-8-2	Baldwin	73352	May 1947	17x22	44"	Operating.
80	2-8-2	Alco	61980	May 1920	19x20	44"	Built for Sumpter Valley RY No. 20 (2nd No. 101), sold 1940; to WP&Y No. 80, sold August 1977; to Sumpter Valley No. 20, on display.
81	2-8-2	Alco	61981	May 1920	19x20	44"	Built for Sumpter Valley RY No. 19 (2nd No. 102), sold 1940; to WP&Y No. 81, sold August 1977; to Sumpter Valley No. 19, on display.

This Brooks 2-6-0 locomotive, the first to arrive in Alaska for the White Pass and Yukon Railroad, is on display in downtown Skagway. Numbered No. 2 and later renumbered to No. 52 when it was rebuilt in 1900, this historic narrow-gauge locomotive also saw service with the Taku Tram before being retired in 1940. (H. Clifford)

USA Engines

U.S. Army Transportation Corps locomotives remaining on the railroad in 1946 were turned over to the White Pass & Yukon.

Road No.	Wheel Arr.	Builder	C/N	Year	Cylinders	Drivers	Notes
10	4-6-0	Baldwin	42766	January 1916	16x22	45"	Built for ET&WNC No. 10, sold 1942, rebuilt at NP S. Tacoma shops; to U.S.A. (WP&Y), damaged by fire, December 1944, scrapped December 1945.
14	4-6-0	Baldwin	52406	September 1919	16x22	45"	Built for ET&WNC No. 14, sold 1942, rebuilt at NP S. Tacoma shops; to U.S.A. (WP&Y), damaged by fire, December 1944, scrapped December 1945.
20	2-8-0	Baldwin	11355	December 1890	16x20	37	Built for Utah & Northern No. 272, sold 1890; to Denver, Leadville & Gunnison No. 272, sold 1898; to Colorado & Southern No. 69, sold April 1943; to U.S.A. No. 3920 (WP&Y), scrapped April, 1945, Seattle, WA.
21	2-8-0	Baldwin	11356	December 1890	16x20	37"	Built for Utah & Northern No. 273, sold 1890; to Denver, Leadville & Gunnison No. 273, sold 1898; to Colorado & Southern No. 70, sold April 1943; to U.S.A. No. 3921 (WP&Y), scrapped January 1945, Seattle, WA; converted to oil burner in 1941.
22	2-8-0	Baldwin	24109	January 1904	16x20	37"	Built for Silverton Northern No. 3, sold 1942; to U.S.A. No. 2922, (WP&Y), retired 1944, scrapped 1945, Seattle, WA.

Two modes of White Pass & Yukon Route transportation are visible here. The Brooks 2-6-0 locomotive No. 51, built in 1881 and acquired in 1898 by the WP&Y from the Columbia & Puget Sound Railroad, was originally No. 1 on the railroad but numbered No. 51 following its reconstruction in 1900. The engine was retired in 1941 and put on display at Whitehorse, along with one of the White Pass horse-drawn sledges, which were used between Whitehorse and Dawson City during the winter months. (H. Clifford)

USA Engines (continued)

Road No.	Wheel Arr.	Builder	C/N	Year	Cylinders	Drivers	Notes
23	2-8-0	Baldwin	27977	April 1906	16x20	37"	Built for Silverton Northern No. 4, sold 1942; to U.S.A. No. 2923, (WP&Y), retired 1944, scrapped 1945, Seattle, WA.
24	2-8-0	Baldwin	24130	December 1904	16x20	37"	Built for Silverton, Gladstone & Northerly No. 34, sold January 1915; to Silverton Northern No. 34, sold October 1942; to WP&Y, unserviceable probably for parts, scrapped 1951, Skagway, AK.
152	4-6-0	Baldwin	53296	June 1920	14x20	44"	Ex–Alaska Railroad No. 152, retired 1930, to Skagway April 1943; probably never operated, to Seattle 1943; to Antelope & Western No. 2; to Camino, Cable & Northern No. 2, Camino, CA; to Keystone Railway Equipment Company; to Huckleberry Railroad, No. 2, Flint, MI, operating.

Locomotive No. 5, a Baldwin built in 1885, saw a lot of action on the White Pass & Yukon Route before being sold to the Klondike Mines Railway in 1904. The locomotive, KMR's No. 2, is now on display at Minto Park in Dawson City. (Clifford Collection)

USA Engines (continued)

Road No.	Wheel Arr.	Builder	C/N	Year	Cylinders	Drivers	Notes
190	2-8-2	Baldwin	69425	February 1943	16x24	48"	Sold 1960; to Tweetsie RR No. 190, "Yukon Queen," operating.
191	2-8-2	Baldwin	69426	February 1943	16x24	48"	Scrapped 1951.
192	2-8-2	Baldwin	69427	February 1943	16x24	48"	Sold 1961; to Rebel RR No. 192, "Klondike Kate;" to Dollywood Park, No. 192, "Klondike Kate."
193	2-8-2	Baldwin	69428	February 1943	16x24	48"	Scrapped 1951.
194	2-8-2	Baldwin	69429	February 1943	16x24	48"	Scrapped 1951.
195	2-8-2	Baldwin	69430	February 1943	16x24	48"	On display at Skagway, AK, 1962.
196	2-8-2	Baldwin	69431	February 1943	16x24	48"	Used as rip rap at Skagway, AK, 1967.
197	2-8-2	Baldwin	69432	February 1943	16x24	48"	Scrapped 1945.
198	2-8-2	Baldwin	69433	February 1943	16x24	48"	To Auburn, WA, sold 1948; to Hacienda Casa Grande Railroad, Chicama, Peru.
199	2-8-2	Baldwin	69434	February 1943	16x24	48"	To Auburn, WA, sold 1948; to Hacienda Casa Grande Railroad, Chicama, Peru.
200	2-8-2	Baldwin	69435	February 1943	16x24	48"	To Auburn, WA, sold 1948; to Hacienda Casa Grande Railroad, Chicama, Peru.

White Pass & Yukon locomotives Nos. 4 and 5, along with some passenger coaches, are awaiting shipment to Skagway on the Seattle docks in 1897. No. 4, a Baldwin built in 1878, came from the Columbia & Puget Sound Railroad and later went to the Tanana Valley Railroad and Alaska Railroad. No. 5 was also obtained from the Columbia & Puget Sound Railroad and eventually went to the Klondike Mines Railway. (Yukon Archives)

An early White Pass & Yukon excursion train stops in at White Pass summit. Sightseeing cars were constructed from flatcars with open sides and a roof. Passengers sat on benches. (Clifford Collection)

This Baldwin 2-6-2 is just out of the WP&Y shops in Skagway, her career in Alaska ended. She was shipped east to a succession of tourist railroads. It was built in 1912 for the Klondike Mines Railway as the No. 4 locomotive and later became White Pass & Yukon No. 4 (2nd). (H. L. Berry Collection)

USA Engines (continued)

Road No.	Wheel Arr.	Builder	C/N	Year	Cylinders	Drivers	Notes
250	2-8-2	Alco	64981	September 1923	18x22	44"	Built for D&RGW No. 470, sold 1942; to U.S.A. (WP&Y), scrapped 1944, Seattle, WA.
251	2-8-2	Alco	64982	September 1923	18x22	44"	Built for D&RGW No. 471, sold 1942; to U.S.A. (WP&Y), scrapped 1945, Seattle, WA.
252	2-8-2	Alco	64983	September 1923	18x22	44"	Built for D&RGW No. 472, sold 1942; to U.S.A. (WP&Y), scrapped 1945, Ogden, UT.
253	2-8-2	Alco	64985	September 1923	18x22	44"	Built for D&RGW No. 474, sold 1942; to U.S.A. (WP&Y), scrapped 1945, Seattle, WA.
254	2-8-2	Alco	64986	September 1923	18x22	44"	Built for D&RGW No. 475, sold 1942; to U.S.A. (WP&Y), scrapped 1945, Seattle, WA.
255	2-8-2	Alco	64988	September 1923	18x22	44"	Built for D&RGW No. 477, sold 1942; to U.S.A. (WP&Y), scrapped 1945, Seattle, WA.
256	2-8-2	Alco	64990	September 1923	18x22	44"	Built for D&RGW No. 479, sold 1942; to U.S.A. (WP&Y), scrapped 1945, Seattle, WA.

The renumbering of locomotives No. 1–No. 8 to No. 51–No. 58 occurred in 1900.

Locomotives No. 190–No. 200, originally ordered as meter-gauge for Iran, were regauged to (or possibly built as) 36" and diverted to WP&Y.

Note 1: This class of locomotives was numbered 23–42 on the U&N. The Brooks builder's numbers for these engines were between 494 and 627 (nonconsecutive).

Note 2: The assets of the Klondike Mines Railway became part of Yukon Consolidated Gold Corporation about 1925. The locomotives were not relettered (KMR previously abandoned).

A trainload of Porter saddle-tankers is en route to Whitehorse on the White Pass & Yukon Route. The little locomotives were used by the Detroit-Yukon Mining Company near Dawson City. The WP&Y locomotive is No. 59, a Baldwin 4-6-0 built in 1900 for the railroad. (Yukon Archives)

Now with the Nebraska Midland, this locomotive is known as Klondike Casey. It was retired from the WP&Y in 1954 after almost a half-century of service, where it was known as the "Gila Monster." (Dedman Photo from the Clifford Collection)

One of the locomotives acquired by the WP&Y during World War II was this Baldwin 2-8-2. This class of locomotives was originally ordered as meter-gauge for export by the Army Corps of Engineers but was converted for use on the White Pass & Yukon. Klondike Kate was retired in 1960 and acquired by the Rebel Railroad as a tourist attraction in 1961. (Dedman Photo from the Clifford Collection)

# White Pass & Yukon Route

Diesel/Gas Locomotive Roster

Road No.	Builder	C/N	Year	Model	Rated HP	Notes
	WIW	68	1937		90 hp	Taku Tram, 1937–1951 (stored).
1	GE	29191	June 1947	25 ton	150 hp	Ex-Colorado Fuel & Iron Co. No. 6, retired 1979, donated 1985 to the B.C. Forest Museum, Duncan, B.C. Canada.
2	GE	29195	June 1947	25 ton	150 hp	Ex-Colorado Fuel & Iron Co. No. 10, retired 1972, scrapped 1985, North Vancouver, B.C.
3 (first)	FOR		1924		27 hp	Shop switcher, ex-Frye-Bruhn Co., scrapped 1946.
3 (second)	PLY	4471	July 1942	20 ton ML-6	175 hp	Ex-U.S. Army No. 7651, renumbered 1946 to WP&Y, No. 3, destroyed in roundhouse fire, 1969.
81	GE	32933	June 1957		800 hp	Ex-U.S. Army No. 3000, loaned to D&RGW for testing at Durango, CO, to WP&Y, sold to Bandegua (Cia de Desarollo Bananero de Guatemala) No. 314.
90	GE	32060	June 1954	GEX3341	800 hp*	Operating, currently rated at 890 hp.
91	GE	32061	June 1954	GEX3341	800 hp*	Operating, currently rated at 890 hp.
92	GE	32709	December 1956	GEX3341	800 hp*	Operating, currently rated at 890 hp.
93	GE	32710	December 1956	GEX3341	800 hp*	Operating, damaged in derailment, June 24, 1965, retrieved, 1966, to CPR Ogden shop, 1967, returned, 1969, currently rated at 890 hp.
94	GE	32711	December 1956	GEX3341	800 hp*	Operating, currently rated at 890 hp.

This was once a very familiar scene on the waterfront at Skagway. Still using the dock area originally developed by Captain Billy Moore, White Pass and Yukon Route trains picked up cruise ship passengers on the dock for a scenic trip over historic White Pass to Lake Bennett and Whitehorse. The steam locomotive, No. 70, a Baldwin 2-8-2 built in 1938 and retired in 1963, was sold to Dollywood Park for restoration and use on its theme park tourist railroad. (Dedman's Photo Shop)

Chapter 1: White Pass & Yukon Route 51

The skeleton of the old log church at Lake Bennett is a constant reminder of the romance and history of the gold rush of 1898. Bennett was the jumping-off point for thousands as they took their boats, scows, and barges into the unknown waters of the north to make their way to the Klondike. The church was a popular visitor's attraction during the luncheon stop at Bennett on WP&Y trains traveling between Skagway and Whitehorse. (Yukon Travel and Information)

White Pass snowplow No. 1 and steam locomotive No. 73 were part of the display of early day railroad equipment at Lake Bennett. Now returned to service, the locomotive is a Baldwin 2-8-2 built in 1947. Lake Bennett was the building and launching point for a fleet of boats and scows that the Klondike stampeders used to make their way down the various lakes to the Yukon River and Dawson City. (H. Clifford)

White Pass & Yukon snowplow No. 2 and locomotive No. 81 are loaded aboard a train in Seattle en route to the Sumpter Valley Railroad in Oregon. No. 81, formerly Sumpter Valley No. 19, was shipped north to Skagway for use on the White Pass & Yukon in 1940. After its retirement in 1957, it was stored and was only recently returned to the Sumpter Valley Railroad—now a tourist operation—where it has been restored and put back into service. The rotary is now in Como, Colorado. (H. Clifford)

Diesel Locomotive Roster (continued)

Road No.	Builder	C/N	Year	Model	Rated HP	Notes
95	GE	34592	March 1963	GEX3341	890 hp	Operating - Damaged in derailment, June 24, 1965, retrieved, 1966, to CPR Ogden shop, 1967, returned, 1969.
96	GE	34593	March 1963	GEX3341	890 hp	Operating.
97	GE	34594	March 1963	GEX3341	890 hp	Operating.
98	GE	35790	May 1966	GEX3341	990 hp	Operating.
99	GE	35791	May 1966	GEX3341	990 hp	Operating.
100	GE	35792	May 1966	GEX3341	990 hp	Operating.
101	Alco/MLW	602301	May 1969	DL535E	1200 hp	Sold to Sociedad Colombiana de Ferroviaro, November, 1992. Repurchased by WP&Y, 1999.
102	Alco/MLW	602302	May 1969	DL535E	1200 hp	Destroyed in roundhouse fire 1969, scrapped 1993.
103	Alco/MLW	602303	May 1969	DL535E	1200 hp	Sold to Sociedad Colombiana de Ferroviaro, November 1992. Repurchased by WP&Y, 1999.
104	Alco/MLW	602304	May 1969	DL535E	1200 hp	Sold to Sociedad Colombiana de Ferroviaro, November 1992. Repurchased by WP&Y, 1999.
105	Alco/MLW	602305	May 1969	DL535E	1200 hp	Destroyed in roundhouse fire 1969, scrapped 1993.
106	Alco/MLW	602306	May 1969	DL535E	1200 hp	Sold to Sociedad Colombiana de Ferroviaro, November 1992. Repurchased by WP&Y, 1999.
107	Alco/MLW	602307	May 1969	DL535E	1200 hp	Sold to Sociedad Colombiana de Ferroviaro, November 1992. Repurchased by WP&Y, 1999.
108	MLW	605401	December 1971	DL535E	1200 hp	Operating.

Today the Skagway waterfront is similar to the scene above. The dock, cruise ship, and train coaches haven't changed much, but a modernized diesel locomotive now provides motive power. The General Electric diesel No. 90 was built in 1954 for the White Pass & Yukon operation. (Dedman's Photo Shop)

Completed in 1901, this steel bridge over Dead Horse Gulch was just one of the many marvels of the White Pass & Yukon Route. The bridge was bypassed by a shorter bridge and tunnel but was in use for more than 65 years. A covered turntable, used while a temporary switchback was in operation, is visible at the far left. (Dedman's Photo Shop)

Brand-spanking new, the first diesel-electric locomotive on the White Pass & Yukon is tested outside the railroad shops at Skagway. Locomotive No. 90 was acquired in June 1954 to allow the retirement of war-weary equipment. (Dedman Photo from Clifford Collection)

These two photos illustrate two different eras in WP&Y history. The upper photo, taken in the late 1940s or early 1950s, depicts the last stand of steam power on the railroad. The lower photo, taken between 1957 and 1967, shows the transition to diesel power. The Skagway depot in the background has changed little. (Dedman Photos from Clifford Collection)

Diesel Locomotive Roster *(continued)*

Road No.	Builder	C/N	Year	Model	Rated HP	Notes
109	MLW	605402	December 1971	DL535E	1200 hp	Operating.
110	MLW	605403	December 1971	DL535E	1200 hp	Operating.
111	BOM	612301	July 1982	DL535E	1200 hp	Never delivered. Sold to U.S. Gypsum, Plaster City, CA to replace No. 113.
112	BOM	612302	July 1982	DL535E	1200 hp	Never delivered. Sold to U.S. Gypsum, Plaster City, CA, 1991.
113	BOM	612303	July 1982	DL535E	1200 hp	Never delivered. Sold to U.S. Gypsum, Plaster City, CA, 1991, destroyed in accident.
114	BOM	612304	July 1982	DL535E	1200 hp	Delivered 1995, operating.

Alco/MLW American Locomotive Company/Montreal Locomotive Works
BOM Bombardier Inc.
FOR Fordson
GE General Electric
MLW Montreal Locomotive Works
PLY Plymouth Locomotive Works
WIW Westminster Iron Works

* The 90-series locomotives are equipped with Alco 251-type prime movers. With minimal modification, the horsepower of these engines can be modified.

A White Pass & Yukon Route train at Carcross (formerly Caribou Crossing) hauls tub-shaped ore containers of lead-zinc concentrate to the terminal at Skagway. From there it was shipped to U.S. and Canadian smelters for processing. (White Pass & Yukon Route)

Passengers in front of the old log depot at Whitehorse await the arrival of the daily White Pass & Yukon Route train from the yards. The railroad connected the two historic gold rush towns with one of the most scenic rail trips in the world. The narrow-gauge trains closely followed the route taken by the gold seekers of 1898. (Yukon Travel and Information)

A White Pass & Yukon Route passenger train along the shores of scenic Fraser Lake (Beernard Lake) in British Columbia. The White Pass & Yukon follows the original Trail of '98 from Skagway to Whitehorse, Y.T. Until 1982, modern diesel locomotives pulled trains formerly headed by small narrow-gauge steam locomotives. (White Pass & Yukon Route)

Chapter 2

Taku Tram

Just as the Atlin gold rush was a spin-off of the Klondike gold rush, the Taku Tram became a spin-off of the White Pass & Yukon Railway.

The Atlin gold strike occurred in July 1898. Fifteen hundred White Pass & Yukon Railway construction workers (and many others) abandoned their jobs with the railroad to join in the rush, taking railroad-owned picks and shovels with them on the stampede.

At first, the Atlin rush seemed like the real thing, and it instigated various railroad construction projects. In January 1899, a group of Victoria businessmen obtained a charter from the British Columbia Legislature to build a tramway or railroad. This tramway, known as the Atlin Short Line Railway and Navigation Company, was to be built across the isthmus from Taku Arm near the mouth of the Atlintoo River to Scotia Bay on the west shore of Atlin Lake. This route was a shortcut from the headwaters of the Yukon River, via the White Pass & Yukon Route from Skagway to the gold fields of the Atlin area. The new company also got permission to construct telegraph lines, to utilize Pine Creek for the production of electric power, and to build wharves and other facilities for steamship services.

Reaching Atlin Lake, the site of the gold strike, had been complicated before the tram was built. Passengers and freight had to be transferred from the White Pass & Yukon Railway to one of the lake steamers at Bennett or Carcross for the trip through Bennett or Nares Lakes. Travel had continued for 70 miles down Tagish Lake to Taku,

Early day transportation across the Taku Isthmus was via horse-drawn cars on wooden rails as seen here. Later the Taku Tram carried passengers and freight across this narrow arm of land between the Taku Inlet (Taku Arm) and Atlin Lake. (University of Washington Library)

where a portage of 2 miles was required before reloading at Scotia Bay aboard another steamer for the trip across the lake to the community of Atlin.

On June 6, 1899, J. H. Brownlee of the Atlin Short Line Railway and Navigation Company officially opened the tramway as a wooden railed tram road for hauling freight across the portage from Scotia Bay to Taku. Brownlee's firm also constructed wharves at Scotia Bay and Taku. The John Irving Navigation Company temporarily took control of the Atlin Short Line during the navigation season of 1899, but Brownlee reassumed direction of the line in the fall of the same year.

Not to be outdone, Captain John Irving planned a second tramway across the peninsula to compete with the Brownlee concern, and in March 1900 construction began. But protests from Brownlee's group caused the work to be temporarily suspended. By May, Irving had acquired the rival tramway. Irving's reign was short-lived: in June of that year, the White Pass & Yukon bought out the Irving Navigation Company's assets, steamers, wharves, and tramway and completed the railroad across the isthmus. The line was known as the Taku Tram or locally as the Taku Central or Taku Limited.

Both the Canadian Development Corporation and the White Pass and Yukon had realized the financial significance of a transportation monopoly in the gold country, so the WP&Y also purchased all remaining independent transportation companies in the area. The WP&Y thus gained control of all transit to the mining camps between Atlin, Carcross, and other areas in British Columbia and the Yukon.

Following these WP&Y acquisitions, a narrow-gauge rail system was completed between Taku and Scotia Bay. On July 18, 1900, the first train ran across the isthmus, over what was probably the shortest railroad in Canada. One-way fare was $2. Passengers sat on limited seating (for 14) or on their baggage during the journey. There was no turntable or wye, so the train had to travel forward from Taku to Scotia Bay and backward on the return trip. Grades on the run reached up to 7 percent, and often the

One of the North Country's most historic locomotives is the little Duchess, which saw service on the Taku Tram. Here the narrow-gauge locomotive is pulling one of the tram's passenger cars. The presence of coach No. 232 dates this photo to mid-1917 and identifies the steamer in the background as the newly constructed "Tutshi." The Duchess is now on display at Carcross. (Canadian Pacific Archives)

locomotive had to take a run at the hill to pull the 12-ton passenger car over the summit. Sometimes the passengers disembarked and helped push.

Another unusual feature of the Taku Tram was that the original passenger car was fully air-conditioned—it was in fact open-air. Swallows built their nests in the inside corners, and when the car moved from one end of the line to the other, they flew alongside it. The moment the train stopped, they reboarded. A swallow sitting on eggs in its nest stayed put when the train set out. When the eggs hatched, the birds flew alongside the moving train catching insects and feeding them to their hatchlings once the train came to a stop.

The first locomotive acquired by the Taku Tram was a little engine that had seen hard usage since its construction 22 years earlier by the Baldwin Locomotive Works in September 1878 (Shop #4424 for Dunsmuir, Diggle & Company). The locomotive became the second purchased for the Wellington Colliery Railway on Vancouver Island and was bought by the Taku Tram in 1899. The 11-ton wood burner, built as a 2-foot, 6-inch gauge, was widened out to 3-foot narrow-gauge. In the conversion, the leading drivers were not reconnected, making the 0-6-0T in effect a 0-(2)4-0T. The little locomotive was originally called Duchess (of Wellington), a name it still carries today.

The other early day Taku Tram equipment consisted of a passenger car seating 14 passengers and six flatcars, each with a 10-ton capacity.

After more than 15 years of use on the Taku Tram, the Duchess was converted to an oil-burner in 1917. In 1921, it was taken out of commission and later moved to Carcross, where it was sidetracked, refurbished with new paint, and put on display for tourists. For years, however, the Duchess still served a useful purpose for the White Pass & Yukon Railroad agent at Carcross, who burned papers and other refuse in its firebox.

WP&Y locomotive No. 51 followed the Dutchess in 1921. It was a Brooks 2-6-0 that had been built in 1881. In 1931, it blew a piece out of its main steam pipe and was replaced by a sister locomotive, the former WP&Y No. 52, also a Brooks 2-6-0 built in 1881. This locomotive served on the Taku Tram until the fall of 1936 when it was replaced by a gasoline-powered, 4-wheeled speeder/locomotive built by the Westminster Iron Works. This locomotive operated until 1950 when Atlin was connected by road to the Alaska Highway.

No. 51 was repaired and used by the White Pass & Yukon Railroad until 1941, when it was retired. In 1958, the locomotive was donated to the McBride Museum and placed on display at Whitehorse. No. 52 was retired in the fall of 1936, but it was not until 1964 that it was recovered (it had been left on a spur at Taku), restored, and put on display. White Pass & Yukon employees, under the direction of Carl Mulvihill, a dispatcher and third-generation White Pass & Yukon man, began the initiative known as Project 52 (named after the locomotive) to purchase, recover, and restore the historic engine. As the drive gained momentum, the White Pass & Yukon donated the locomotive to the project.

Project 52 was lengthy and difficult. It required transporting the 29-½-ton locomotive over the frozen surface of Lake Atlin to Whitehorse using a low-boy truck, and then moving it by train to Skagway, where it was restored. Unfortunately, the locomotive was damaged in a fire that destroyed the Skagway roundhouse and yards in October 1969. The roundhouse repairs and other urgent projects delayed its final restoration until late 1971, when it was moved to its current location in downtown Skagway.

In 1956, the Tutshi was pulled up on the beach at Carcross. The rails at Taku-Scotia Bay were removed, leaving the rolling stock in the bush. Today the Duchess and one of the White Pass & Yukon stages are on display at Carcross, mementos of the early days of transportation in the area.

Other railroads for Atlin were proposed originally, but none of them materialized. In 1899 the Atlin Southern Railway Company proposed—and had a charter granted—to build a line from Log Cabin via Atlin to Telegraph Creek. Between 1900 and 1902, the Pacific Northern and Omineca Railway Company developed plans to construct a railroad from Kitimat Inlet via Hazelton, Teslin, and Atlin to Dawson City. The Atlin Claim, the community newspaper, repeatedly urged both the provincial and federal governments to support these railroad projects. The Claim argued that an all-Canadian railroad route to the Yukon was essential and that any of the proposed routes would keep northern trade in the hands of Canadian businesses. But the Claim's protests were in vain: the period between 1900 and 1915 was a booming one for railroad construction in Canada, but the major routes ran east to west rather than to the northland. None of the railroads that planned to originate from or pass through Atlin ever materialized. The only railroad to Atlin was the Taku Tram.

Taku Tram

Steam Locomotive Roster

Road No.	Wheel Arr.	Builder	C/N	Year	Cylinders	Drivers	Notes
Duchess	0-6-0T	Baldwin	#4424	1878	10x12	27"	Built for Dunsmuir, Diggle & Co. "Duchess" (30" gauge) converted to 36" gauge, 0(2)-4-0T in 1879, forward axle not connected, sold in 1883 to Wellington Colliery Railway "Duchess," sold in 1899, Taku Tram (WP&Y), retired in 1919, on display at Carcross, Y.T.
1	2-6-0	Brooks	Note 1	1881	14-½ x18	42"	New boiler and cylinders, 1900, built for Utah & Northern, sold in November 1889 to Columbia & Puget Sound 2nd No. 3, sold in 1897 to WP&Y, renumbered 51, Taku Tram 1919–1931, retired in 1941, on display in Whitehorse, Y.T.
2	2-6-0	Brooks	Note 1	1881	14-½ x18	42"	New boiler and cylinders, 1900, built for Utah & Northern, sold in 1890 to Columbia & Puget Sound 2nd No. 4, sold in 1898 to WP&Y, renumbered 52, Taku Tram 1931–1937, on display in Skagway, AK.

Note 1: This class of locomotives was numbered 23 to 42 on the U&N. The Brooks builder's numbers for these engines were between 494 and 627 (nonconsecutive).

Gas Locomotive Roster

Builder	C/N	Year	Rated HP	Notes
WIW	68	1937	90 hp	Taku Tram, 1937–1951 to WP&Y (stored).

Chapter 3

Whitehorse Tramways

The gold rush in the Klondike brought thousands of prospectors to the north, and whether they traveled through Chilkoot Pass out of Dyea or over White Pass from Skagway, they eventually found their way through the lake country and down the Yukon River.

One of the major hazards of this route was Miles Canyon, a danger few chose to risk their lives or possessions to tackle. On top of that, the Northwest Mounted Police had ruled that stampeders had to hire experienced pilots to take them through the canyon and fixed a fee of $20—so that they would not be fleeced. One of those early day pilots was Jack London, who is reported to have made $3,000 in 1897 before continuing on to the Klondike.

In the spring of 1897, Norman D. Macaulay arrived at White Horse Rapids. A year later, he and five other men constructed a tramway known as the Canyon & White Horse Rapids Railway on the east side of the Yukon (also known at that time as the

A group of stampeders with a horse-drawn tramcar move their goods over the wooden rails of the Miles Canyon and Lewes River Tramway, Inc. This tramline was constructed by John Hepburn on the east side of the river and extended about half a mile above the Macaulay Tramline in hopes of tapping the river traffic. The Northwest Mounted Police buildings and stacks of freight awaiting transportation are visible in the background. The trams operated in 1897–98, prior to the building of the White Pass & Yukon Railway. (Yukon Archives)

Lewes or Fifty Mile River) from Canyon City, 1 mile above Miles Canyon. Macauley operated a roadhouse there about 4 miles downstream from the canyon, where a community eventually known as White Horse (Whitehorse) was under construction. (The town moved across the river to its present site when the White Pass and Yukon Railway came down the west side of the river.)

The tramway was constructed of rough-hewn poles about 8 inches in diameter, laid 3 feet apart. At intervals of from 5 to 12 feet, ties were placed. A tramcar with concave-surfaced iron wheels was drawn by a horse. Thus, boats, supplies, and so on were transferred past the treacherous rapids.

Macaulay did a land-office business, charging 3¢ a pound and $25 for boats. The little wagons or cars were not steady on the rails, and many old timers recall riding high on top of a load of freight on one of the cars, watching with bated breath as boats and barges zoomed through the canyon.

Shortly thereafter, another tramway, this one on the west side of the river, was constructed by John Hepburn. This tramway was about 6-½ miles in length and was designed to tap the river traffic about half a mile above Macaulay's. A crude windlass was rigged to hoist the gear from boats to the top of the bank. Hepburn's route was along the line of the old portage trail and was known as the Miles Canyon and Lewes River Tramway, Inc.

Loaded horse-drawn tramcars are pulled along the Miles Canyon–Whitehorse tramline dock, with piles of freight awaiting transport seen in the background. The stern-wheeler Bailey is docked nearby. The line, known as the Macaulay Tramline, was on the east side of the river and later became known as the Canyon and Whitehorse Rapids Railway. The tramline enabled stampeders to bypass the treacherous White Horse Rapids, one of the most dangerous spots en route to the Klondike. (Yukon Archives)

Hepburn eventually sold to Macaulay for a reported $60,000, and he successfully operated both tramways until the White Pass & Yukon tracks neared Whitehorse. Macauley sold both rights-of-way to the Canadian Development Company, a subsidiary of the Alaska Steamship Company, (C. E. Peabody and Associates) who later sold to the White Pass & Yukon.

Macaulay later operated three roadhouses on the route between Whitehorse and Dawson City, which he eventually sold to the Canadian Development Company. Later on he built the White Horse Hotel.

Chapter 4

Klondike Mines Railway

In 1899, in answer to a petition, the government of the Dominion of Canada in Ottawa determined that the proper development of the Klondike mining district depended on the incorporation of the Klondike Mines Railway and Stage Company (KMR). On July 10, it passed an act that incorporated the company. Thomas W. O'Brien of Dawson City, James A. Seybold of Ottawa, William R. Rose of New Glasgow, N.S., Llewellyn N. Bates of Ottawa, and Harold McGiverin of Ottawa were involved in the decision. The act incorporated

the company for $1 million and gave it the right to build a single or double-line railroad, tramway, or both. The company was allowed to build a route that extended from Klondike City to Bonanza Creek, along the divide to Dominion Creek, to Indian River, to the Yukon, and then back to Dawson City. Branch lines on the Klondike River to Hunker Creek, Bear Creek, Quartz Creek, Sulphur Creek, Eldorado Creek, and other

Jerome Chute's KMR construction crew poses for the photographer on the Klondike River Bridge in 1905. Dawson City is visible in the background. The railroad eventually ran from Dawson City to Sulphur Springs, a distance of 31 miles. (Yukon Archives)

creeks were also provided for, along with telegraph, telephone, and electric power lines. Shortly after these papers were granted, Thomas O'Brien submitted a personal application to lease waterfront lots in Klondike City for the terminus of the railroad. These rights were ultimately transferred to the Klondike Mines Railway in 1905.

In 1902 William White started negotiations on behalf of the railroad to acquire property for the construction of railway shops at Ogilvie Bridge, but these too were dropped because the railroad was unable to obtain surface rights to the property from the owners of placer claims. In the same year, Thomas O'Brien, W. H. Parsons, and E. C. Hawkins (who was well known in railroad construction circles for his work on the White Pass & Yukon) made an application to the Dawson City Council for a railroad right-of-way. These three men represented Dawson City business owners who believed they would lose money if the terminus stayed in Klondike City as originally planned. The right-of-way entered the city via First Avenue to Queen Street, where a passenger depot was to be constructed. The proposed right-of-way continued along the waterfront to King Street, back to First Avenue, and then to Albert Street, where the terminus was to be located. In 1905 further negotiations occurred between the railroad contractor Jerome A. Chute and the Klondike City Council regarding the use of

The photographer labeled this as the first excursion train on the Klondike Mines Railway, but it was actually the second. It is shown here making its way out of Klondike City on September 5, 1905. The locomotive is a Brooks 2-6-0, acquired from the White Pass & Yukon. The first train actually ran on Labor Day, September 4, from Dawson City to 96 Below, on Bonanza Creek. It used only a single coach and carried a few select passengers. The train was under the direction of Dave Curry, road construction superintendent. (H. L. Berry Collection)

One of the major operations for the Klondike Mines Railway was hauling cordwood to the mining areas where large boilers generated steam to thaw the permafrost. This train, headed by KMR No. 3, a Vauclain compound Baldwin, is en route through Klondike City to the gold field. Dawson City is located across the river. (H. L. Berry Collection)

waterfront property as a railroad terminus in that community. The leases were finally granted, first at $1 per year per front foot and later at $10 per year for all the property required. The mad rush of the early day excitement in the Klondike temporarily died down from 1901 to 1903. Then on May 23, 1903, the Yukon Council sent a communication to the governor general of Canada in which it reported that cheap transportation (rail) would allow the reworking of claims at a profit if large machinery could be brought in. The report emphasized that at present such transportation in the Klondike was inadequate.

Following the Yukon Council letter, 6 or 7 miles of grading was done and 3 or 4 miles of track laid. The portion of the grade located above Milepost 5 was abandoned afterward, and work started on a new grade in May 1906, with construction and operation financing provided by a

THE KLONDIKE MINES RAILWAY COMPANY

Operating daily trains between **Dawson** and **Sulphur Springs** and connecting with our own stages running on **Sulphur, Dominion** and **Quartz Creeks**.

We operate our own freighting outfits in connection with the railway and quote passenger and freight rates to any claim on Bonanza, Eldorado, Hunker, Sulphur, Dominion, Gold Run and Quartz Creeks, or any of their tributaries. For rates or other information address

E. A. MURPHY, Manager
Dawson, Y.T.

An advertisement for the Klondike Mines Railroad Company as it appeared in the July 21, 1909, edition of the Dawson Daily News. This was the peak of the Klondike Mines operation. (Clifford Collection)

Klondike Mines Railway locomotive No. 1, a Brooks 2-6-0 acquired from the White Pass & Yukon, is on display at Minto Park in Dawson City.

British company, the Dawson, Grand Forks & Stewart River Railway Company of London. Construction was completed, and steel was laid to Grand Forks (at Milepost 13) by July 18.

On August 16, 1906, the railroad applied to open the first 15 miles of the line out of Klondike City. At that time, the first 13 miles of narrow-gauge track had been constructed using 52-pound rails and then tapered off to 45-pound rails for the remainder of the trackage. The first 13 miles of track (Dawson City to Grand Forks) was opened to traffic in mid-July 1906 after various government agencies certified that the railroad was finished and built to standard.

Eventually, 31 miles of track was laid to Sulphur Springs (Sulphur) at a cost of $2 million. Work on this line was completed on October 16, 1906, and from then on the railroad hauled large amounts of cord wood, freight, and mining equipment to the creeks. Passengers were also transported, and the cargo was handled by the company's own freighting outfits from the railroad to its various destinations. The train operated daily for the first three years after it was built. Horse-drawn stages picked up the service from 1909 to 1911.

The Klondike Mines Railway acquired its first locomotive in 1902, a 2-6-0 Brooks freight engine known as a Mogul, from the White Pass & Yukon. The second locomotive was also acquired from the White Pass & Yukon. It was a 2-8-0 Consolidation-type freight engine built by Baldwin Locomotive Works. The Klondike Mines No. 3 was also a 2-8-0 built by Baldwin as a Vauclain compound. Unique on the KMR but common with many narrow-gauge locomotives of the period, the No. 3 had an outside frame, in which the wheels are placed inside the frame for increased stability and to allow a larger firebox and lower (or larger) boiler. These three locomotives are now on display at Minto Park in Dawson City, where they were moved from Klondike City in the early 1960s.

The Klondike Mines No. 4 locomotive was built new for the railroad by Baldwin. It was a 2-6-2

Three locomotives from the Klondike Mines Railway, plus a small Porter tank engine, are on display at Dawson City's Minto Park. They are a vivid reminder of early day railroading in the Yukon. (H. Clifford)

Prairie type and was used extensively during its two years of service (1912 and 1913). The locomotive was later sold to the White Pass & Yukon.

From the beginning of service in 1906 until May 31, 1908, the KMR lost $121,596.65 on revenue of $128,058.82. The loss was caused mostly by a lack of business during the winter months. After only a single winter's (1906–1907) operation, the railroad settled down to a five- to six-month-per-year operation from May to October.

Dawson City looking north from Queen Street at midnight on June 10, 1904. The Klondike Mines Railway started operating about two years later from Dawson City to the gold fields. (Clifford Collection)

The barge section of a giant gold dredge under construction is seen in the center of this photo of a Canadian Klondyke Mining Company construction camp at Bonanza Creek. The photograph was taken in August 1912. The railroad ceased operation two years later when the level of traffic fell off. (Yukon Archives)

The last KMR train operated in late October 1913. The Yukon Consolidated Gold Corporation acquired the line's assets when it was chartered in 1925. Trackage was later removed, and on September 6, 1928, the government was given permission to use several hundred feet of the right-of-way from Six Below to Bonanza as a highway. That highway is still in use today.

Klondike Mines Railway

Locomotive Roster

Road No.	Wheel Arr.	Builder	C/N	Year	Cylinders	Drivers	Notes
1	2-6-0	Brooks	522	1881	14x18	41"	Built as Kansas Central Railway No. 7 (UP No. 102, 1885) "Sidney Dillon," sold in 1890 to Trail Creek Tramway, sold in 1896 to Columbia & Western Railway, sold in 1899 to Canadian Pacific Railway, sold in 1900 to WP&Y No. 63, sold in 1902 to Klondike Mines Railway No. 1, on display in Dawson City Y.T., 1961.*
2	2-8-0	Baldwin	7597	May 1885	15x18	36-½"	Built as Columbia & Puget Sound No. 8, sold in 1897 to WP&Y No. 5, renumbered 55, sold in 1905 to Klondike Mines Railway No. 2, on display in Dawson City Y.T., 1961.*
3	2-8-0	Baldwin	16456	January 1899	11-½ & 19x20	38"	Built as WP&Y No. 7. Renumbered 57, sold in 1906 to Klondike Mines Railway No. 3, on display in Dawson City Y.T., 1961.*
4	2-6-2	Baldwin	37564	March 1912	15x20	37"	Built as Klondike Mines Railway No. 4, sold in July 1942 to WP&Y, retired in 1952, sold in 1955 to Oak Creek Central, transferred in 1960 to Peppermint & Northwestern RR, sold in 1964 to Petticoat Junction RR, sold in 1972 to Gold Nugget Junction RR, sold in September 1984 to Midwest Central RR, sold in October 1984 to Steve Wild, stored.*

* The assets of the Klondike Mines Railway became part of Yukon Consolidated Gold Corporation about 1925. The locomotives were not relettered.

Chapter 5

Klondike Short Lines

In addition to the relatively well-known Klondike Mines Railway, the Dawson area spawned a trio of short, narrow-gauge railways, which operated under half a dozen corporate names.

The earliest of these was the North American Transportation and Trading Company (NAT&TCo.), which in 1899 established a 1-1/2-mile railroad along Cliff Creek, 58 river miles downstream from Dawson. The railroad's purpose was to connect the company's coal mine to transshipment facilities on the bank of the Yukon River. The narrowness of the canyon and the steepness of the creek required a track alignment with average grades of 5 percent. Only the short distance of the line and a modest train size would have made this operationally practical.

A little Porter saddle-tank 0-4-0 is shown hauling coal from the North American Transportation and Trading Company mine to the transfer facility on the Yukon River. The photo was taken in 1902 or 1903 when business had begun to taper off a bit. (Yukon Archives)

Locomotives from the Klondike Mines Railway and the Detroit Yukon Mining Company are on display at Minto Park in Dawson City, along with other mining equipment from the Klondike gold rush. (Blaine Freer)

The company was the brainchild of John J. "Captain" Healy, whose checkered past involved infamous trading posts in Montana, southern Canada, and Dyea, Alaska, and a fleet of stern-wheelers that traveled the lower Yukon River.

While there is little doubt that the energy needs of the Klondike were significant—and were outstripping the cordwood supply—the relatively poor quality and small supply of coal in the area west of Dawson would not provide long-term financial success for the captain.

The company operated its railroad until 1903, when the mines became depleted and there was no further need for the operation. The locomotive and cars were sold to the Coal Creek Coal Company (CCCCo.), which, fortuitously for Healy, was just starting its operation. The company's fleet of river steamers was active until 1906 and its mercantile business until 1912. Ironically, the railroad itself outlasted the entire company, finally succumbing to a scrapper in 1918.

Around the same time as the demise of the Healy coal enterprise, a second railroad was established to access the lignite deposits in the area. On Coal Creek (also a tributary to the Yukon River), just 4 miles upstream from Cliff Creek, the Coal Creek Coal Company was starting construction of its own railroad to serve the company's mine. The company had been patented early in 1903 by Falcon Joslin, James Williams, Henry Siemer, August Carlson of Dawson, and Carl Johanson of Circle City, Alaska.

Construction of the railroad proceeded through the summer of 1903. By September, the 11-1/2-mile line had been completed from the Yukon River to the mine. Unlike the NAT&TCo. railroad, the CCCCo. roadbed followed a relatively level drainage, which kept gradients to approximately 1 percent.

At the completion of railroad construction, three second-hand locomotives were on the property, together with sufficient cars to start train operations, if only for a few weeks before the winter shutdown. The company's goal was to ship 10,000 tons of coal to Dawson during the 1904 season, with the majority of the product going to the Dawson Electric Light and Power Company (DEP&LCo.)—a firm with many shareholders in common with the coal company.

Production from the mines continued through 1905 and 1906, with coal by then coming from both the Coal Creek mine and the adjacent Sourdough Mine. By the end

Carrying No. 1 on its spotplate, this Porter saddle-tanker, which saw service with the Detroit Yukon Mining Company near Dawson City, is pictured on its way south to Vancouver, B.C. It was acquired by Roger Brammall of Vancouver from the Yukon Consolidated Gold Corporation, which took over the Detroit Yukon Gold Mining Company (and its successor's) properties. Brammall retrieved the locomotive from YCGC's Bear Creek Camp. (Whitehorse Star)

of the 1906 season, however, changes were in the wind and control of the DEP&LCo. passed to N. A. Fuller and Dr. A. S. Grant. In October, the pair also acquired the Coal Creek properties and its associated railroad, henceforth to be operated under the name Sourdough Coal Company.

Production from the mines continued in 1907, but by 1908 the coal veins were starting to play out and the Coal Creek mine remained closed through the summer. The mine's big customer, DEP&LCo., turned to a cordwood contract for 1909.

The final incarnation of the Coal Creek railway was in the form of the Northern Light, Power, and Coal Company, a firm backed by English capital that contemplated diverse holdings, including power generation, water supply, mining, and transportation. The NLP&CCo. reopened the Coal Creek mine when a new vein was discovered in 1909 and rebuilt the railroad, which was damaged annually by spring runoff. Additionally, the company ordered a new locomotive, a Shay from the Lima Locomotive Works, to provide heavier motive power. The locomotive had the dubious distinction of being the only one of its type to be used in either the Yukon or Alaska.

Plans were immediately made to construct a power plant near the mine. In 1910, the plant was constructed and began operation. Power was generated for a few months in 1911, but not at all in 1912. It was never used significantly after that. Coal was still being shipped upriver to Dawson, but the higher quality Tantalus coal from east of Dawson was gaining a significant competitive edge.

The mine operated some in 1914 and possibly in 1915, but the end was at hand. In 1917 the power plant was dismantled, and it was shipped out in 1918. The three Porters were left on the site—the Shay having been sold earlier. Thus the railway era on Coal Creek came to an end.

The third short line in the area was located several miles up the Klondike River from Dawson at Bear Creek. In 1904, the Detroit Yukon Mining Company (DYMCo.) constructed a short railroad to bring gold-bearing gravel to the Klondike River for washing. During the fall of 1903, the company had imported a pair of Marion steam shovels, which were to be used to load the railcars. Mid-1904 saw the delivery of four identical Porter 0-4-0Ts and 24 side dump gravel cars.

Operations on the railroad started in the summer of 1904 and continued through the work season of 1905. Early 1905 brought several significant changes to DYMCo. The company obtained mining rights to approximately 40 square miles of the Klondike River valley and as a result embarked on a plan to construct large dredges to efficiently extract and wash the gravel. This plan would rapidly eliminate the need for a railroad.

With this property acquisition, DYMCo. was reorganized and taken over by the just-created Canadian Klondyke Mining Company. CKMCo. made swift progress on the construction of its dredges. With the railroad scarcely a year old, it became obsolete. The cars and locomotives stayed in the Dawson area until at least 1912, assisting with dredge construction, minor excavation, and freight-moving projects.

The year 1921 marked the end of CKMCo. After several years of financial troubles, Burrall and Baird Limited foreclosed upon it and seized its assets. Within four years, the assets were transferred to the Yukon Consolidated Gold Corporation. It is doubtful that either of these two firms ever operated any of the railroad equipment.

The three rail lines featured in this chapter are remarkable in that, despite having operated so long ago and in an area so forbidding, six of the eight locomotives shared by the lines have survived to the present.

… Chapter 5: Klondike Short Lines

Coal Creek Coal Company

Locomotive Roster

Road No.	Wheel Arr.	Builder	C/N	Year	Cylinders	Drivers	Notes
	0-6-0T	Porter		Ca. 1890	7x12	25"	Built for: unknown, sold in 1903 to Coal Creek Coal Company, sold in 1906 to Sourdough Coal Company, sold in 1909 to Northern Light, Power & Coal Company. Abandoned June 1918 to March 1969. To Gunnar Nilsson, donated in 1993 to Yukon Transportation Museum, on display.
	0-6-0T	Porter		Ca. 1890	8x14	27"	Built for: unknown, sold in 1903 to Coal Creek Coal Company, sold in 1906 to Sourdough Coal Company, sold in 1909 to Northern Light, Power & Coal Company. Abandoned June 1918 to March 1969, to Harry Cooper, sold in 1992 to Dick Gilbert, preserved.
1	0-4-0T	Porter	1972	1899	6x10	24"	Built for North American Transportation & Trading Company No. 1, sold in 1903 to Coal Creek Coal Company, No. 1, sold in June 1905 to Tanana Mines Railroad, No. 1, old in 1907 to AEC No. 1, transferred in 1923 to Tanana Valley Railroad, No. 1, sold in 1917 to Alaska Railroad, No. 1, retired before 1929, on display in 1930, to Friends of the Tanana Valley Railroad, No. 1, preserved.

Detroit Yukon Mining Company

Locomotive Roster

Road No.	Wheel Arr.	Builder	C/N	Year	Cylinders	Drivers	Notes
1	0-4-0T	Porter	3022	1904	6x10	24"	Sold in June 1905 to Canadian Klondyke Mining Company, No. 1, sold in 1921 to Burrall & Baird, No. 1, 1925 to Yukon Consolidated Gold Corporation, No. 1, sold in 1965 to Roger Brammall, No. 1, on display.
2	0-4-0T	Porter	3023	1904	6x10	24"	Sold in June 1905 to Canadian Klondyke Mining Company, No. 2. Disposition unknown.
3	0-4-0T	Porter	3024	1904	6x10	24"	Sold in June 1905 to Canadian Klondyke Mining Company, No. 3, sold in July 1913 to Northern Light, Power & Coal Company, No. 3, abandoned June 1918 to March 1969, to Dan Nowlan, No. 3, sold in 1983 to Kieth Christenson, No. 3, preserved.

Detroit Yukon Mining Company *(continued)*

Road No.	Wheel Arr.	Builder	C/N	Year	Cylinders	Drivers	Notes
4	0-4-0T	Porter	3025	1904	6x10	24"	Sold in June 1905 to Canadian Klondyke Mining Company, No. 4, sold in 1921 to Burrall & Baird, No. 4, 1925 to Yukon Consolidated Gold Corporation, No. 4, sold in 1961 to Dawson City Museum, No. 4, on display.

Northern Light, Power & Coal Company

Locomotive Roster

Road No.	Wheel Arr.	Builder	C/N	Year	Cylinders	Drivers	Notes
	0-6-0T	Porter		Ca. 1890	7x12	25"	Built for: unknown, sold in 1903 to Coal Creek Coal Company, sold in 1906 to Sourdough Coal Company, sold in 1909 to Northern Light, Power & Coal Company, abandoned June 1918 through March 1969, to Gunnar Nilsson, donated in 1993 to Yukon Transportation Museum, on display.
	0-6-0T	Porter		Ca. 1890	8x14	27"	Built for: unknown, sold in1903, to Coal Creek Coal Company, sold in 1906 to Sourdough Coal Company, sold in 1909 to Northern Light, Power & Coal Company, abandoned June 1918 through March 1969, to Harry Cooper, sold in 1992 to Dick Gilbert, preserved.
1	2-truck	Lima	2190	1909	8x12	26-½"	Built for: unknown, sold in 1913 to Alaska-Gastineau Mining Company, No. 2 (Salmon Creek Dam Railroad), sold in March 1921 to Puget Sound Machinery Depot, sold in 1921 to Biles-Coleman Lumber Company, No. 2, No. 101, scrapped in 1940.

Chapter 6

Alaska Central Railway

During the first years of the 20th century, the Klondike was booming at a rate of $20 million per year. This sparked interest among American business developers in the construction of an all-American route that would eliminate some of the many days of travel between the Klondike gold fields and the United States proper. A variety of natural resources supporting a permanent population were already in place, and the increased traffic to the area was considered potentially very profitable.

John F. Ballaine initiated primary investigations into the feasibility of a trans-Alaska route in 1900. His reconnaissance led him to believe that Resurrection Bay would provide the best saltwater terminus for the railroad. This decision would plague the Alaska Central operation and its successors for many years.

The Alaska Central Railway Company was organized with capital of $30 million by a group of Seattle business owners on March 31, 1902. Five hundred and fifty thousand shares of common stock were created at par value of $50 a share, along with 50,000 shares of 5-percent preferred stock. General headquarters was located in the Denny Building in Seattle, and C. W. Dickinson, former general manager of the Northern Pacific Railroad, took on leadership of the company as president and general manager. John H. McGraw, former governor of Washington, served as vice president; J. W. Godwin, president of the Alaska Fisheries Union, was treasurer; George Turner, a U.S. Senator from Washington State, was made general counsel; and John F. Ballaine, a Spanish-American war veteran and a former secretary to Governor McGraw, who had

The construction headquarters of the Alaska Central Railway in 1904 when work started on the railroad. The company was headquartered in Seattle. The Alaska Central later became the Alaska Northern, then the U.S. Government Railroad, and finally the Alaska Railroad (ARR). Today ARR trains operate over practically the same route surveyed by early Alaska Central crews. (University of Washington Library, Northwest Collection)

Seward was a booming seaport town during the construction of the Alaska Central Railway and later the Alaska Northern Railway. A bright summer day finds citizens strolling out on the city's dock. (Seattle Historical Society)

assisted with the initial groundwork on the project, became secretary and auditor. Charles W. Peck of Omaha, Captain E. C. Caine, Charles L. Denny, and C. M. Andrews, all of Seattle, also became involved in the project.

The projected route extended from the present site of Seward on Resurrection Bay through the Susitna Valley and Broad Pass to the Tanana River, where Nenana has since been built. The distance of this route was 412 miles. The plan was to reach the rich coal fields of the Matanuska Valley as soon as possible. Fairbanks did not enter into the program until 1903, and only then as the result of the 1902 gold strike.

The route followed a preliminary survey completed earlier under the supervision of C. M Andrews, a civil engineer from Seattle. The survey was adopted and approved by the board of directors and filed with the interior department in Washington D.C. This route was much the same as that used by the present-day Alaska Railroad.

The site on Resurrection Bay selected as the terminus and seaport for the railroad was in essentially the same location used by Russians in 1767 to establish a shipbuilding facility in Alaska. From native timber, they built one of the largest frigates in the Russian navy prior to 1800.

The original American surveyors for Seward, as the town site was to be named, arrived in midsummer 1903. In the survey of the town, Alaskan ingenuity was used in place of a surveyor's measurement chain that had been lost in shipment; links were cut from baling wire using a tailor's measuring tape as a standard. Later, when the proper equipment arrived, the measurements were found to be only a few inches off.

An early locomotive on the Alaska Central Railway was this 4-4-0 Baldwin built in 1881 for the Northern Pacific Railroad. Three of the locomotives obtained by the Alaska Central came from the Northern Pacific, which also supplied the railroad's first president and general manager, C. W. Dickinson. This locomotive later became No. 11 on the Alaska Railroad roster. (University of Washington, Northwest Collection)

Prior to the establishment of the town, a settler named Mrs. Lowel had homesteaded on the site. John Ballaine acquired the homestead for $4,000 cash and $2,000 in soldier's scrip. Ballaine and his brother, Frank, along with W. M. Whittlesey, laid out the city. Ballaine's background in real estate taught him the importance of controlling the land at a railhead.

The panic of 1901 made it impossible to sell Alaska Central bonds or have them underwritten as was planned, so in July 1903 the Tanana

Early day cheesecake. Even in the early 20th century, a pretty young lady added much to a promotional photograph for a growing railroad. Here one is pictured with the Alaska Central Railway locomotive No. 1. (University of Washington Library, Northwest Collection.)

An Alaska Central work train with the reliable old locomotive No. 1, a Portland 4-4-0 built in 1883 for the Northern Pacific, pulling flatcars loaded with ties. (University of Washington Library, Northwest Collection.)

The rotary snowplow operated by the Alaska Central Railway was kept in storage at Seward during the summer months. During the winter, heavy snowfall made it necessary to use the large snowplow in some areas to keep the right-of-way open. (Oregon Historical Society)

Construction Company was organized. John Ballaine took ownership of all of the stock except for qualifying shares for the other directors. Ballaine was made president and manager. The Tanana Company agreed on a contract with the Alaska Central to build the railroad from Resurrection Bay to the Tanana River in exchange for $35,000 per mile in Alaska Central bonds and a majority of the Alaska Central stock.

E. A. and C. B. Shedd and four of their Chicago associates provided Ballaine with

Work continued at a fast pace on the Alaska Central during the summer of 1905. Locomotive No. 1 is seen pulling a work train along the water's edge with the snow-capped mountains along Turnagain Arm in the background. Rails and supplies for 70 to 80 miles of track were on hand by this time, along with 1,800 workers and 170 horses. (University of Washington Library, Northwest Collection)

$200,000 in funds to construct the first 20 miles, with a tentative agreement to finance additional sections, based on mileage actually built. Ballaine was required to put up $50,000, which he raised in Seattle. He later raised another $75,000 in Chicago to supplement the original $200,000.

On August 23, 1903, about 30 workers landed at Seward, along with horses and supplies. On August 28, the town of Seward was officially founded. The advance construction crew built a dock and collected bridge timbers during the fall and winter months in preparation for construction beginning in the spring.

Construction on the standard-gauge line started on April 16, 1904, with the driving of the first spike on the completed dock. Additional workers arrived that week, and the first locomotive for the railroad was landed from the Pacific Navigation Company's *Santa Ana* a few days later. Frank Ballaine was placed in charge of business management, and Colonel A. W. Swartz was

The loop trestle was used by the Alaska Central, Alaska Northern, the U.S. Government Railroad, and the Alaska Railroad until 1951. It was one of the great scenic attractions on the route. (University of Alaska Archives, McKeown Collection)

named chief engineer. The Shedd syndicate designated E. R. Kesler as treasurer. The Tanana Company awarded a contract to the Seward Construction Company of Chicago for railroad construction and to J. M. Moore of Seattle for right-of-way clearing. The general manager for the project was John Dowdle of the contracting firm Nash and Dowdle.

In the early days of construction—prior to the arrival of rails and locomotives—laborers built wooden rails and set up dog-pulled cars to carry supplies. The first tunnel was driven by hand at a per-foot cost less than those driven by machinery later on. Beginning wages were $2 per day, with board figured at an additional $1 per day. There was a medical plan that cost $1.50 per month.

Cost of the first 20 miles of track, including some heavy rock work, was $16,000 per mile, including rolling stock and equipment. This was considered tremendously high at the time. It cost over $50 per ton to buy rails and ship them to Seward. Labor rates rose to $4 and $5 per day, and even at these figures workers would stay on the job only long enough to earn "grub stakes" so they could go prospecting nearby and perhaps discover ground that would pay them $20 a day.

For the first several years, the railroad workers filled the town. There were churches, stores, a hospital, schools, restaurants, bakeries, and saloons where the hardworking laborers could get rest, refreshment, and entertainment. From the beginning,

The first locomotive for the Alaska Central arrived in Seward in mid-April 1904 aboard the Pacific Navigation Company's Santa Ana. The locomotive was later used by Alaska Northern Railway and then transferred to the Alaskan Engineering Commission. (Anchorage Historical and Fine Arts Museum, Alaska Railroad Collection)

With a full head of steam and smoke pouring from the stack, a northbound special highballs along the rickety tracks of the Alaska Central Railway. This photo was taken in 1906 before the economic panic brought an end to the dreams of the Alaska Central backers. (Alaska Railroad Archives)

Seward, which by now had a population of 4,500, was a social town with parades, parties, picnics, and ball games shared by all.

Some 20 miles of trackage was completed during the first year of construction. During 1904, John Ballaine negotiated with several groups of capitalists for money to complete the road to the Tanana Valley. Two eastern financiers, A. C. Frost of Chicago and H. C. Osborne of Toronto, made a survey of the company and routing and started negotiations for $2.5 million. The easterners offered to purchase Ballaine's stock in the Tanana Construction Company, which also owned and controlled Alaska Central. Ballaine sold out in 1905 after Frost and Osborne had secured backing of $3.5 million from the Sovereign Bank of Canada with a contingent promise of up to $18 million. The Shedds and all other original investors were paid off in full.

Frost and Osborne agreed to a contract with Ballaine to complete the Alaska Central Railway. Frost became president of both the Alaska Central and the Tanana Construction Company, and Frost was made vice president. Ballaine continued to hold a minority share of stock.

Additional construction contracts were let, one to P. Welch & Company of Spokane, Washington, in the amount of $1.2 million for construction of 30 miles of track along Turnagain Arm; the other contract went to Rich Harris of Prosser, Washington, for $300,000 to build a 2,500-foot tunnel at Placer River Canyon, about 50 miles from Seward. Rails and supplies for 70 to 80 miles of track were on hand

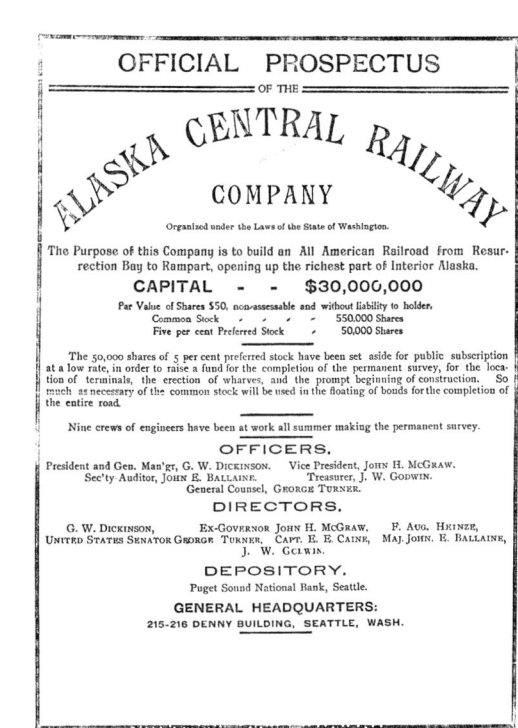

Title page for the prospectus of the Alaska Central Railway Co. C. W. Dickson of Seattle was the company's first president. He was formerly general manager of the Northern Pacific Railroad. Initial financing was furnished by the Shedd Brothers of Chicago, who with their associates provided $200,000 to construction. (Clifford Collection)

for the project, along with 1,800 workers and 170 horses. By June 1906, the Alaska Central Railway had four locomotives, 30 flatcars, 10 boxcars and cabooses, a snowplow, a large number of side dump construction cars, and 350 horses.

The panic of 1907 saw the failure of the Sovereign Bank of Canada and with it the failure of Frost and Osborne and their Alaska Central, as well as their Chicago and Milwaukee Electric railroads. Over the next three years, bank receivers tried to reorganize the Alaska Central without success. The railroad operated in receivership until October 1909, when its assets were sold and it was finally reorganized as the Alaska Northern Railway.

By that time, the line had been extended 51 miles from Seward and included grades over two passes at 705 and 1,063 feet elevation, considerable trackage with grades of 2.2 percent, and numerous trestles and curves. At one point, between Miles 50 and 51, the track passed near Bartlett Glacier and made a complete loop, a marvelous engineering feat for that day. During the construction of the Alaska Railroad years later, an old plaque making note of a location survey for the Alaska Central Railway was found carved in a spruce tree near Mile 245 of the government railroad. The names of several members of the survey party were inscribed on the plaque, among them Slumgullion Joe, stomach robber (cook); Moose Liver Jackson, dog musher; Long Shorty, dog musher; and Long Shafter Murphy, dog musher. There were others too, such as Cy Perkins and Al Miller.

Alaska Central Railway

Locomotive Roster

Road No.	Wheel Arr.	Builder	C/N	Year	Cylinders	Drivers	Notes
1	4-4-0	Portland	499	September 1883	18x24	63"	Built for Northern Pacific, No. 784, sold in 1904, to Alaska Central, No. 1, sold in 1909, to Alaska Northern, No. 1, sold in 1915, to Alaskan Engineering Commission, No. 10, retired in 1920, to Alaska Railroad, No. 10, scrapped in 1930
2	4-4-0	Baldwin	5880	October 1881	18x24	63"	Built for Northern Pacific, No. 846, sold in 1904, to Alaska Central, No. 2, sold in 1909, to Alaska Northern, No. 2, sold in 1915, to Alaskan Engineering Commission, No. 11, to Alaska Railroad, No. 11, scrapped.
3	4-6-0						Original owner unknown, to Alaska Central, No. 3, sold in February 1907, to Copper River & Northwestern No. 51.
4	4-6-0	Baldwin	9696	1889	17x24	55"	Built for Northern Pacific, No. 374, No. 436, sold to Alaska Central, No. 4, sold in 1909, to Alaska Northern, No. 4, sold in 1915, to Alaskan Engineering Commission, destroyed in fire in May 1916, scrapped.

Chapter 7

Alaska Northern Railway

The Alaska Northern Railway Company was chartered on October 28, 1909. The company bought out the Alaska Central Railway Company, whose properties were sold under foreclosure on October 11, 1909. The successful bidder was F. C. Jemmett of Toronto, who represented the Sovereign Bank of Canada, former owner of the majority of the $4 million in Alaska Central bonds. Officers of the new company included O. G. Larabee of Seattle, president; J. D. Williams of Seattle, vice president; and J. A. Haight of Seattle, secretary. Jemmett was named treasurer, and A. H. Weatly of Seward was named auditor. The Company's general offices were located in the Alaska Building in Seattle.

The Alaska Northern took over three operational locomotives from the Alaska Central. Other property included two baggage or mail cars; 33 freight cars, including seven boxcars and 26 flatcars; and one service car; plus other rolling stock. The Alaska Central had slightly more than 50 miles of operational trackage when ownership was transferred.

Construction resumed on the single-track standard-gauge line using 65-pound rails, and another 21 miles of track was added to the old Alaska Central. Near the end of the Alaska Central trackage was the "loop"—an engineering feature designed to allow the climb over the Kenai Mountains at a reasonable gradient. The wooden trestle

Seward was headquarters for the Alaska Central and Alaska Northern railroad construction and later served as the initial operations base for the U.S. Government Railroad. This is Seward pictured sometime during the first decade of the 1900s when construction was at its height. (Anchorage Historical and Fine Arts Museum, Alaska Railroad Collection)

Alaska Northern Railway construction headquarters at Seward. This facility also served as temporary headquarters for the Alaskan Engineering Commission (Alaska Railroad) before the offices were moved to Anchorage. (Anchorage Historical and Fine Arts Museum, Alaska Railroad Collection)

supporting the upper track of the loop was nearly 100 feet high when it was taken over by the reorganized Alaska Northern Railway. Alaska Northern finished the loop and brought the track 52 miles from Seward to Kern Creek, to Tunnel Siding, and another 19 miles from Tunnel Siding. In addition, there were 16 miles of sidetracks—with another 40 miles partially completed.

This section of track was put into operation. Arriving trains were met by boats that came up Turnagain Arm, and freight went out over the Iditarod Trail from this point. The railroad would be constructed north to the Fairbanks area on the Tanana River—a total distance of 450 miles. Another division of 300 miles of track was also planned through the Kuskokwim country in the new field at Iditarod, leaving the main line at Susitna. Stock on hand included an additional 10 miles of graded right-of-way, 40 miles of ties, and 10 miles of rails. The survey had been completed to the Tanana River. The railroad optimistically projected completion of this work by 1912.

However, it ran short of money. John F. Ballaine (of the Alaska Central) tried to regain control by requesting funds from J. P. Morgan. His request was denied on the grounds that J. P. Morgan was in partnership with the Guggenheim Syndicate in the

An Alaska Northern gravel train at Mile 71 at the height of construction. Alaska Northern took over from Alaska Central on April 15, 1910, and completed construction to Mile 71 where travelers could meet boats that came up Turnagain Arm. Freight also went over the Iditarod Trail from this point. (Clifford Collection)

development of the Copper River & Northwestern Railway to the copper holdings in the Kennecott district, which planned an extension to the Tanana.

With no money forthcoming, trackwork and equipment began to deteriorate, and for a time a gasoline-powered speeder was about the only rolling stock operating on the track.

By now, all of Alaska was pleading for help with the railroad, and Walter Fisher, secretary of the interior, made a visit to the territory in 1911 to examine the routes from Valdez, Cordova, and Seward. In his yearly report, Fisher officially recommended that the government purchase the Alaska Northern and complete it to the Yukon River.

President William Howard Taft sent a special message to Congress in February 1912 asking for authorization of $35 million to carry out Secretary Fisher's recommendation. But opponents attached a rider to the Alaska Territorial Act creating an Alaska Railroad Commission to investigate the program, thereby delaying the government's purchase of the Alaska Northern and forcing an evaluation of the Copper River and Northwestern as an alternative.

In 1915, the government first leased and finally purchased the Alaska Northern's 71 miles of standard-gauge track, advance gradings and surveys, and shops and equipment under the government's own appraisal (as provided in the Alaska Railroad Act). The railroad was rehabilitated and operated by the Alaskan Engineering Commission.

The Canadian owners of the railroad had offered the Alaska Northern for $6 million, but the government set the price at $1,150,000, which was approximately the amount finally paid. The cash cost of the property, including advance work, surveys,

Alaska Northern motor car No. 2 at Mile 52 in 1913. Such cars were used for passenger service when light traffic did not warrant steam train operation. (Alaska Railroad Archives)

and seven tunnels at Mile 48 and 52, had been $4,125,000. The government purchase price was 25¢ on the dollar. The Canadian owners had previously frozen all interests in the railroad except those held by the defunct Sovereign Bank.

The cost to the government—despite the poor condition of the road and the money needed to bring it up to standard—was less than it would have been for new construction on another route.

By the end of 1916, the line was in very good condition as far as Mile 45, having been considerably improved and many of the old trestles renewed or filled in. In January and February 1917, there were three trains per week operating from Seward to Mile 40, and by June with the reconstruction completed on the old Alaska Northern Railway, one train a week ran to Kern at Mile 71.

In September 1917, a destructive storm hit Seward and washed out most of the year's work. Losses were estimated at $100,000. The line was closed down for several weeks, but by November two trains a week were again operating between Seward and Kern Creek.

When the Alaska Northern became part of the Alaskan Engineering Commission (AEC), it transferred three operational locomotives, a rotary snowplow, two cabooses, five boarding cars, one observation car, three boxcars, 24 flatcars, one large Fairbanks Morse gasoline car (No. 22) with a Sheffield motor, and one Fairbanks Morse gasoline car (No. 24A) with a Sheffield motor. One other locomotive and six flatcars were destroyed in a fire at Seward shortly before the property was turned over to the Alaskan Engineering Commission.

Alaska Northern Railway

Locomotive Roster

Road No.	Wheel Arr.	Builder	C/N	Year	Cylinders	Drivers	Notes
1	4-4-0	Portland	499	September 1883	18x24	63"	Built for Northern Pacific, No. 784, sold in 1904 to Alaska Central, No. 1, sold in 1909 to Alaska Northern, No. 1, sold in 1915 to Alaskan Engineering Commission, No. 10, retired in 1920, to Alaska Railroad, No. 10, scrapped in 1930.
2	4-4-0	Baldwin	5880	October 1881	18x24	63"	Built for Northern Pacific, No. 846, sold in 1904 to Alaska Central, No. 2, sold in 1909 to Alaska Northern, No. 2, sold in 1915, to Alaskan Engineering Commission, No. 11, to Alaska Railroad, No. 11, scrapped.
3	4-6-0	Baldwin	11280	October 1890	17x24	55"	Built for Port Townsend Southern No. 3, to Northern Pacific No. 369, to Alaska Northern, No. 3, sold 1915 to Alaskan Engineering Commission, No. 20, to Alaska Railroad, No. 20, scrapped in 1930 (leased to Healy Coal Corp., ca. 1920s).
4	4-6-0	Baldwin	9696	1889	17x24	55"	Built for Northern Pacific, No. 374, No. 436, sold to Alaska Central, No. 4, sold in 1909 to Alaska Northern, No. 4, sold in 1915 to Alaskan Engineering Commission, destroyed in fire in May 1916, scrapped.

Chapter 8

The Alaska Railroad Commission and the Birth of the AEC

By the early 20th century, Alaskans had become discouraged at the continued failure of companies such as the Alaska Central and Alaska Northern, as well as others that had proposed and begun railroad construction from such places as Katalla and Valdez to the interior. As these failures continued, Alaska began pleading for federal help. At the same time, Congress, which had become disillusioned by private railroad financing, was unwilling to continue the policy of land grants to pioneer railroads and refused to come to the fiscal aid of distressed Alaskan ventures.

Lawmakers, on the other hand, believed it an outrage that a territory more than twice the size of Texas and with great mineral resources but a sparse population should for all practical purposes be without a railroad. The first efforts to get the government to take over the financially plagued Alaska Northern resulted in a visit in 1911 from Walter Fisher, secretary of the interior. He examined the routes from Valdez, Cordova, and Seward and in his report for the year officially recommended that the government purchase the Alaska Northern and complete it to the Yukon River. The army and the navy departments were also interested in the project as a military measure, with coal an all-important factor for the navy and its ships on patrol in northern waters.

President William Howard Taft sent special messages to Congress in February 1912 asking for an authorization of $35 million to carry out Secretary Fisher's recommendations. Opponents to government railroads in Alaska, however, attached a rider to the Alaska Territorial Act on August 2, 1912, creating an Alaska Railroad Commission and appropriating $25,000 for expenses. This rider provided for examining routes for the government railroad from the coast to the interior.

The Alaska Railroad Commission (also known as the Taft Commission) was made up of four men, three of whom were appointed by President Taft—Major J. J. Morrow from the U.S. army corps of engineers (who later served as governor of the Panama Canal Zone) was chairman; Leonard M. Cox, a U.S. navy engineer; and Colin M. Ingersoll, a consulting railroad engineer from New York. They were joined by Dr. Alfred H. Brooks, vice chairman, who was geologist in charge of the division of Alaska mineral resources and had been designated by Congress.

The Alaska Railroad Commission was created by the Alaska Territorial Act of August 2, 1912. Members of the commission appointed by President William Howard Taft are pictured here as they arrived in Cordova: Alfred H. Brooks and Leonard M. Cox are standing; John M. Ingersoll and Major J. J. Morrow, chairman, are seated. (Seattle Historical Society)

The Commission submitted a voluminous report to the president on January 20, 1913, on the advantages and disadvantages of the various routes, but its overall recommendation was for the construction of two railroads. One route would extend from Cordova to Chitina following the route of the Copper River & Northwestern. From Chitina the line would be extended to Fairbanks. The other route would stretch from Seward along the Alaska Northern route, around Cook Inlet, through the Matanuska-Susitna Valley, across the Alaska Range, and into the Iditarod mining area.

The Commission studied other routes and commented on them briefly in the report. These routes included White Pass, which was traversed by the White Pass & Yukon Railroad and lay almost completely in Canadian territory; and the Chilkoot route, almost adjacent the White Pass & Yukon, which was higher in altitude and not feasible for railroad development. A route was also considered from the Pyramid Harbor/Haines route up the Chilkat River to the Alsek, over passes some 3,200 feet high, through the flat divide between the White and Tanana basins, and then to Fairbanks. This was the longest of all proposed routes, and it also lay in foreign territory for more than half its distance.

Another route that the commission studied extended from Yakutat Bay to the mouth of the Alsek and then up the Alsek valley to the Pyramid Harbor/Haines route 200 miles from the coast. This route also passed through Canadian territory and was not as favorable as the Pyramid Harbor/Haines route over the same area.

The Copper River Valley route was considered next, with three alternatives. One was from either Cordova or Katalla directly up the river; the second extended from Valdez over 1,800-foot-high Marshall Pass and down the Tusnuna to the Copper River Valley; the third was from Valdez over 2,750-foot-high Thompson Pass and a lower summit at Ernestine, and from there to the Copper River at a point near Copper Center. Along this route, the Copper River & Northwestern Railway had already been constructed to Chitina from Cordova, 132 miles apart. This was the longest of the three, but it didn't surmount any grades until the divide between the Copper River and the Yukon Basins.

The next possible route was from Seward on Resurrection Bay over the route started by the Alaska Central and Alaska Northern Railways. This route also presented the promise of allowing for a connection with the great Kuskokwim Basin through one of the passes leading from the headquarters of the Yentna, a tributary of the Susitna. Rainy Pass, about 2,900 feet in elevation, was the most promising way through.

Upper Cook Inlet is closed due to ice during the winter season, which was the only downside the commission saw to constructing a railroad based at some harbor in the inlet. West of Cook Inlet, high, rugged mountains prevent direct access to the Kuskokwim from the west side. The Iliamna Lake Region offered a possible route from a terminal point such as Iliamna Bay into the Kuskokwim, and from that great valley possibly on into the lower Yukon, from which it is separated only by a low watershed.

The Alaska Railroad Commission effectively came to an end after the submission of its report.

In 1914, two bills were introduced in Congress, one by Senator Chamberlain of Oregon that provided $40 million for completion of the road. The other bill was presented by House delegate James Wickersham of Alaska and was identical in most respects to the first bill except in calling for $35 million in construction costs. The later bill was passed by both House and Senate and was approved on March 12, 1914. It authorized the president to "locate, construct and operate a railroad in the Territory of

The various railroads planned, under construction, or completed by 1916 are shown on the map of Alaska. The map was prepared by the Alaska Bureau of the Seattle Chamber of Commerce prior to the Chamber's trip to Alaska. (Seattle Historical Society)

Alaska." The bill also gave the president the authority to select the route, restricted the total mileage of the railroad to 1,000 miles, and specified that the railroad must connect a port to an interior navigable river and one or more coal fields.

Less than two months later, on May 2, 1914, President Woodrow Wilson directed Secretary of the Interior Franklin K. Lane to proceed with surveying routes for the railroads in Alaska. The president appointed the Alaskan Engineering Commission (AEC) under the authority of the interior secretary. Three men were named to the commission: William C. Edes, chairman and chief engineer, who had more than 30 years experience in locating and constructing railroads in the West; Lt. (later Colonel) Frederick J. Mears of the army, who had been engaged in railroad building in the West and in Panama; and Thomas Riggs, Jr, who had served as chief surveyor on the Alaska Boundary Commission and who had spent many years in Alaska. He later became governor of the territory.

An appropriation of $1 million was made by Congress to defray preliminary expenses of the commission, which on May 8, 1914, received instructions to employ assistants, purchase supplies and equipment, and proceed to Alaska at the earliest possible date. On May 22, members of the commission arrived in Seattle, rented offices, and set machinery in motion to accomplish a survey of the routes and study conditions connected with the project. The party left Seattle on May 26, and 11 survey parties under the direction of competent engineers were organized and in the field by the middle of June. The main bases for supplies were established, one at Ship Creek on Knik Arm, Cook Inlet, and the other in Fairbanks.

During the summer of 1914, practically every available route from the coast to the Tanana and Yukon Rivers was examined and surveys made, including examination of the Copper River & Northwestern route, which was then operating from Cordova to Kennecott (this railroad had recently been offered for sale to the government), the route from Valdez paralleling the Valdez-Fairbanks Military Road, and the Alaska Northern Route from Seward.

In February 1915, the commission presented its complete report to the secretary of the interior, with the remarks that "in presenting this report the Commission has not deemed it necessary or proper to make any recommendation as to the best route to follow. This Commission is essentially an engineering one, organized to handle the subject along technical lines. In selecting the route, other questions besides strictly engineering ones are to be considered."

With all the surveys before him and with the facts of the possibilities and needs of the territory delineated, on April 10, 1915, President Wilson issued an executive order selecting the western or Susitna route. This route commenced at the town of Seward, passed around Turnagain Arm across the Matanuska Valley, continued up the Susitna Valley over Broad Pass and then along the Nenana River to the Tanana, where it proceeded across the Tanana and then northeast to Fairbanks. This planned route measured approximately 467 miles in length with a branch line of about 40 miles to the Matanuska coal fields. The first 72 miles of this route would be over the rails of the extant Alaska Northern.

The president also authorized the purchase of the Alaska Northern at a price of $1,150,000 set under government appraisal as provided for by the Alaska Railroad Act, giving it power of appraisal and condemnation. (Opponents to this route and many others expressed the opinion that President Wilson selected this course over the Copper River route due to his intense opposition to the Morgan-Guggenheim financial interests.) The M-G financial syndicate already controlled the Copper River & Northwestern, much of the copper basin it served, and a significant portion of the gold resources in Alaska and the Yukon. In essence, the Alaska Syndicate—as it was called—manipulated the finances of the entire region and was the dominant fiscal and political force in the area during the first decade of the 20th century. The Canadian owners of the Alaska Northern were asking for $6 million, and an investigation by the commission demonstrated that the Alaska Northern had cost the original owners and builders $5,250,000. The owners claimed that they had $4,125,000 invested in the property, including advance work and surveys; and the Interstate Commerce Commission (ICC) reported a total investment in road and equipment of $3,616,800.81 as of June 30, 1912.

The actual payment price of $1,157,339.49 (another government report placed the figure at $1,154,188.48) was slightly below the value of the property as established by the engineers of the commission and as certified by the valuation experts of the ICC. Both figures showed the value of the railroad to be roughly $16,000 per mile.

Although the government took over the Alaska Northern properties almost immediately, the first installment of $504,188.49 was not paid until August 15, 1915, when litigation on ownership had ceased. The remainder was paid on June 30, 1916, when the government came into full possession of the Alaska Northern and its route.

It was not until the completion of the railroad and the driving of the Golden Spike by President Warren G. Harding on July 15, 1923, that the railroad officially became the Alaska Railroad, and the names under which construction had gone ahead and equipment had been marked—"U.S. Government Railroad," and Alaska Northern Railway—were finally dropped.

Alaskan Engineering Commission

Narrow-Gauge Locomotive Roster

Road No.	Wheel Arr.	Builder	C/N	Year	Cylinders	Drivers	Notes
1	0-4-0T	Porter	1972	1899	6x10	24"	Built as North American Transportation & Trading Co., No. 1, sold 1903 to Coal Creek Coal Company No. 1, sold in June 1905 to Tanana Mines Railway No. 1, sold in January 1907 to Tanana Valley Railroad No. 1, sold in December 1917 to Alaskan Engineering Commission No. 1. Transferred in 1923 to Alaska Railroad No. 1, retired before 1929, on display 1930, to Friends of the Tanana Valley Railroad, preserved.
4	0-4-0T	Baldwin	34957	1910	7x12	23"	Possibly built as USACOE. Scrapped, boiler used at Nenana.
5	0-4-0T	Baldwin		1910?			Possibly built as USACOE. Used at AEC coal mine. Leased to mine at Moose Creek in the 1920s. To Premier Mine No. 5, on display in Palmer, AK.
6	0-4-0T	Baldwin	34982	1910	7x12	23"	Possibly built as USACOE. Scrapped, boiler used as air reservoir, 1924.
19	0-4-0T	Alco or Vulcan			11x16		Built as USACOE, Portland, OR, sold in 1916 to AEC, No. 19, retired by 1924.
20	0-4-0T	Vulcan		1908	11x16		Built as USACOE, Portland, OR, sold in 1916 to AEC, No. 20, retired by 1924.
21	0-4-0T	Davenport		1908	10x16	29"	Built as USACOE, Portland, OR, sold in 1916 to AEC, No. 21, leased to coal mine as of 1924.
22	0-4-0T	Davenport		1908	10x16	29"	Built as USACOE, Portland, OR, sold in 1916 to AEC, No. 22, leased to coal mine as of 1924.
50	4-4-0	Baldwin	4294	March 1878	12x16	42"	Built as Olympia & Chehalis Valley No. 1 "E.H. Quimette," sold in May 1891 to Columbia & Puget Sound No. 10, sold in 1898 to WP&Y No. 4, renumbered 54, sold in 1905 to Tanana Mines Railway No. 50, sold in January 1907 to Tanana Valley Railroad No. 50, sold in December 1917 to Alaskan Engineering Commission No. 50, transferred in 1923 to Alaska Railroad No. 50, retired before 1924, scrapped in 1930.

Narrow Gauge Locomotive Roster *(continued)*

Road No.	Wheel Arr.	Builder	C/N	Year	Cylinders	Drivers	Notes
51	2-6-0	Brooks	578	1881	14x18	42"	Built as Kansas Central Railway No. 8 (UP No. 103, 1885), sold in 1890,* to Trail Creek Tramway No. 3, sold in April 1896 to Columbia & Western Railway No. 3, sold in 1898 to Canadian Pacific Railway, sold in August 1900 to WP&Y No. 65, sold in September 1906 to Tanana Mines Railway No. 51, sold in January 1907 to Tanana Valley Railroad No. 51, sold in December 1917 to Alaskan Engineering Commission No. 51, transferred in 1923 to Alaska Railroad No. 51, retired before 1924, scrapped 1930.*
52	2-6-0	Baldwin	10880	May 1890	11x18	38"	Built as Alberta Railway & Coal Co. No. 12, sold in 1906 to Tanana Mines Railway No. 52, sold in January 1907 to Tanana Valley Railroad No. 52, sold in December 1917 to Alaskan Engineering Commission No. 52, transferred in 1923 to Alaska Railroad No. 52, scrapped in 1930.
151	2-8-0	Baldwin	11073	July 1890	16x20	37"	Built as Alberta Railway & Coal Co., No. 5, sold in 1917 to Alaskan Engineering Commission No. 151, transferred in 1923 to Alaska Railroad No. 151, scrapped in 1936.
152	4-6-0	Baldwin	53296	June 1920	14x20	44"	To Alaska Railroad No. 152, retired in 1930, to Skagway in April 1943. Probably never operated, to Seattle in 1943. To Antelope & Western, No. 2. To Camino, Cable & Northern, No. 2, Camino, CA. To Keystone Railway Equipment Company. To Huckleberry Railroad, No. 2, Flint, MI, operating.
802	0-4-0T	Davenport	764	October 1907	10x16		Built as Isthmian Canal Commission, No. 802, sold in 1917 to AEC, No. 802, out of service by 1924. Rebuilt to standard gauge as ARR, No. 6, by 1927. Renumbered No. 1 (2nd) 1947, on display in Anchorage.
830	0-6-0T	Porter	4302	1910	8x14	24"	Built as Isthmian Canal Commission, No. 830, sold in 1917 to AEC, No. 830, out of service by 1924.

* Initial owner and construction specifications are unconfirmed.
** The AEC obtained seven small locomotives from the Isthmian Canal Commission. One was unnumbered, the others were No. 802, No. 823, No. 824, No. 830, No. 833, and No. 851. The unnumbered, No. 823, No. 824, No. 833, and No. 851 were never used by the AEC.

Chapter 9

Alaska Railroad

On April 10, 1915, President Woodrow Wilson formally announced his decision to adopt the Susitna Route for the Government Railroad. At the same time, the duties of the Alaskan Engineering Commission (AEC) were extended by executive order to include the construction of the proposed railroad. Engineers and workers were on the ground and attacking the job of laying out the first construction camp 16 days after the president signed the order. William C. Edes, chairman of the commission, became chief engineer on the project and managed all the commission's activities. The administrative offices were set up in Seward, and the head of the various divisions reported to Edes there.

Frederick Mears took charge of work on the new line from Ship Creek (Anchorage) northward. He left Seattle on April 18, arrived in Ship Creek on April 26, and proceeded with construction. Thomas Riggs Jr. continued to Fairbanks and made additional surveys and relocations of the line between Fairbanks and Broad Pass during the summer. There was no actual construction work done on the north section in 1915.

On April 29, 1915, three days after Mears arrived at the Ship Creek Camp, the ceremonial first spike was driven—not by a high government official as might be expected, but by Babe White, whose mother ran the Whitehouse bunkhouse in the construction camp. During the summer, 34 miles of line were cleared and graded, and by the end of 1915, 20 miles of track had been laid. Repairs on the Alaska Northern trackage and dock at Seward and the building of a new machine shop to replace the one that had burned during the summer were the main order of business in the Seward area.

The Alaskan Engineering Commission was faced with the problem of how to compensate workers at the Alaskan wage scale—and allow them to work the extended daylight hours—while complying with federal standards for both compensation and hours of work. Hiring independent contractors to perform the work solved the problem.

The basic, generally unskilled work of preparing the roadbed was allocated by the station (a "station" in engineering terms is generally 100 feet). The work consisted of clearing, grubbing (removing stumps and roots), excavation and fill, and grading. This class of work, which started in May 1915, was performed by independent contractors.

Construction workers watch as Babe White, daughter of the Whitehouse bunkhouse operator at Ship Creek (Anchorage), drives the ceremonial first spike in the construction of the Government Railroad (Alaska Railroad) on April 29, 1915. (Seattle Historical Society)

The contractors would band together and apply for a contract to perform a specified job on a length of railroad defined by a number of stations. The clearing and grubbing would generally be measured by the acre, the excavation and fill by the cubic yard, and the grading by the foot or station. The crew would then complete the work at a pace that the contractors chose. The incentive to the individuals was that the sooner they completed the contract, the higher per-hour profit there was to be shared—and if they

The first new locomotive brought to Alaska for the Alaska Railroad was this Alco-Rogers 0-4-2T purchased by the AEC in 1915. The engine was later used for roundhouse switching in Anchorage. It was eventually retired, sold to Bethlehem Steel Company in Seattle, and scrapped in 1947. (Seattle Historical Society)

were still interested, they could attempt another contract. Upon completion of the work, the construction items were measured and each of the employees was paid.

Contractors were not boarded by the commission, but they were allowed to purchase supplies and provisions from the commissary at reasonable prices. Ordinary day laborers received about $3 for an 8-hour day and were charged a dollar a day for good board at the construction camp. Medical care was provided for free, and ill or injured workers were moved to Seattle for special treatment at government expense.

Workers endured rugged living conditions during the construction of the railroad from 1915 to 1923. Accommodations consisted of tents with no floors, pole bunks covered with wild hay for mattresses, and no bedding. (You packed your own.) There was no smiling camp steward to direct the new arrivals to their quarters. New arrivals generally had to provide or build their own quarters.

In some areas, log cabins chinked with moss were hastily constructed. Roofs were constructed of strong poles

This railcar, No. 2, was operated by the U.S. Government Railroad in the summer of 1915 after the operation was taken over from Alaska Northern. This photo was taken somewhere along Turnagain Arm. (Clifford Collection)

laid with little pitch or slope and then covered with birch bark, hay, and moss and capped with an overall covering of 2 or 3 feet of topsoil. Ingenious carpenters fashioned door hinges out of bent nails or leather from old boot tops, and homemade wooden latches held the doors shut. Empty flour sacks covered openings where windows should have been.

Bunks at both ends of a typical bunkhouse were similar to post office boxes—they were made out of poles much like honeycomb cells. These bunks were usually 4 feet square and 8 feet deep and were aptly called muzzle loaders. The extra 2 feet of depth in the bunks was for duffel storage. Two coal oil lamps suspended from the ceiling provided light, and a central stove heated the structure. A person should not claim to be an Alaska Railroad pioneer until after spending at least one night in a muzzle loading bunkhouse.

Ship Creek soon developed into a community of 2,000 or more, and on June 10, 1915, under the direction of the general land office, a new town site was surveyed and 1,407 lots were put up for sale. Citizens soon voted to change the name of the new town to Anchorage. The town was governed by a commission-appointed town site manager. Certain restrictions were placed on the purchase of lots—prohibiting their use for the sale of liquor, gambling, or other "immoral" activities. Noncompliance with these restrictions resulted in the lots being forfeited. Lots sold for a minimum of $75 and for as high as $1,100, for a total of $147,235 for the entire town site, a record for such government sales at the time.

The land auction at Ship Creek (Anchorage) on July 10, 1915, attracted many of the construction workers from the U.S. Government Railroad. Lots sold for a minimum of $75 and for as high as $1,100, bringing in a total of $147,235 for the entire town site. Certain restrictions were placed on the use of the lots, including prohibition of liquor sales, gambling, and other "immoral" activities. (Anchorage Historical and Fine Arts Museum, Alaska Railroad Collection)

The first business established in Anchorage was the Montana Cafe. The Anchorage sale was followed by a similar sale at Seward on September 11 and 12, 1915. The

---

The Panama Connection

A federal act in March 12, 1914, made mandatory the use of any "machinery, equipment, instruments, material and other property of any sort whatsoever" that was no longer needed for construction of the Panama Canal. As a result, a representative of the AEC went to Panama and arranged for the shipment (by chartered vessel) of steam shovels, derricks, locomotives, flatcars, structural steel, shop machinery, and other construction and railroad equipment.

At the time the French started work on the digging of the Panama Canal, they used a variety of gauges, although a significant amount of the equipment was 5-foot–gauge. When Americans took over the project, they continued use of the broad gauge. The Alaska Railroad was built to North American standard gauge—4 feet, 8-1/2 inches—so it was necessary to convert the locomotives acquired from the Isthmian Canal Commission by installing extra-wide steel tires on the wheels. This was accomplished at an estimated cost of $775 for each locomotive. The 24 available locomotives, M-1, 2-6-0s, had been built by the American Locomotive Company in 1906 at a cost of $11,000 each. The AEC eventually acquired a total of 18.

The commission also bought several narrow-gauge locomotives from the Isthmian Commission for construction and mine use. A total of 22 of these little saddle-tankers, built by H. K. Porter Company, Davenport Locomotive Company, and the Vulcan Iron Works, were declared surplus and eventually disposed of. They were originally purchased at prices ranging from $2,950 to $3,163 each. Two of the locomotives have survived.

The conversion of freight cars was carried out at a cost of approximately $28.50 each. All of the equipment was made available at no cost to the commission other than transportation and modification.

This Alco-Brooks 2-8-2 No. 31 was obtained by the Alaska Railroad after service with the Buffalo & Susquahana, Pittsburg & West Virginia, and an equipment dealer, Southern Iron & Equipment Company. Built in 1903, it was purchased by the Alaska Railroad in 1927 and retired during the 1930s. (Clifford Collection)

lots were sold outright with half the purchase price paid at the time and the balance within one year. There were no restrictions on the use of the property.

During the first summer the Government Railroad was in service, the line also operated gasoline motorcars over the first 34 miles of track from Seward, charging passengers 12-1/2¢ a mile and freight service at 1-1/2¢ per pound for the entire distance. The Government Railroad got its feet wet in river navigation in 1916 when the Alaskan Engineering Commission built docks and various terminal facilities on the Tanana River at the native village of Tortella, which was almost immediately renamed Nenana.

At the same time dock facilities were under construction at Nenana, a construction camp was established there and in August 1916 the first lots were sold, bringing in a revenue of $129,705. On October 24, 1916, Mrs. Emma Duke drove the first spike when trackage commenced on the Fairbanks division. She was the first white woman to reach the settlement at Nenana when the trading post was established in 1906 by her husband James Duke.

One of 18 American Locomotive Company's 2-6-0s built in 1906 to 5-foot gauge for the Isthmian Canal Commission for the building of the Panama Canal. This one, No. 285, was shipped to Alaska for use on the U.S. Government Railroad (ARR). These locomotives were narrowed to standard gauge by adding wide steel tires and were used into the 1940s. (Clifford Collection)

In the spring of 1916, the reconstruction of the Alaska Northern continued, consisting of the rebuilding of bridges, the elimination of trestles with fills, improvement of alignment, and some slight reduction in grades. Seventy-five thousand new ties were laid. By September 1916, a total of 3,582 workers were on the job, including 300 imported from Seattle for special tasks. During the year, 60 miles of mainline track and 100 miles of additional grade were completed, and the right-of-way was cleared for 230 miles. Work progressed well on rebuilding the old Alaska Northern trackage, and work south of Fairbanks was making good

The Alaska Railroad on the Water

Until 1920, materials were brought in through St. Michaels and Whitehorse for railroad construction between McKinley Park and Fairbanks. Vessels operated by Northern Commercial Company and American Yukon Navigation Company handled this cargo.

By 1921, the American Yukon Navigation Company had purchased the Northern Commercial Company river lines and various independents and become virtually the only operator on the river. Alaska Yukon Navigation eliminated operation below Fort Yukon, and service became so chaotic that immediate action was necessary to reestablish operations to out-of-the-way points and to prevent the collapse of the entire river economy. The only service still available was by two small stern-wheelers and two barges operated and maintained by the Army Transport Service to Forts Egbert, Hamlin, and Gibbon. The Service also maintained the military telegraph service along the Tanana and Yukon Rivers. The war department discontinued this operation when it abandoned all installations in Alaska except for Chilkoot Barracks at Haines, a small detachment at Anchorage, and a few Signal Corps locations.

The equipment from these installations was turned over to the Government Railroad by executive order in the fall of 1922. In May 1923, the interior department established a passenger, mail, and freight service between Nenana and Holy Cross, a distance of 642 miles. In 1925, the route was extended to Marshall, 132 miles below Holy Cross, in 1946 to Circle, and in the next year to Fort Yukon.

During the following years, the original equipment was replaced. A rehabilitated vessel (the steamer Alice) was put into operation in 1929 and retired in 1953. The steamer Nenana, built at Nenana in 1932, was acquired in 1933. Other vessels used included the Yukon and the Barry K, which were retired in 1946 and 1947. Various other barges were purchased and later retired. In the years 1947 and 1951, a number of steel barges were built by the railroad at Nenana. In 1953, the motor vessels Tanana and Yukon and the barges OB-2 and OB-3 were acquired. These hulls were of modern design for river operation and met the demands of difficult service without failure.

On March 1, 1955, the Alaska Railroad awarded a contract to the B&R Tug and Barge Company to operate the river transportation system on the Tanana and Yukon Rivers. B&R in turn transferred interest to the Yutana Barge Lines. The railroad's last stern-wheeler, the Nenana, was declared surplus and turned over to the Fairbanks Chamber of Commerce in 1956. It is now is a tourist attraction at Alaskaland.

The last of the stern-wheelers operated by the Alaska Railroad was the Nenana, which was put into service in 1933 and retired and turned over to the Fairbanks Chamber of Commerce in 1956. The vessel is now on display at Alaskaland in Fairbanks. (Western Airlines)

progress. The first two passenger coaches for the railroad arrived in Anchorage on September 23, 1916.

There were new problems for the railroad in 1917. The U.S. went to war, and material and labor costs jumped. Much controversy centered on the relocation of railroad headquarters from Seward—originally designated as the permanent headquarters for the railroad—to Anchorage. The year also saw the narrow-gauge Tanana Valley Railroad purchased for $300,000 and the branch line to the Matanuska coal fields completed. A chamber of commerce had been organized in Anchorage, and in one of its bulletins (apparently attempting to bring new people to town) it printed a list of typical wages. Unskilled labor earned 50¢ an hour, or $4 a day; cooks earned $100 to $125 per month plus board; locomotive engineers made $204 per month; and steam shovel engineers $210 per month—the highest rate.

By the end of the year, 121 miles of railroad was in operation. A year later this had been extended to 168 miles. The average monthly number of workers in 1917 was 4,466, but this dropped to 2,550 in 1918 because of the draft.

The AEC purchased several narrow-gauge saddle-tankers from the Army Corps of Engineers in 1916 and leased them to various coal mine operations in the Matanuska Valley. One is visible in operation here. Bearing the No. 22, this little Davenport was built in 1908 and was in coal mine service by 1924. (Clifford Collection)

During 1919, little work was done on the railroad until late summer due to a lack of appropriation from Congress. Some work was done on both the lines, but by the end of the year there was still a gap of 122 miles between the two divisions. A general reorganization to consolidate construction and operational divisions was developed.

Following his return from service in France, Colonel Frederick Mears, formerly in charge of railroad construction in Anchorage, was appointed chairman and chief engineer for the AEC. He succeeded William C. Edes, chairman since its organization in 1914. Edes was appointed consulting engineer with headquarters in Washington D.C. He retired in 1920. Shortly after Colonel Mears's reappointment, cash began to flow in from Congress and construction work was resumed on the railroad.

In 1920, for the first time since construction had started, there was ample funding available in advance for the summer working season. The year also marked the successful mining of coal for use of the railroad at Eska, with the average

A former Isthmian Canal Commission 2-6-0 built to 5-foot gauge is being used as a work locomotive during the construction of the U.S. Government Railroad. Built by the American Locomotive Company in 1906, the engines were converted to standard gauge by adding wide steel treads to the wheels. No. 225 was retired and scrapped in 1936. (Anchorage Historical and Fine Arts Museum, Alaska Railroad Collection)

One of several locomotives acquired from the Isthmian Canal Commission upon completion of the building of the canal. The 2-6-0 locomotives were built by Alco-Brooks in 1905–6 to 5-foot gauge and converted for use on Alaska's standard-gauge trackage by adding wide steel treads to the wheels. These steel treads are visible on the drivers of No. 605. (Anchorage Historical and Fine Arts Museum, Alaska Railroad Collection)

cost of $6 per ton. Some 32,276 tons of coal were mined.

On November 2, 1920, the city of Anchorage was incorporated, and the operation and maintenance of the city were turned over to local authorities on December 1, 1920. By the end of the year, the gap between the Northern and Southern Divisions of the railroad was closed to 84 miles for steel and 50 miles for grading. Moreover, the original 31.9 miles of narrow-gauge trackage on the Tanana Valley Railroad had been supplemented by 48.5 miles of narrow-gauge track, temporarily laid on a standard-gauge roadbed to carry the rails to the Tanana River.

Dining car service was in full operation during 1920, with lobster, combination, tuna, and Alaska salmon salads at $1 per portion; fried or baked halibut at $1; mountain trout with bacon at $1.25; roast leg of pork at $1.25; prime rib of beef at $1.50; and chili con carne at 75¢. Pie cost 20¢, cold drinks 25¢, coffee a dime, and tea 25¢.

November 1921 saw the Northern and Southern Divisions of the railroad as such abolished and all divisions changed to departments.

One of the more difficult construction projects involved in the building of the railroad was the Hurricane Gulch Bridge, a marvel in engineering. It was completed in 1921. Construction of the bridge was done by the American Bridge Company (one of the occasions in which work was turned over to an outside contracting firm). A construction camp was set up at Mile 285 in May 1920 for preliminary clearing and grading, and actual construction work started in March 1921. Two hinged spandrel arches spanning 384 feet in length each were constructed for a total overall span of 918 feet,

Work is nearing completion on the Hurricane Gulch Bridge at Mile 385 of the Alaska Railroad as this photo was taken on August 8, 1921. The bridge was completed a week later, and the first official train crossed the structure three days after that. (Clifford Collection)

2 inches. Work was completed on August 15, 1921, and a work train tested the span on that date. The first passenger train crossed the span on August 18, 1921.

With trackage (except that over the Tanana River) completed, the following winter saw narrow-gauge rails laid on the ice and passengers and freight carried across the river for transfer to standard-gauge trains at the opposite bank. The narrow-gauge rails were removed from the river on April 19, and for a short time transfers were made by horse team. All transfers were discontinued on May 1, and boats were used to cross the river starting on May 9.

A contract was awarded to the American Bridge Company to construct the Tanana River Bridge, and on June 15, 1922, all narrow-gauge trackage was supplemented by standard gauge. This was accomplished by adding a third rail on the section between Happy and Fairbanks, permitting narrow-gauge trains as well as standard-gauge equipment over this section. The third rail was used until 1930 when service to Chatanika was terminated. The bridge over the Tanana was completed on February 27, 1923, with a 700-foot span, the second largest truss bridge in the country.

On Sunday, July 15, 1923, at a ceremony on the north end of the Nenana Bridge, President Warren G. Harding drove the golden spike connecting 471 miles of railroad

This was the first regular train to cross the Hurricane Gulch Bridge on the Alaska Railroad. The date was August 18, 1921. The bridge was constructed by the American Bridge Company, one of the outside contracting firms hired to work on the railroad. Construction on the 918-foot, 2-inch span began in March 1921 and was completed on August 15, 1921. The two-hinged spandrel arch spans 384 feet. (Clifford Collection)

President Warren G. Harding came a great distance to drive the golden spike marking the completion of the U.S. Government Railroad (Alaska Railroad). The ceremony took place at Nenana on July 15, 1923, with a host of dignitaries on hand. (Alaska Railroad Archives)

The golden spike ceremony was reenacted on the 50th anniversary of the completion of the railroad. One of the special guests at that time was Sam Chiamis, a retired gandy dancer. Chiamis was at North Nenana when President Harding took part in the initial ceremony and watched the president drive the final spike of the railroad Chiamis had helped build. At the anniversary ceremony, Chiamis placed the duplicate gold spike (actually just gold-plated) in place to be driven by John W. Ingram, chief of the Federal Railroad Administration, who was representing President Richard Nixon. Those invited to the ceremony were presented with this golden spike plaque. (Clifford Collection)

from Seward to Fairbanks. The official party included the first lady Mrs. Harding, Secretary of the Interior Hubert Work, Secretary of Commerce Herbert Hoover, Secretary of Agriculture Henry Wallace, Alaska Territorial Governor Scott C. Bone, and many others. Colonel Frederick Mears, who had been chairman of the Alaskan Engineering Commission during the final years of construction but who had returned to the army for a short tour of duty, was not present.

To start the ceremony, Governor Scott Bone carefully inserted the golden spike in a prepared hole and the president tapped it lightly. The golden spike was then removed and an iron spike substituted. The president missed it twice and then finally drove it home. The Alaska Railroad was officially completed. The Alaskan Engineering Commission was dissolved, and the designation "Government Railroad" was replaced with "Alaska Railroad."

Actually, there were two official golden spikes driven on the Alaska Railroad. One spike is now owned by the Southern California Arms Collectors Association. This spike was presented to Colonel Mears by the city of Anchorage for his work as chairman of the Alaskan Engineering Commission. He designed and built the Alaska Railroad and served as the railroad's general manager from 1919 to 1923. Reportedly, this spike was driven upon completion of the Seward-Anchorage section of the railroad on September 10, 1918.

The second golden spike was the one driven by President Harding at Nenana upon completion of the railroad. This spike is on display in the Harding Museum Home in Marion, Ohio. The California-owned spike was returned to Alaska for the 1967 Centennial and was on display in Fairbanks—improperly described as the spike that President Harding drove at Nenana.

The years from 1924 to 1945 were difficult ones for the Alaska Railroad. Though the line was officially completed, much of the construction was temporary. Over the years, general managers of the railroad repeatedly recommended that permanent structures be constructed and partially completed work be finished, but proposed budgets for improvements were slashed or ignored. At first some improvements and repairs were made only as needed to keep the railroad in operation. The true purpose of the Alaska Railroad—to aid in the development of the territory of Alaska—was forgotten. The annual operating deficit became a red flag to the appropriations committees. Making the railroad profitable was the goal, and all else was ignored. The railroad was forced to use outdated equipment and at times to do without needed supplies and necessary maintenance; yet there was still an annual deficit until 1938.

The original construction appropriation was $35 million, but the project had cost $70 million, partially because of high prices during and after World War I. No one charged that there had been fraudulent use of funds, and no shrewd promoter made a million dollars or even a single dollar. Every cent was properly accounted for. After completion, however, the first investigator arrived. After a hurried 36-hour visit, he declared that the railroad was a failure, the country in which it was built worthless, and the money spent constructing it wasted. He advocated tearing up the rails and junking the whole project.

A railroad track was constructed across the frozen Tanana River during the winter of 1921 to tie together the southern standard-gauge and northern narrow-gauge sections of the AEC (Alaska Railroad). Narrow-gauge locomotive No. 151, purchased by the AEC for use on the Tanana Valley section, and one of the little saddle-tankers are shown testing the river ice in this photo. (Anchorage Historical and Fine Arts Museum, Alaska Railroad Collection)

General Simon B. Buckner leads a group of military and railroad dignitaries after "holing through" on the secret Portage-Whittier tunnel constructed during World War II. The project, completed in the spring of 1943, was to make a safe southern terminus for the railroad at Whittier—assumed to be protected from Japanese attack. The 14,410-foot tunnel was dedicated to Anton Anderson, chief engineer of construction, in December 1976. (Anchorage Historical and Fine Arts Museum, Alaska Railroad Collection)

The colonization of the Matanuska Valley, a movement sponsored by the Federal Emergency Relief Administration and later turned over to the Alaska Rural Rehabilitation Corporation, brought more than 200 colonists with families to the Palmer area and gave additional travel impetus to the railroad. Another boost came as a result of the building of the Mount McKinley Park Hotel, which was turned over to the railroad by the National Park Service on December 8, 1938, and which was completed and opened for business on June 1, 1939.

In 1941, the United States was on the threshold of World War II, and the Alaska Railroad was ill-prepared for the burden of increased tonnage imposed by preparation for war. Instead of a seasonal operation, the railroad was faced with the problem of carrying more tonnage every month than it had previously carried in its peak months. Total tonnage rose from 157,000 in fiscal year 1939 to 627,000 tons in 1944.

To safeguard the flow of military supplies and personnel during the war, a branch called the Whittier Cutoff was constructed in 1942–43 under the supervision of the U.S. Army Corps of Engineers. This part of the main line extended from Whittier on Passage Canal, Prince William Sound, to Portage Station. The new line was 12.4 miles long and included two tunnels through the mountains, one 13,090 feet long and the other 4,910 feet long. The construction of the cutoff shortened the distance from a deep-water port to Fairbanks by 51.5 miles and gave the railroad two terminal points where connections could be made with ocean vessels—Seward and Whittier. A branch line was also constructed from the northern terminus in Fairbanks to Ladd Field.

Because of a reduction in personnel due to the draft and to the construction industry in Alaska and elsewhere during the early days of the war, outside assistance was necessary for the railroad to transport military supplies. The 714th Railroad Operating Battalion was assigned to the Alaska Railroad in 1943. The battalion departed from Camp Clayborne, Louisiana, on March 14, 1943, and moved onto the railroad on April 3, 1943. The unit was commanded by Lieutenant Colonel Herbert S. Huron, who was later succeeded by Lieutenant Colonel W. Hastedt. The 714th was on the railroad for more than two years, augmenting the civilian personnel in all departments. The members of the military integrated easily with the regular railroad employees, and the two groups worked side by side for the two-year period. It was not uncommon for an engine crew to consist of one civilian and one enlisted man. The unit was relieved on May 7, 1945, and departed for the Lower 48 three days later.

Following the war, the rehabilitation and reorganization of the railroad began, including the replacement of 70-pound rails with 115-pound rails. The railroad's first

These former "troop sleepers" are reminders of World War II. They are now on display at MATI. (Western Airlines)

streamliner, the Aurora, made its shakedown run to Palmer on October 16, 1947, and formal service was inaugurated to Mt. McKinley on Alaska Day, October 18, 1947. The year also marked the completion of new terminal facilities in Anchorage and Fairbanks worth $9.5 million.

On January 15, 1951, one of the most disastrous blazes in the history of the railroad destroyed the Anchorage machine shop and coach shed and along with it equipment and maintenance records from the railroad's inception on.

The longest freight train in the history of the railroad made its way from Whittier to Anchorage on June 25, 1951. This train was 108 cars long, carried 5,200 tons of freight, and was powered by five diesels, three on the head and two cut in 60 cars back. During the months of May and June of that year, a total of 270,000 tons of freight were handled—also a record. On August 31, the railroad had its biggest payday when 6,200 paychecks totaling $1,350,000 were handed out.

The scenic but costly Loop, constructed by the Alaska Central and Alaska Northern between Miles 47.5 and 50.8, was eliminated in a $1 million improvement program during the fall of 1951. A golden spike was driven to mark the occasion, which cut 1.1 miles off the Seward-Anchorage run. This also resulted in the elimination of five bridges, a heated tunnel (to keep out the ice), and a snow shed, thus saving $36,000 in maintenance costs each year.

The new grade curved close to the base of the snubbed and muddy nose of the Bartlett Glacier. The relocation was completed over ground that had been covered with 75 to 100 feet of ice 30 years earlier. The Bartlett Glacier had retreated nearly a

The Moose Gooser

Probably one of the most unusual days in the history of the railroad was February 24, 1944, when a moose delayed five trains for nearly five hours in the area of Curry and Mile 255. The first train was delayed for an hour and a half before the moose allowed it to pass. A short time later, the same moose stood off a rotary snowplow crew for almost three hours before he was shot. Three more trains were thrown off schedule and held on siding awaiting the two delayed trains.

An extremely stubborn animal, the moose prefers walking along railroad tracks because they are usually free of snow. Today the railroad still has to coax moose off the right-of-way and continues to be ignominiously unsuccessful—many methods and many, many colorful curses later. Some tactics used against the moose have been oscillating lights, high-pitched whistles, hot steam fusees, rocket pistols, aluminum sheeted bridges, snow balls, and shots of hot coffee from the pots of certain railroad cooks.

Another strategy was to carve out turnouts along the track through the snow banks. Section workers and bulldozer operators sliced turnouts and "parking lots" at 45-degree angles that they thought might entice the moose, which unfortunately had no effect on the animals. Alaska Railroad locomotives still carry the nickname Moose Goosers. Meanwhile, trains still chug into stations hours late, and the obstinate moose still choose to meet their fate by challenging the right-of-way of 2,000-ton trains.

In 1954, one stunt finally worked. A large moose was found sound asleep on the track, and an exasperated brakeman walked up and placed a flare under its tail. The brakeman lit the flare and hopped back on the train. Needless to say, the moose left the tracks pronto and headed for the nearest snow bank. After publicizing this incident, the ARR received so many letters of protest from animal lovers that orders were issued to use the red flares only for standard purposes. The winter kill of moose by the Alaska Railroad has been cut back considerably in recent years by turning off the oscillating light on the locomotives when approaching a moose. The animals are apparently hypnotized by the light and are unable to move.

In one of the worst winters for the large grazing animals (1989–1990), 749 moose were killed on the railroad. In the same winter, another 1,200 were killed on Alaska's highways. Altogether, it was a bad winter to be a moose.

This Porter 0-4-0T saw service on several railroads during its long and busy life. Built in 1899, it served with the North American Transportation and Trading Company near Dawson City, Y.T.; the Coal Creek Coal Company, Dawson City, Y.T.; the Tanana Mines Railway; the Tanana Valley Railroad and eventually the Alaskan Engineering Commission; and the Alaska Railroad. The little workhorse was retired in 1929 and is now being restored in Fairbanks.

mile in 30 years, exposing a hillside that permitted a track location that would have been impossible when the right-of-way was first laid out.

The postwar rehabilitation program cost $75 million, and on November 17, 1952, a ceremony and dedication of a monument at the Anchorage headquarters of the railroad marked the occasion.

Up until 1953, all of the general managers, their expertise gained in military railroading, had been federally appointed. A change came with the first Republican administration in 23 years. Presidents of U.S. railroads and officials of the Association of American Railroads were asked to submit names of likely candidates for the job. For eight years, Alaska became a training ground for private stateside railroad companies. The system worked well inasmuch as it removed the railroad from local politics and provincialism.

General managers of the Alaska Railroad and their appointment dates are contained in the following table:

Lee H. Landis	October 1, 1923
Noel W. Smith	December 19, 1924
Colonel Otto F. Ohlson	August 1, 1928; reappointed August 12, 1943

Colonel John P. Johnson	January 1, 1946
Frank E. Kalbaugh	September 1, 1953
Reginald N. Whitman	April 16, 1955
John H. Lloyd	August 16, 1956
Robert H. Anderson	August 16, 1958
Donald J. Smith	September 21, 1960
John E. Manley	March 1, 1962
Walter S. Johnson	January 1, 1972
William Dorcy	April 1, 1976
Stephen A. Ditmeyer (interim)	July 4, 1979
Frank H. Jones	January 30, 1980
Frank Turpin	1985–90
Robert Hatfield	1990–96
William Sheffield	1997–

In May 1968, one of the major branches of the Alaska Railroad, first put into service in August 1916, was closed down when the military facilities at Elmendorf and Richardson changed from coal to oil. The line ran from the main line at Matanuska Junction, about 26 miles north of Anchorage, through Palmer and up the Matanuska River to the Sutton Y and the Eska and Evans Jones Coal Company mines. There were also other mines in the area such as the Buffalo Coal Mine and Premier Coal Company properties, which had been served by narrow-gauge track and small tank locomotives obtained from various sources.

The Alaska Railroad became a full-fledged bureau in the Department of the Interior. In October 1966, Congress established the Department of Transportation and within it the Federal Railroad Administration, which became responsible for operating the Alaska Railroad.

Almost all steam locomotives were retired from the Alaska Railroad in November 1956, although No. 557 was kept on standby basis for several years. In 1964, No. 557 was finally sold to a scrapper who in turn sold it to Monte Holm of Moses Lake, Washington, where it is on display.

A special Alaska Railroad train provided transportation to the Hatcher Pass area for the filming of The Cheechakos by the Alaska Moving Picture Corporation. Filmed in 1923, The Cheechakos was the first motion picture made in Alaska by an Alaskan company. Prints of the film are still available and are often shown at gatherings of Alaskan sourdoughs in many parts of the country. (Anchorage Historical and Fine Arts Museum, Alaska Railroad Collection)

In 1962, the first car barge arrived at Whittier, thus eliminating the need to transfer freight from railcars to ships and then back again. In 1964, the barge operation was supplemented by train-ship service. Rail-marine service continued to be improved with the addition of Canadian National's 56-car barge in 1983. Direct, efficient connections with the railroads in the South 48 or Canada continue to be available through Whittier to either the ports of Seattle or Prince Rupert.

Disaster hit the Alaska Railroad when a great earthquake struck south central Alaska at 5:36 p.m. on Good Friday, March 27, 1964. The quake was measured at 8.4 to 8.6 on the Richter scale and released twice as much energy as the 1906 quake that wrecked San Francisco. It was felt on land over almost half a million square miles. For

A scenic attraction no longer beheld. An Alaska Railroad train on the famous Loop, with snow-covered mountains in the background. Riding the Loop, which was constructed by the Alaska Central and Alaska Northern crews, was quite a thrill since in its later years the wooden structure began to sag and passengers experienced terror along with the thrill and beauty of crossing the structure as it swayed in the wind. At the time the railroad was constructed, the Loop was necessary because of the nearness of the Bartlett Glacier, which since has receded nearly a mile. The Loop, located between Mile 47.5 and Mile 50.8, was eliminated in a 1951 improvement plan. (Anchorage Historical and Fine Arts Museum, Alaska Railroad Collection)

the Alaska Railroad, that 3.5-minute disaster cost $27 million—sections of track that had been twisted like pretzels had to be completely rebuilt. Other sections and the entire dock facilities at Seward slid into Resurrection Bay, and the tsunami that accompanied the quake ruptured two tank farms, which resulted in widespread fire.

In other areas, the tsunami hit standing freight cars so hard that the flanges on their wheels ripped the rails loose, popping spikes out of ties. After the disaster, Alaska Railroad inspectors found ties still in place, with little other than the empty spike holes to indicate that there had been rails there. The entire town of Portage dropped so that the tracks were under water at high tide. In the 185 miles from Seward to the Matanuska Valley, most of the bridges buckled; in short, they were "cambered from compression."

There was one bright spot in the whole picture—technological advances that changed the whole pattern of train maintenance. Gone were the crack all-woman section crew from Cantwell and the gandy dancer, along with the requisite hand tools and reliance on brawn. Earth-moving equipment; power shovels; tie tampers; and caterpillar tractors for spreading ballast, inserting ties, and laying rails enabled eight section workers to accomplish the same amount of track work that 80 workers had done 15

It was a thrilling adventure to ride the Loop until 1920, when it was redesigned. As it aged, the wooden structure started to sag. Terror became an ingredient in the thrill and beauty of a crossing because the structure would sway with the wind. At times the swaying became so pronounced that the engines jumped the track and had to be replaced using crowbars and frogs. Repairs were carried out in the winter by Alaska Railroad workers. The Loop was one of the most interesting attractions on the Alaska Railroad in the early days. (Anchorage Historical and Fine Arts Museum, Alaska Railroad Collection)

years earlier. Service north from Anchorage to Fairbanks was restored in about a week. Within about three weeks, trains were again rolling to Whittier—on a slow-order basis. In all, about 186 miles of the total 536 was damaged and 110 bridges structurally compromised, with 71 needing immediate repairs.

In 1969, President Nixon suggested selling the Alaska Railroad to cut down on government expenditures, but nothing came of the proposal. Other efforts were made to sell the railroad for more than $100 million, but no private parties were interested. The railroad was withdrawn from the market in 1975.

Alaska Railroad steam locomotive shops in Anchorage. The various steam locomotives operated by the Alaska Railroad were rebuilt, modified, and repaired here. (Anchorage Historical and Fine Arts Museum, Alaska Railroad Collection)

Premier Mine No. 5., one of several Baldwin 0-4-0 narrow-gauge saddle-tankers obtained by the Alaska Railroad. It was used in the railroad's Moose Creek coal mining operations. (Clifford Collection)

The early 1970s brought the construction of the trans-Alaska oil pipeline. As a result of additional traffic, a 10.2-mile extension from the city of Fairbanks to the Fairbanks International Airport was constructed in the spring of 1972 at a cost of $800,000.

In 1975, the railroad, finding itself short of equipment as a result of pipeline construction, purchased three new 3000-hp locomotives and borrowed 12 locomotives from the U.S. Army.

The year 1983 was pivotal for the Alaska Railroad. In January, President Reagan signed a bill that authorized the transfer of the ARR from the federal government to the state of Alaska. Later in the year, Governor Sheffield and Secretary of Transportation Dole agreed on the assets that were to be included in the sale. Subsequently, the U.S. Railway Association established a valuation for the railroad—$22.3 million. These actions set the stage for the actual sale of the railroad.

Negotiations between Alaska and the Department of Transportation continued through 1984. By mid-year, the state was confident enough of the eventual transfer that a quasi-public corporation was formed—the Alaska Railroad Corporation—to be run by a board of seven directors. On January 5, 1985, amid multiple ceremonies, the Alaska Railroad officially became the property of the state of Alaska.

The change of ownership resulted in a change in management. Since 1985, literally hundreds of millions of dollars have been poured into the railroad. New freight and passenger equipment has been purchased, and new-generation diesels appear to be

Earthquake and tsunami damage to Alaska Railroad facilities from the Good Friday 1964 earthquake. Damage to railroad in south-central Alaska ran into the millions of dollars (Anchorage Historical and Fine Arts Museum—Alaska Railroad collection)

constantly on order. Facility and trackage improvements have also been made, with 87,000 new ties installed in 1996 alone.

The physical plant was not all that improved. Overnight piggyback service was instituted between Anchorage and Fairbanks. Coal and gravel trains became major bulk commodity movers. Passenger service reached new heights, and special tour cars were added to the daily train between Anchorage and Fairbanks.

The changes were reflected in the financial bottom line. The railroad remained in the black for most years and for 1996 posted a record profit of $8,000,000. There were those who did not appreciate even this level of success, and the 1996 State Legislature voted to have the railroad appraised for sale. The governor vetoed the bill.

The Alaska Railroad is no Toonerville Trolley, although it does offer services not found on any other railroad. It is a messenger service, a grocery delivery service, a hunter taxi service, a riverboat company, and a scenic tour and Izaak Walton guide, pointing out the best streams in the area. You can often see the engineer deliver groceries to people along the track on the more remote sections of the line. The engineer has been known to run other errands too—delivering notes into town or to other mileposts and other residents, for example. The train stops anywhere on the line for hunters and fishermen and will stop at the same point days later to pick them up with their bag or catch. That's the Alaska Railroad for you.

The tracks of the Alaska Railroad disappeared into the waters of Turnagain Arm near Portage following the earthquake of March 27, 1964, which did millions of dollars' worth of damage to the ARR. In many areas, the land mass dropped 15 to 20 feet; in other areas it rose out of the nearby waters about the same amount. (Clifford Collection)

Chapter 9: Alaska Railroad 113

These rails led nowhere after the earthquake and tsunami on Good Friday 1964. This is part of the Seward waterfront, where damage was extensive. Overall damage ran into the millions of dollars. (Anchorage Historical and Fine Arts Museum, Alaska Railroad Collection)

Alaska Railroad locomotive No. 610, one of the 2-6-0 600s built in 1906 by Alco-Brooks as 5-foot gauge for use on the Panama Canal construction. They were converted to standard gauge before being shipped north by adding extra-wide treads to the wheels at a cost of approximately $775 per engine. They arrived in Alaska in 1922 and were put into service at that time. (Anchorage Historical and Fine Arts Museum, Alaska Railroad Collection)

Alaska Railroad railcar No. 215, a 26-passenger car used on shorter runs and during periods of light traffic. (Anchorage Historical and Fine Arts Museum, Alaska Railroad Collection)

AEC locomotive No. 151 heads a train moving freight and passengers across the Nenana River ice during the winter of 1921–22. The ice crossing tied together the northern and southern sections of the railroad prior to the completion of the bridge at Nenana. (Alaska Railroad Archives)

Alaska Railroad

Steam Locomotive Roster

Road No.	Wheel Arr.	Builder	C/N	Year	Cylinders	Drivers	Notes
1	0-4-2T	Alco-Rogers	47317	July 1915	14x22	44"	Retired in 1946, scrapped in 1947, Bethlehem Steel, Seattle.
2	0-4-0						Operated as AEC No. 1, gone before 1924.
5	0-4-0T	Alco-Rogers	6438	November 1917	14x22	44"	Retired in 1947.
10	4-4-0	Portland	499	September 1883	18x24	63"	Originally Northern Pacific No. 784, sold in 1904, to Alaska Central, No. 1, sold in 1909 to Alaska Northern, No. 1, sold in 1915, to AEC, No. 10, retired in 1920. To Alaska Railroad, No. 10, scrapped in 1930.
11	4-4-0	Baldwin	5880	October 1881			Originally Northern Pacific No. 846, sold in 1904, to Alaska Central, No. 2, sold in 1909, to Alaska Northern, No. 2, sold in 1915, to AEC, No. 11, to Alaska Railroad, No. 11, scrapped.
20	4-6-0	Baldwin	11280	October 1890	17x24	55"	Originally Port Townsend Southern, No. 3, to Northern Pacific, No. 369, to Alaska Northern, No. 3, sold in 1915, to AEC, No. 20, to Alaska Railroad, No. 20, scrapped in 1930 (Leased to Healy River Coal Corp., ca. 1920s).
21	4-6-0	Baldwin	30606	January 1906	16x24	46"	Originally Peninsular Rwy. Co., No. 1, to Simpson Timber Co., No. 7 "Sol Simpson," to Climax Manufacturing Co. (Dealer), sold in 1917, to AEC, No. 21, to Alaska RR, No. 21, stationary boiler at Curry, AK, by 1924, scrapped.
31	2-8-2	Alco-Brooks	27796	July 1903			Originally Buffalo & Susquahana, No. 121, to Pittsburgh & West Virginia, No. 118, to Southern Iron & Equipment, No. 2137, to Alaska Railroad, No. 31, 1927 (retired 1930s). Rebuilt from 2-8-0 to 2-8-2 by Southern Iron & Equipment. Boiler used at Marine Ways in Nenana, AK, until 1948.
101	2-8-0	Alco-RI	44600	November 1907	20x26	56"	Originally Copper River & Northwestern No. 23, to U.S. Army, No. 23 (Cordova), transferred 1945–6 to Alaska Railroad, No. 101, scrapped in 1947, Bethlehem Steel, Seattle.
208	2-6-0	Alco/Cooke	39099	January 1906	19x24	54"	Originally Isthmian Canal Commission, No. 208, to AEC No. 208, to Alaska Railroad, No. 208, 1915–16, scrapped in 1930.
221	2-6-0	Alco/Cooke	39112	January 1906	19x24	54"	Originally Isthmian Canal Commission, No. 221, to AEC No. 221, to Alaska Railroad, No. 221, 1915–16, scrapped in 1936.
224	2-6-0	Alco/Cooke	39115	January 1906	19x24	54"	Originally Isthmian Canal Commission, No. 224, to AEC No. 224, to Alaska Railroad No. 224, 1915–16, retired in July 1946, scrapped in 1947.

Steam Locomotive Roster (continued)

Road No.	Wheel Arr.	Builder	C/N	Year	Cylinders	Drivers	Notes
225	2-6-0	Alco/Cooke	39116	January 1906	19x24	54"	Originally Isthmian Canal Commission, No. 225, to AEC No. 225, to Alaska Railroad No. 225, 1915–16, scrapped in 1936.
239	2-6-0	Alco/Cooke	39150	September 1906	19x24	54"	Originally Isthmian Canal Commission, No. 239, to AEC No. 239, to Alaska Railroad, No. 239, 1915–16, rebuilt into 0-6-0, retired in July 1946.
242	2-6-0	Alco/Cooke	39153	September 1906	19x24	54"	Originally Isthmian Canal Commission, No. 242, to AEC No. 242, to Alaska Railroad, No. 242, 1915–16, scrapped in 1947.
247	2-6-0	Alco/Cooke	39158	September 1906	19x24	54"	Originally Isthmian Canal Commission, No. 247, to AEC No. 247, to Alaska Railroad, No. 247, 1915–16, scrapped in 1930.
264	2-6-0	Alco/Cooke	39175	September 1906	19x24	54"	Originally Isthmian Canal Commission, No. 264, to AEC No. 264, to Alaska Railroad, No. 264, 1915–16.
265	2-6-0	Alco/Cooke	39176	September 1906	19x24	54"	Originally Isthmian Canal Commission, No. 265, to AEC No. 265, to Alaska Railroad, No. 265, 1915–16, scrapped in 1930.
266	2-6-0	Alco/Cooke	39177	September 1906	19x24	54"	Originally Isthmian Canal Commission, No. 266, to AEC No. 266, to Alaska Railroad, No. 266, 1915–16, retired in January 1946.

This little Davenport 0-4-0T built in 1907 now carries Alaska Railroad's No. 1 and is on display at the Anchorage headquarters for the railroad. It is the former Isthmian Canal Commission No. 802, brought to Alaska in 1917 by the Alaskan Engineering Commission (AEC) as its No. 802. It was converted from narrow gauge to standard gauge in 1927 and used as a shop switcher, carrying No. 6. Following World War II, it was renumbered No. 1 and placed on display. (Western Airlines)

Steam Locomotive Roster *(continued)*

Road No.	Wheel Arr.	Builder	C/N	Year	Cylinders	Drivers	Notes
270	2-6-0	Alco/Cooke	39181	September 1906	19x24	54"	Originally Isthmian Canal Commission, No. 270, to AEC No. 270, to Alaska Railroad, No. 270, 1915–16, retired in 1946, scrapped in 1947.
272	2-6-0	Alco/Cooke	39183	September 1906	19x24	54"	Originally Isthmian Canal Commission, No. 272, to AEC No. 272, to Alaska Railroad, No. 272, 1915–16, scrapped in 1947.
275	2-6-0	Alco/Cooke	39185	December 1906	19x24	54"	Originally Isthmian Canal Commission, No. 275, to AEC No. 275, to Alaska Railroad, No. 275, 1915–16, scrapped in 1930.
277	2-6-0	Alco/Cooke	39187	December 1906	19x24	54"	Originally Isthmian Canal Commission, No. 277, to AEC No. 277, to Alaska Railroad, No. 277, 1915–16, scrapped in 1936.
278	2-6-0	Alco/Cooke	39188	December 1906	19x24	54"	Originally Isthmian Canal Commission, No. 278, to AEC No. 278, to Alaska Railroad, No. 278, 1915–16, scrapped in 1936.
280	2-6-0	Alco/Cooke	39190	December 1906	19x24	54"	Originally Isthmian Canal Commission, No. 280, to AEC No. 280, to Alaska Railroad, No. 280, 1915–16, scrapped in 1930.
285	2-6-0	Alco/Cooke	39195	December 1906	19x24	54"	Originally Isthmian Canal Commission, No. 285, to AEC No. 285, to Alaska Railroad, No. 285, 1915–16, retired in 1946, scrapped in 1947.
287	2-6-0	Alco/Cooke	39198	December 1906	19x24	54"	Originally Isthmian Canal Commission, No. 287, to AEC No. 287, to Alaska Railroad, No. 287, 1915–16, scrapped in 1947.
301	0-6-0	Alco-Man	39530	May 1906	20x26	51"	Originally Northern Pacific, No. 1042, to Alaska Railroad, No. 301, February 1943, scrapped in 1947.
310	0-6-0	Lima	8390	February 1944	21x28	50"	Originally U.S., No. 4056, to ARR, No. 310, retired in April 1954.
311	0-6-0	Lima	8402	February 1944	21x28	50"	Originally U.S., No. 4068, to ARR No. 311, retired in April 1954.

No. 312 and No. 315 were two of the 300 series locomotives acquired by the Alaska Railroad from the military. The class was used as switchers and was retired in the mid-1950s. (Anchorage Historical and Fine Arts Museum, Alaska Railroad Collection)

Steam Locomotive Roster *(continued)*

Road No.	Wheel Arr.	Builder	C/N	Year	Cylinders	Drivers	Notes
312	0-6-0	Lima	8407	March 1944	21x28	50"	Originally U.S., No. 4073, to ARR No. 312, retired in April 1954.
313	0-6-0	Lima	8406	March 1944	21x28	50"	Originally U.S., No. 4072, to ARR No. 313, retired in April 1954.
314	0-6-0	Lima	8408	February 1944	21x28	50"	Originally U.S., No. 4074, to ARR, No. 314.
315	0-6-0	Lima	8391	February 1944	21x28	50"	Originally U.S., No. 4057, to ARR No. 315, retired in April 1954.
316	0-6-0	Lima	8379	January 1944	21x28	50"	Originally U.S., No. 4045, to ARR, No. 316, retired in April 1954.
317	0-6-0	Lima	8393	February 1944	21x28	50"	Originally U.S., No. 4059, to ARR No. 317, retired in April 1954.
318	0-6-0	Lima	8392	January 1944	21x28	50"	Originally U.S., No. 4058, to ARR No. 318, retired in April 1954.
319	0-6-0	Lima	8382	January 1944	21x28	50"	Originally U.S., No. 4048, to ARR No. 319, retired in April 1954.
320	0-6-0	Lima	8383	January 1944	21x28	50"	Originally U.S., No. 4049, to ARR, No. 320, retired in April 1954.
401	2-8-0	Lima	7879	February 1942	21x26	50"	Originally U.S. TC, No. 6998, to Alaska Railroad, No. 501, to Alaska Railroad, No. 401, sold to F. C. deLargero in January 1958.
402	2-8-0	Lima	7880	February 1942	21x26	50"	Originally U.S. TC, No. 6999, to Alaska Railroad, No. 502, to Alaska Railroad, No. 402, sold to F. C. deLargero in January 1958.

ARR No. 502 was one of the 500 series Lima 2-8-0 locomotives acquired by the Alaska Railroad from the U.S. Army. The 500s were renumbered into the 400s after being put into service. Four of the six 400s went to Spain following retirement from the Alaska Railroad. (Anchorage Historical and Fine Arts Museum, Alaska Railroad Collection)

Steam Locomotive Roster *(continued)*

Road No.	Wheel Arr.	Builder	C/N	Year	Cylinders	Drivers	Notes
403	2-8-0	Lima	7881	March 1942	21x26	50"	Originally U.S. TC, No. 10 (Claiborne & Polk Military RR No. 10), to Alaska Railroad, No. 503, to Alaska Railroad, No. 403, destroyed in fire in January 1951, used as rip-rap at Matanuska River.
404	2-8-0	Lima	7877	February 1942	21x26	50"	Originally U.S. TC, No. 6996, to Alaska Railroad, No. 504, to Alaska Railroad, No. 404.
405	2-8-0	Lima	7875	February 1942	21x26	50"	Originally U.S. TC, No. 6994, to Alaska Railroad, No. 505, to Alaska Railroad, No. 405, sold to F. C. deLargero in January 1958.
406	2-8-0	Lima	7876	February 1942	21x26	50"	Originally U.S. TC, No. 6995, to Alaska Railroad, No. 506, to Alaska Railroad, No. 406, sold to F. C. deLargero in January 1958.
501 (see 401)							
502 (see 402)							
503 (see 403)							

Baldwin No. 551 was the first of the G.I. 2-8-0s acquired from the army by the Alaska Railroad in 1943. The locomotive was of the standard Gypsy Rose Lee type—stripped down for action. This locomotive was retired in 1956. (Anchorage Historical and Fine Arts Museum, Alaska Railroad Collection)

Steam Locomotive Roster *(continued)*

Road No.	Wheel Arr.	Builder	C/N	Year	Cylinders	Drivers	Notes
504 *(see 404)*							
505 *(see 405)*							
506 *(see 406)*							
551	2-8-0	Baldwin	69636	June 1943	19x26	57"	Originally U.S., No. 2379, to Alaska Railroad, No. 551, in September 1943, retired in November 1956.
552	2-8-0	Baldwin	69637	June 1943	19x26	57"	Originally U.S., No. 2380, to Alaska Railroad, No. 552, in September 1943, sold to F. C. deLargero in January 1958.
553	2-8-0	Baldwin	69638	June 1943	19x26	57"	Originally U.S., No. 2381, to Alaska Railroad, No. 553 in September 1943, wrecked in 1943 and scrapped.
554	2-8-0	Baldwin	69639	May 1943	19x26	57"	Originally U.S., No. 2382, to Alaska Railroad, No. 554, September 1943, retired in November 1956, sold to F. C. deLargero in January 1958.
555	2-8-0	Baldwin	69854	August 1943	19x26	57"	Originally U.S., No. 2626, to Alaska Railroad, No. 555, in October 1943, retired in April 1954.

Alaska Railroad No. 562 was the last of the G.I. Consolidations obtained by the Alaska Railroad. The 2-8-0 was built in 1942 by Alco and acquired by the ARR from the military following World War II. No. 562 was retired in 1956 and is shown with a snowplow over the pilot. (Anchorage Historical and Fine Arts Museum, Alaska Railroad Collection)

Steam Locomotive Roster (continued)

Road No.	Wheel Arr.	Builder	C/N	Year	Cylinders	Drivers	Notes
556	2-8-0	Baldwin	69855	August 1943	19x26	57"	Originally U.S., No. 2627, to Alaska Railroad, No. 556, in October 1943, retired in November 1956, on display at Anchorage.
557	2-8-0	Baldwin	70480	December 1944	19x26	57"	Originally U.S., No. 3523, to Alaska Railroad, No. 557, retired in June 1963, sold in 1964. To Michelson Steel, to Monte Holm, on display at Moses Lake, WA.
558	2-8-0	Baldwin	70478	December 1944	19x26	57"	Originally U.S., No. 3521, to Alaska Railroad, No. 558, sold to F. C. deLargero in January 1958.
559	2-8-0	Baldwin	70479	December 1944	19x26	57"	Originally U.S., No. 3522, to Alaska Railroad, No. 559, retired in April 1954, sold to F. C. deLargero in January 1958.
560	2-8-0	Baldwin	70367	December 1944	19x26	57"	Originally U.S., No. 3410, to Alaska Railroad, No. 560, retired in April 1954, sold to F. C. deLargero in January 1958.
561	2-8-0	Baldwin	70366	December 1944	19x26	57"	Originally U.S., No. 3409, to Alaska Railroad, No. 561, retired in November 1956.
562	2-8-0	Alco-Sch	70431	November 1942	19x26	57"	Originally U.S., No. 1600, to Alaska Railroad, No. 562, retired in November 1956.
601	2-6-0	Alco-Brooks	39122	January 1906	20x26	63"	Originally Isthmian Canal Commission, No. 601, to AEC No. 601, January 1922. To Alaska Railroad, No. 601, January 1923, rebuilt with 54" drivers.
605	2-6-0	Alco-Brooks	39126	January 1906	20x26	63"	Originally Isthmian Canal Commission, No. 605, to AEC, No. 605, in January 1922, to Alaska Railroad, No. 605, in January 1923.

Locomotive No. 556, a Baldwin 2-8-0 acquired from the U.S. Army in 1943 and retired in November 1956 was one of the last steamers used on the Alaska Railroad. A sister locomotive, No. 557, was retained an additional number of years as a backup for use during flood conditions and was the last steamer on the ARR. No. 556 was donated to the city of Anchorage and is on display. (Western Airlines)

Steam Locomotive Roster *(continued)*

Road No.	Wheel Arr.	Builder	C/N	Year	Cylinders	Drivers	Notes
606	2-6-0	Alco-Brooks	39127	January 1906	20x26	63"	Originally Isthmian Canal Commission, No. 606, to AEC, No. 606, January 1922, to Alaska Railroad, No. 606 in January 1923, scrapped in 1947.
610	2-6-0	Alco-Brooks	39131	January 1906	20x26	63"	Originally Isthmian Canal Commission, No. 610, to AEC, No. 610, in January 1922, to Alaska Railroad, No. 610, in January 1923.
614	2-6-0	Alco-Brooks	39135	January 1906	20x26	63"	Originally Isthmian Canal Commission, No. 614, to AEC, No. 614, in January 1922, to Alaska Railroad, No. 614, in January 1923, wrecked in March 1932, scrapped in 1947.
618	2-6-0	Alco-Brooks	39137	January 1906	20x26	63"	Originally Isthmian Canal Commission, No. 618, to AEC, No. 618, in January 1922, to Alaska Railroad, No. 618, in January 1923.
620	2-6-0	Alco-Brooks	39141	January 1906	20x26	63"	Originally Isthmian Canal Commission, No. 620, to AEC, No. 620, in January 1922, to Alaska Railroad, No. 620, in January 1923, wrecked in February 1938.
701	2-8-2	Baldwin	59605	October 1926	22x28	54"	Built as Alaska Railroad, No. 701, retired in April 1954, sold to F. C. deLargero in January 1958.
702	2-8-2	Baldwin	59606	October 1926	22x28	54"	Built as Alaska Railroad, No. 702, retired in April 1954, sold to F. C. deLargero in January 1958.

The last steam locomotive in service on the Alaska Railroad was No. 557. Seldom used after 1956, it was retained by the railroad because it could pull trains through water, which diesels could not do when tracks were flooded during spring runoff. The 557 was finally retired in 1963. The locomotive was acquired in 1966 by Monte Holm of Moses Lake, Washington, where it is currently displayed. (Anchorage Historical and Fine Arts Museum, Alaska Railroad Collection)

Steam Locomotive Roster (continued)

Road No.	Wheel Arr.	Builder	C/N	Year	Cylinders	Drivers	Notes
703	2-8-2	Baldwin	60689	December 1928	22x28	54"	Originally Alaska Railroad, No. 703, retired in April 1954, sold to F. C. deLargero in January 1958.
751	2-8-2	Alco-Sch	46856	November 1909	27-1/2x30	63"	Originally Northern Pacific, No. 1676, to Alaska Railroad. No. 751, in February 1942, scrapped in 1947.
752	2-8-2	Alco-Sch	46872	November 1909	27-1/2x30	63"	Originally Northern Pacific, No. 1692, to Alaska Railroad, No. 752, February 1943 scrapped in 1947.
801	4-8-2	Baldwin	61736	May 1932	22x30	63"	Wrecked in 1942 and 1951, to Dulien Steel Products, 1953, scrapped.
802	4-8-2	Baldwin	64366	July 1942	22x30	63"	To Dulien Steel Products, 1953, scrapped.
901	4-6-2	Baldwin	62515	December 1940	22x28	63"	Sold to F. C. deLargero in January 1958.
902	4-6-2	Baldwin	70336	June 1945	22x28	63"	
	2-8-2	Alco-Brooks	55491	November 1915	20x28	48"	Originally CR&NW, No. 71, to Alaska Railroad, never used after WWII.
4015 (U.S.)	0-6-0	Alco		1942	21x28	50"	Originally U.S., No. 4015, used for parts.

Notes:
Locomotives in the 200 and 600 series were originally built as 5-foot gauge and received wider tires when acquired by the Alaska Railroad.
Baldwin 2-8-2T+T (c/n 6159, 12/1929) ex-Comox Lumber Co., No. 16, operated on the Alaska Railroad during the summer of 1967.

Alaska Railroad locomotive No. 556, one of the last steamers to see service on the railroad, is shown here in passenger service. No. 556 was obtained from the U.S. Army in 1943 and retired from service in 1956. The Baldwin 2-8-0 is now on display in the Anchorage City Park. (Anchorage Historical and Fine Arts Museum, Alaska Railroad Collection)

Alaska Railroad

Diesel Locomotives

Road No.	Builder	Model	Date Built	C/N	History	Acq.	Ret.	Notes
Mate 1	Alco/ARR	slug	1971	71320	Built as ARR 1001	1971	1983	Scrapped
Mate 2	Alco/ARR	slug	1972	70670	Ex-ARR 1027 Built as USA 8049	1972	1983	Scrapped
50	GE	25-ton	1944	27501	Built as USA 7769	1946	1956	To Schnitzer Steel, to Northwest Steel Rolling Mills 27501, c. 1961, to Salmon Bay Steel 27501, to Oregon Electric Railway Museum.
51	GE	23-ton	1941	13146	Ex-Oregon Shipbuilding Built as Todd-California ship-building 50	1946	1956	To Schnitzer Steel L-1, 1961, to Inter-City Metals 737, to Oregon Steel Mill 737, renumbered 372–500.

This locomotive, No. 801, a Baldwin 4-8-2 built in 1932, could be called one of the tough-luck engines on the Alaska Railroad. It was wrecked in 1942 when it hit a slide between Potter and Indian. It was rebuilt, only to be wrecked again in 1951. The 1951 wreck marked the end of its career. (Anchorage Historical and Fine Arts Museum, Alaska Railroad Collection.)

Diesel Locomotive Roster (continued)

Road No.	Builder	Model	Date Built	C/N	History	Acq.	Ret.	Notes
60	Whit.	20GM15	1940	13179	Built as USWD 2022	1946?	195?	To USA 7654.
61	Whit.	20GM15	1940	13180	Built as USWD 2023	1946?	195?	To USA 7655, to Bunker Hill & Sullivan Mining, to Lewiston Grain Growers 7. (Note: c/n's on 60/61 may be interchanged.)
115	Plym.	HLC-3	1927	2635	Built as Standard Steel Car Co.	1927	1930	To Great Southern RR to National Lime & Stone Co. 3, renumbered 0605.
243	Plym.	ML8/2	1943	4494	Built as USA 7613	1946?	?	Scrapped
701	Budd	RDC-3	January 1953	5703	Ex-SEPTA 9171 Ex-PC 93 Built as NH 126	1986	-	In service
702	Budd	RDC-3	May 1952	5819	Ex-SEPTA 9170 Ex-PC 96 Built as NH 129	1986	-	In service
711	Budd	RDC-2	May 1952	5609	Ex-AMTRAK 36 Ex-PC 82 Built as NH 121	1987	-	In service
712	Budd	RDC-2	July 1951	5420	Ex-AMTRAK 34 Ex-PC 80 Built as NYC M480	1987	-	In service

Locomotive No. 701 was the first of three sister engines acquired by the Alaska Railroad in 1926 to 1928. These Baldwin 2-8-2s were retired in 1954 and were shipped to F. C. deLargero in Spain in 1958. (Anchorage Historical and Fine Arts Museum, Alaska Railroad Collection)

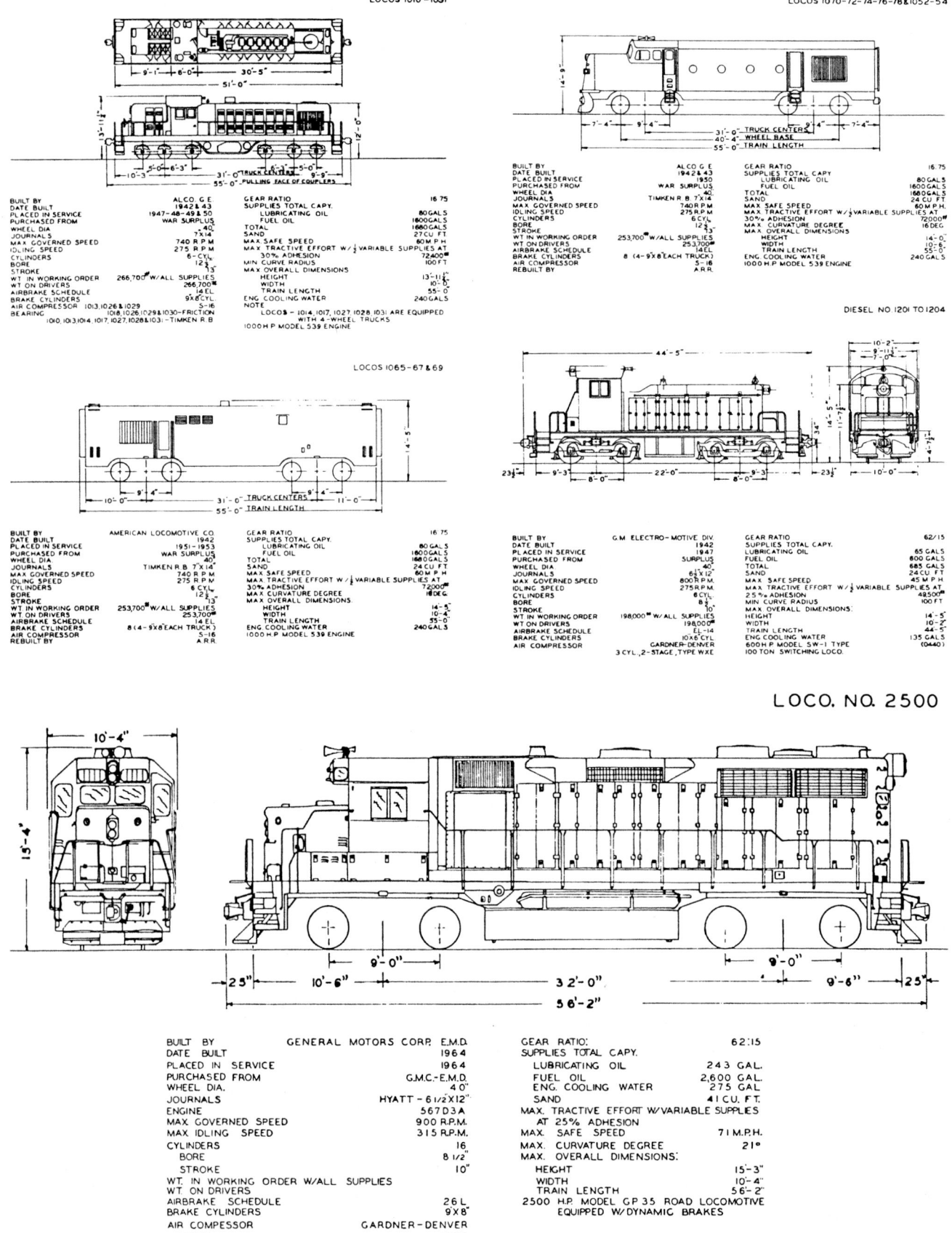

Diagrams of the various 1000 series, 1200 series, and 2500 series diesel electric locomotives on the Alaska Railroad. (Anchorage Historical and Fine Arts Museum, Alaska Railroad Collection)

Diesel Locomotive Roster (continued)

Road No.	Builder	Model	Date Built	C/N	History	Acq.	Ret.	Notes
721	Budd	RDC-1	March 1952	5802	Ex-AMTRAK 15 Exx PC 44 Built as NH 44	1987	-	Used for parts. Never run, number assigned for accounting purposes only.
1000	Alco	RS-1	1944	71319	Acquired new	1944	1973	To MATI
1001	Alco	RS-1	1944	71320	Acquired new	1944	1971	To ARR slug Mate 1, 1971.
1002	Alco	RSD-1	1943	70659	Built as USA 8038	1949	1950	To ARR RF1B 1055, 1950.
1010	Alco	RSD-1	1943	70662	Built as USA 8041	1947	1965	Scrapped, 1960s.
1011	Alco	RSD-1	1943	70672	Built as USA 8051	1947	1950	To ARR RF1B 1075, 1950.
1012	Alco	RSD-1	1943	70664	Built as USA 8043	1947	1950	To ARR RF1B 1077, 1950.
1013	Alco	RSD-1	1943	70665	Built as USA 8044	1947	1965	Scrapped, 1966–68.
1014	Alco	RSD-1	1943	70666	Built as USA 8045	1947	1970	Was to become Mate 3; scrapped, 1973.
1015	Alco	RSD-1	1943	70656	Built as USA 8035	1948	1952	Damaged by fire; to ARR RF1B 1065, 1952.
1016	Alco	RSD-1	1942	70647	Built as USA 8026	1949	1953	To ARR RF1B 1067, 1953.
1017	Alco	RSD-1	1945	72157	Built as USA 8664	1949	1964	Scrapped, 1965–67.
1018	Alco	RSD-1	1943	70669	Built as USA 8048	1949	1965	Scrapped, 1966–68?
1019	Alco	RSD-1	1943	70674	Built as USA 8053	1949	1949	To ARR RF1A 1078, 1949.
1020	Alco	RSD-1	1943	70676	Built as USA 8055	1949	1949	To ARR RF1A 1052, 1949.
1021	Alco	RSD-1	1941	69567	Ex-USA 8002; Built as MILW RS-1 1678	1949	1950	To ARR RF1B 1069, 1950.
1022	Alco	RSD-1	1943	70668	Built as USA 8047	1950	1950	To ARR RF1A 1070, 1950.
1023	Alco	RSD-1	1943	70673	Built as USA 8052	1949	1950	To ARR RF1A 1072, 1950.

The first diesel on the Alaska Railroad was No. 1000, an Alco-GE purchased new in 1944. The locomotive was retired and is on display at the Museum of Alaskan Transportation and Industry. (Western Airlines)

Diesel Locomotive Roster (continued)

Road No.	Builder	Model	Date Built	C/N	History	Acq.	Ret.	Notes
1024	Alco	RSD-1	1943	70657	Built as USA 8036	1949	1950	To ARR RF1A 1074, 1950.
1025	Alco	RSD-1	1943	70667	Built as USA 8046	1949	1950	To ARR RF1A 1076, 1950.
1026	Alco	RSD-1	1943	70663	Built as USA 8042	1949	1964	Scrapped, 1965–67.
1027	Alco	RSD-1	1943	70670	Built as USA 8049	1949	1971	To ARR slug Mate 2, 1972.
1028	Alco	RSD-1	1942	70640	Built as USA 8019	1950	1972	Scrapped, 1973.
1029	Alco	RSD-1	1942	70641	Built as USA 8020	1950	1964	Scrapped, 1965–67.
1030	Alco	RSD-1	1942	70644	Built as USA 8023	1950	1964	Scrapped, 1967.
1031	Alco	RSD-1	1941	69424	Ex-USA 8005; Built as CRIP RS-1 748	1950	1964	Scrapped.
1032	Alco	RSD-1	1942	70645	Built as USA 8024	1951	1956	Returned to USA 8024, 1956; To Tenn. Valley Auth. 39.
1033	Alco	RSD-1	1943	70660	Built as USA 8039	1951	1956	Returned to USA 8039, 1956; To Tenn. Valley Auth. 38. Sold 1993, scrapped.
1034	Alco	RSD-1	1941	69427	Ex-USA 8011; Built as ASAB RS-1 902	1951	1956	Returned to USA 8011, 1956; to FRA 8011, DOT/FRA 013, to Smithsonian Institution, 1983, loaned to RR Museum of Pennsylvania

Two of the Alaska Railroad's aging steamers alongside one of the new diesels, No. 1001, which arrived in 1944. The two steamers are of the 200 series, 2-6-0 American Locomotive Company engines built in 1906 to 5-foot gauge for use on the Panama Canal and then converted to standard gauge for use on the Alaska Railroad. (Anchorage Historical and Fine Arts Museum, Alaska Railroad Collection)

Diesel Locomotive Roster *(continued)*

Road No.	Builder	Model	Date Built	C/N	History	Acq.	Ret.	Notes
1035	Alco	RSD-1	1942	70634	Built as USA 8013	1951	1956	To USA 8013, 1956; To Tenn. Valley Auth. 43.
1036	Alco	RSD-1	1945	72143	Built as USA 8650	1951	1956	To USA 8650, 1956; To Tenn. Valley Auth. 36. Sold in 1993, scrapped.
1041	Alco	RSD-1	1941	69570	Ex-USA 8004; Built as CRIP RS-1 747	1951	1956	To USA 8004, 1956; to FRA 8004, to DOT/FRA 011; to Mt Rainier Scenic 41.
1042	Alco	RSD-1	1941	69425	Ex-USA 8006; Built as CRIP RS-1 749	1951	1956	To USA 8006, 1956; To Tenn. Valley Auth. 400, 48
1043	Alco	RSD-1	1941	69568	Ex-USA 8003; Built as MILW RS-1 1679	1951	1956	To USA 8003, 1956; To DOT/Pueblo, 1974; destroyed.
1050	Alco	RF1A	1943	70661	Ex-ARR 1050A; Built as USA 8040	1949	1963	Scrapped, 1963.
1050A	Alco	RF1A	1943	70661	Built as USA 8040	1947	1949	To ARR 1050, 1949.
1050B	Alco	RF1A	1943	70675	Built as USA 8054	1947	1949	To ARR 1051, 1949.
1051	Alco	RF1A	1943	70675	Ex-ARR 1050B; Built as USA 8054	1949	1964	Scrapped, 1965–67.
1052	Alco	RF1A	1943	70676	Ex-ARR 1020; Built as USA 8055	1949	1956	Scrapped, 1966–68.

Decked out in Alaska Railroad colors is the ex-U.S. Army Alco-GE diesel No. 8040, renumbered No. 1050 after extensive rebuilding for the ARR. The Alaska Railroad acquired the locomotives following World War II and used them into the 1960s (Anchorage Historical and Fine Arts Museum, Alaska Railroad Collection)

Diesel Locomotive Roster (continued)

Road No.	Builder	Model	Date Built	C/N	History	Acq.	Ret.	Notes
1053	Alco	RF1B	1942	70642	Ex-ARR 1089; Built as USA 8021	1950	1965	Scrapped, 1966–68.
1054	Alco	RF1A	1943	70677	Ex-ARR 1087; Built as USA 8056	1950	1964	Scrapped, 1965–67.
1055	Alco	RF1B	1943	70659	Ex-ARR 1002; Built as USA 8038	1950	1965	Scrapped, 1966–68.
1057	Alco	RF1B	1942	69993	Ex-ARR 1085; Ex-USA 8001; Built as NYSW RS-1 233:1	1950	1965	Scrapped, 1965–67.
1065	Alco	RF1B	1943	70656	Ex-ARR 1015; Built as USA 8035	1952	1972	Scrapped, 1973.
1067	Alco	RF1B	1942	70647	Ex-ARR 1016; Built as USA 8026	1953	1965	Scrapped, 1966?.
1069	Alco	RF1B	1941	69567	Ex-ARR 1021; Ex-USA 8002; Built as MILW RS-1 1678	1950	1963	Scrapped, 1963?.
1070	Alco	RF1A	1943	70668	Ex-ARR 1022; Built as USA 8047	1950	1973	Scrapped, 1973.
1072	Alco	RF1A	1943	70673	Ex-ARR 1023; Built as USA 8036	1950	1973	Scrapped, 1973.

This is one of a series of EMD diesel-electrics obtained by the Alaska Railroad in 1953. It is shown here ready to depart on a passenger train on the Anchorage-Fairbanks run. (Anchorage Historical and Fine Arts Museum, Alaska Railroad Collection)

Diesel Locomotive Roster *(continued)*

Road No.	Builder	Model	Date Built	C/N	History	Acq.	Ret.	Notes
1074	Alco	RF1A	1943	70657	Ex-ARR 1024; Built as USA 8052	1950	1960s	Scrapped, 1966–7.
1075	Alco	RF1B	1943	70672	Ex-ARR 1011; Built as USA 8051	1950	1964	Scrapped, 1964–65.
1076	Alco	RF1B	1943	70667	Ex-ARR 1025; Built as USA 8046	1950	1973	Scrapped, 1973.
1077	Alco	RF1B	1943	70664	Ex-ARR 1012; Built as USA 8043	1950	1965	Scrapped, 1965–66.
1078	Alco	RF1A	1943	70674	Ex-ARR 1019; Built as USA 8053	1949	1972	Scrapped, 1973.
1085	Alco	RSD-1	1942	69993	Ex-USA 8001; Built as NYSW RS-1 233:1	1950	1950	To ARR RF1B 1057, 1950.
1087	Alco	RSD-1	1943	70677	Built as USA 8056	1950	1950	To ARR RF1A 1054, 1950.
1089	Alco	RSD-1	1942	70642	Built as USA 8021	1950	1950	To ARR RF1B 1053, 1950.
1100	Porter	65-ton	1943	7438	Ex-USA 7157; Built as Navajo Ordnance Depot	1947	1954	To Sherwood-Templeton Coal 7438, to Yankeetown Docks 3; scrapped.
1101	Porter	65-ton	1943	7439	Ex-USA 7158; Built as Navajo Ordnance Depot	1947	1954	To East St Louis Stone; scrapped 1978.

One of several diesel-electrics purchased from the Denver & Rio Grande Western Railroad in 1970 was ARR No. 1526. Here it is pictured alongside No. 2502, an EMD built in 1965. (Anchorage Historical and Fine Arts Museum, Alaska Railroad Collection)

Diesel Locomotive Roster (continued)

Road No.	Builder	Model	Date Built	C/N	History	Acq.	Ret.	Notes
1102	Porter	65-ton	1942	7392	Ex-USA 7033; Built as Sierra Ordnance Depot	1947	1954	To Swift & Co. 300; to Tampa Port 300; scrapped late 1970s.
1103	Porter	65-ton	1942	7403	Ex-USA 7034; Built as Tooele Ordnance Depot	1947	1954	to Dewey Portland Cement 7034; scrapped 1975.
1104	Porter	65-ton	1942	7425	Ex-USA 7024; Built as San Jacinto Ordnance Depot	1947	1954	To South Dakota Cement Plant 7425; renumbered 4202 to Dacotah Cement 4202.
1105	Porter	65-ton	1942	7404	Ex-USA 7150; Built as Lake Ontario Ordnance Depot	1947	1954	Wrecked as USA 7150; never used by ARR.
1106	Porter	65-ton	1941	7317	Ex-USA 7187; Built as Jefferson Proving Grounds 1	1947	1954	To American Aggregates 6816.
1107	Porter	65-ton	1941	7318	Ex-USA 7188; Built as Jefferson Proving Grounds 2	1948	1954	To American Aggregates 4323.
1201	EMD	SW1	1942	2000	Built as USA 7003	1947	1965	To Prescott Equip. (D), 1968.

This narrow-gauge railcar was used on the AEC between Nenana and Fairbanks during the early days of the operation. (Clifford Collection)

One of the many diesels obtained from the military by the Alaska Railroad was this one. It went into service without a visible number. (Anchorage Historical and Fine Arts Museum, Alaska Railroad Collection)

This is one of several ARR steam locomotives shipped to Spain in 1958 for use by F. C. deLargero. The transfer took place through the American Aid Mission. Giant cranes were used to hoist the locomotives aboard ship. (Anchorage Historical and Fine Arts Museum, Alaska Railroad Collection)

(right) *Route map of the Alaska Railroad. The track runs from Seward on Resurrection Bay on the south to Eielson AFB, east of Fairbanks on the north. Also shown is the Whittier cutoff from Portage. (Clifford Collection)*

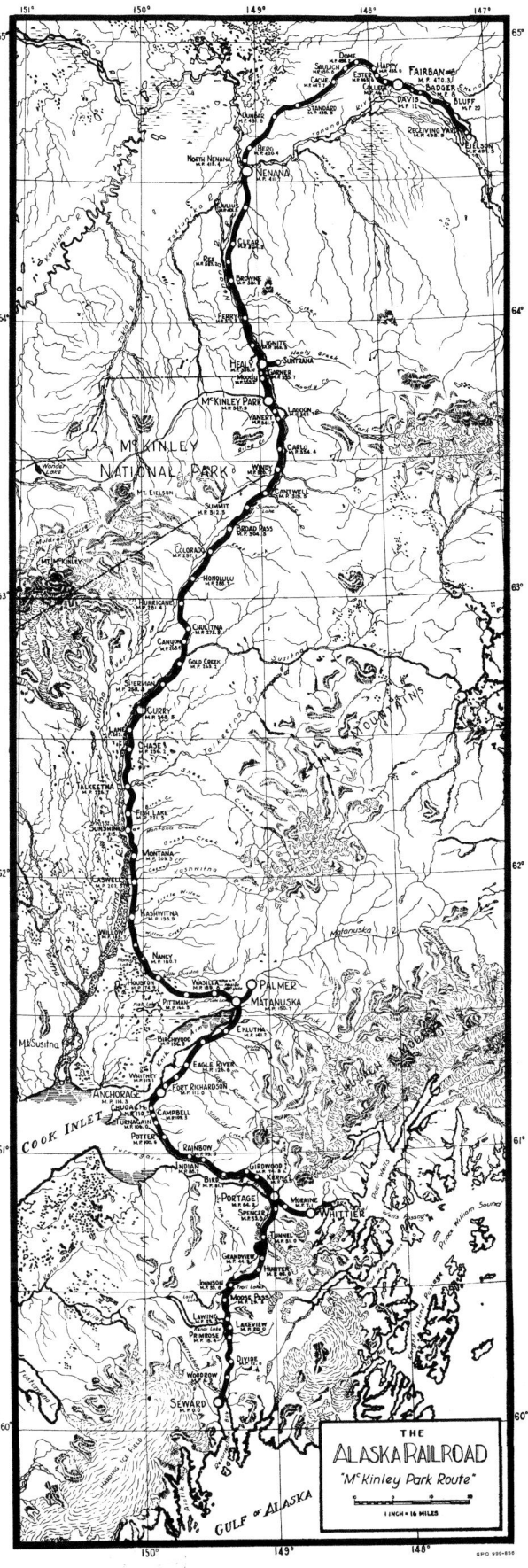

Diesel Locomotive Roster *(continued)*

Road No.	Builder	Model	Date Built	C/N	History	Acq.	Ret.	Notes
1202	EMD	SW1	1942	2001	Built as USA 7004	1947	1965	To Prescott Equip. (D), 1968; To Hercules Powder 69, 1969; To ADM 69, 1976.
1203	EMD	SW1	1942	1990	Built as USA 7001	1947	1957	Scrapped late 1950s.
1204	EMD	SW1	1942	2012	Built as USA 7002	1947	1965	Scrapped, 1973.
1300	Baldwin	VO-1000	1945	71745	Ex-USA V1801; Built as U.S. Atomic Energy Commission 3724	1949	1957	Scrapped, 1968.
1500	EMD	F7A	1952	17710	Acquired new	1952	1985	To MATI.
1501:1	EMD	F7B	1952	17713	Acquired new	1952	Mar62	Wrecked and Retired; Traded in to EMD, 1963.
1501:2	EMD	F7B	1949	8516	Built as GN 444C	1969	1976	Traded in to EMD, 1976.
1502	EMD	F7A	1952	17711	Acquired new	1952	1985	To Purdy Co., 1986 To Americana, Yakima, WA.
1503	EMD	F7B	1952	17714	Acquired new	1952	-	In service.
1504	EMD	F7A	1952	17712	Acquired new	1952	1983	To Seattle Iron & Metal, 1986. To MDT, scrapped 1990.
1505	EMD	F7B	1952	17715	Acquired new	1952	1985	To Seattle Iron & Metal. Scrapped 1986, Seattle.
1506	EMD	F7A	1953	19045	Acquired new	1953	1986	To MDT, wrecked.
1507	EMD	F7B	1953	19047	Acquired new	1953	1983	To Seattle Iron & Metal, to MDT; scrapped.
1508	EMD	F7A	1953	19046	Acquired new	1953	1986	To MDT; to private owner; leased to Massachusetts Central, September 1993; leased to Adirondack Scenic RR, 1998.
1509	EMD	F7B	1949	8515	Built as GN 444B	1969	1975	Traded in to EMD, 1975.
1510	EMD	FP7A	1953	19064	Acquired new	1953	1986	To MDT; to WYCO 1510 To VCRR 1510, 1996.
1511	EMD	F7B	1950	9551	Built as GN 450C	1969	1978	Traded in to EMD, 1978.
1512	EMD	FP7A	1953	19065	Acquired new	1953	1986	To MDT; to WYCO 1512, to VCRR 1512, 1996.
1514	EMD	FP7A	1953	19066	Acquired new	1953	1983	Retired, stripped, stored in Anchorage (privately owned).
1515	EMD	F7B	1950	9550	Built as GN 450B	1969	1975	Scrapped, 1984.
1516	EMD	F3A	1948	8015	Built as GN 438D	1969	1978	Traded in to EMD, 1978.
1517	EMD	F7B	1949	5868	Ex-DRGW 5552; Built as DRGW 555B	1970	1986	To MDT. To Wyoming & Colorado 1511.
1518	EMD	F7A	1949	8513	Built as GN 446A	1969	1975	Traded in to EMD, 1975.
1519	EMD	F7B	1952	16537	Built as DRGW 5732	1970	1975	Traded in to EMD, 1975.
1520	EMD	F7A	1952	16519	Built as DRGW 5711	1970	1976	Traded in to EMD, 1976.
1521	EMD	F7B	1952	16540	Built as DRGW 5743	1970	1976	Traded in to EMD, 1976.
1522	EMD	F7A	1952	16526	Built as DRGW 5744	1970	1978	Traded in to EMD, 1978.
1523	EMD	F9Bm	1952	16542	Built as DRGW F7B 5753	1970	1975	Traded in to EMD, 1975.

Diesel Locomotive Roster *(continued)*

Road No.	Builder	Model	Date Built	C/N	History	Acq.	Ret.	Notes
1524	EMD	F9Am	1949	5866	Ex-DRGW 5571; Built as DRGW F7A 557A	1970	1975	Traded in to EMD, 1975.
1525	EMD	F7B	1950	11416	Built as DRGW 5653	1970	1976	Traded in to EMD, 1976.
1526	EMD	F7A	1952	16522	Built as DRGW 5724	1970	1978	Traded in to EMD, 1978.
1528	EMD	F7A	1952	16520	Built as DRGW 5714	1970	1976	Traded in to EMD, 1976.
1530	EMD	F7A	1950	11406	Built as DRGW 5654	1970	1986	To Purdy Co., 1986 to MDT, scrapped 1990.
1532	EMD	F7A	1950	11408	Built as DRGW 5664	1970	1975	Traded in to EMD, 1975.
1551	EMD	MP15	1976	756146-1	Ex-LEF 25	1992	-	In service.
1552	EMD	MP15	1977	776021-1	Ex-LEF 26	1992	-	In service.
1553	EMD	MP15	1976	766006-1	Ex-KCNW 1	1993	-	In service.
1554	EMD	MP15	1980	796358-1	Ex-KCNW 2	1993	-	In service.
1601	Alco/GE	MRS1	1953	80365/ 31604	Built as USA B-2049	1974	1983	Retired.
1602	Alco/GE	MRS1	1953	80366/ 31605	Built as USA B-2050	1974	1983	Retired.

The rail bus "Ice Worm" of the Alaska Railroad. The vehicle was brought to Alaska and used to carry passengers between Whittier and Portage in 1965–66. The bus was owned and operated by the owners of a sportman's lodge in Whittier. It hauled passengers to the lodge on a regular schedule. It was later taken over by the Alaska Railroad (Western Airlines)

Diesel Locomotive Roster *(continued)*

Road No.	Builder	Model	Date Built	C/N	History	Acq.	Ret.	Notes
1603	Alco/GE	MRS1	1953	80369/31608	Built as USA B-2053	1974	1984	Retired.
1604	Alco/GE	MRS1	1953	80370/31609	Built as USA B-2054	1974	1984	Retired.
1605	Alco/GE	MRS1	1953	80371/31610	Built as USA B-2055	1974	1984	Retired.
1606	Alco/GE	MRS1	1953	80375/31614	Built as USA B-2059	1974	1984	Retired.
1607	Alco/GE	MRS1	1953	80372/31611	Built as USA B-2056	1975	1976	May never have been used or renumbered by ARR.
1608	Alco/GE	MRS1	1953	80377/31616	Built as USA B-2061	1975	1983	Retired.

Alaska Railroad passenger train with Mt. McKinley in the background. The ARR operates on a regular schedule between Anchorage and Fairbanks and is one of the favored tourist attractions in the 49th State. (Anchorage Historical and Fine Arts Museum, Alaska Railroad Collection)

Chapter 9: Alaska Railroad

Diesel Locomotive Roster (continued)

Road No.	Builder	Model	Date Built	C/N	History	Acq.	Ret.	Notes
1609	Alco/GE	MRS1	1953	80383/ 31622	Built as USA B-2067	1975	1983	Retired.
1610	Alco/GE	MRS1	1953	80389/ 31628	Built as USA B-2073	1975	1984	Retired.
1611	Alco/GE	MRS1	1953	80391/ 31630	Built as USA B-2075	1975	1983	Retired.
1612	Alco/GE	MRS1	1953	80393/ 31632	Built as USA B-2077	1975	1983	Retired.
Parts	Alco/GE	MRS1	1953	80333/ 31655	Ex-USN 65-00586 Built as USA 2100	1975	1975	Acquired for parts.
1714	EMD	MRS1	1952	15879	Ex-USN 65-00570 Built as USA 1814	1977	1985	Scrapped.
1715	EMD	MRS1	1952	15880	Ex-USN 65-00571 Built as USA 1815	1977	1983	Scrapped.
1716	EMD	MRS1	1952	15881	Ex-USN 65-00572 Built as USA 1816	1977	1983	Scrapped.
1717	EMD	MRS1	1952	15882	Ex-USN 65-00573 Built as USA 1817	1977	1983	Scrapped.
1718	EMD	MRS1	1952	15883	Ex-USN 65-00574 Built as USA 1818	1977	1985	To USAF 1718 Clear Air Force Base. Retired 1999.
1801	EMD	GP7u	1951	15708	Ex-ARR 1838; Built as USA 1838	1976	1998	To AMR, 1998, to BLDX, August 1998.
1802	EMD	GP7u	1951	15695	Ex-ARR 1825; Built as USA 1825	1976	–	In service
1803	EMD	GP7u	1951	15696	Ex-ARR 1826; Built as USA 1826	1976	1998	To AMR, 1998, to BLDX, August 1998.
1804	EMD	GP7u	1951	15704	Ex-ARR 1834; Built as USA 1834	1976	1986	To private owner, to McCloud River Rwy. To SCRX 1804. To Nevada Industrial Switching.
1805	EMD	GP7u	1951	15709	Ex-ARR 1839; Built as USA 1839	1976	1985	Wrecked, scrapped.
1806	EMD	GP7u	1951	15697	Ex-ARR 1827; Built as USA 1827	1977	–	In service.
1807	EMD	GP7u	1951	15701	Ex-ARR 1831; Built as USA 1831	1977	1984	Wrecked; retired, March 1, 1984.
1808	EMD	GP7u	1951	15706	Ex-ARR 1836; Built as USA 1836	1977	1998	To AMR, 1998, to BLDX, August 1998.
1809:2	EMD	GP7u	1951	15707	Ex-ARR 1837; Built as USA 1837	1977	?	To AMR, 1998, to BLDX, August 1998.
1810	EMD	GP7u	1951	15691	Ex-ARR 1821; Built as USA 1821	1976	1986	To private owner, to McCloud River Rwy., to SCRX.
1809:1	EMD	MRS1	1952	15874	Built as USA 1809	1952	1955	To USA 1809, 1955, to Tooele Army Depot, to Vandenburg AFB, 1969, retired 1979; to Pacific Southwest Rwy. Museum.
1821	EMD	GP7L	1951	15691	Built as USA 1821	1960	1976	To ARR GP7u 1810, 1976.

Diesel Locomotive Roster (continued)

Road No.	Builder	Model	Date Built	C/N	History	Acq.	Ret.	Notes
1825	EMD	GP7L	1951	15695	Built as USA 1825	1960	1976	To ARR GP7u 1802, 1976.
1826	EMD	GP7L	1951	15696	Built as USA 1826	1960	1976	To ARR GP7u 1803, 1976.
1827	EMD	GP7L	1951	15697	Built as USA 1827	1960	1977	To ARR GP7u 1806, 1977.
1828	EMD	GP7L	1951	15698	Built as USA 1828	1960	March 1964	Destroyed by tsunami during earthquake; scrapped, 1964.
1829	EMD	GP7L	1951	15699	Built as USA 1829	1960	1962	Wrecked before receipt; never used on ARR. To USA.
1830	EMD	GP7L	1951	15700	Built as USA 1830	1960	1972	Wrecked; scrapped, 1973.
1831	EMD	GP7L	1951	15701	Built as USA 1831	1960	1977	To ARR GP7u 1807, 1977.
1834	EMD	GP7L	1951	15704	Built as USA 1834	1960	1976	To ARR GP7u 1804, 1976.
1836	EMD	GP7L	1951	15706	Built as USA 1836	1960	1977	To ARR GP7u 1808, 1977.
1837	EMD	GP7L	1951	15707	Built as USA 1837	1960	1977	To ARR GP7u 1809:2, 1977.
1838	EMD	GP7L	1951	15708	Built as USA 1838	1960	1976	To ARR GP7u 1801, 1976.
1839	EMD	GP7L	1951	15709	Built as USA 1839	1960	1976	To ARR GP7u 1805, 1976.
2000	EMD	GP30	1963	28171	Acquired new	1963	1974	To ARR GP30u 2504, 1974.

One of the first switching locomotives obtained by the Alaska Railroad was this Lima 0-6-0, which is being unloaded at Whittier in this photo. The locomotives were purchased from the military in 1947. (Anchorage Historical and Fine Arts Museum, Alaska Railroad Collection)

Diesel Locomotive Roster *(continued)*

Road No.	Builder	Model	Date Built	C/N	History	Acq.	Ret.	Notes
2001	EMD	GP38-2	1977	766008-1	Ex-RARW 108; Built as BAP 108	1986	–	In service.
2002	EMD	GP38-2	1978	786138-1	Ex-RARW 109; Built as BAP 109	1986	–	In service.
2003	EMD	GP38u	1969	35441	Ex-CR 7812; Built as PC 7812	1986	–	In service.
2004	EMD	GP38u	1969	35402	Ex-CR 7773; Built as PC 7773	1986	–	In service.
2005	EMD	GP38u	1969	35381	Ex-CR 7752; Built as PC 7752	1986	–	In service.
2006	EMD	GP38u	1969	35383	Ex-CR 7754; Built as PC 7754	1986	–	In service.
2007	EMD	GP38u	1969	35409	Ex-CR 7780; Built as PC 7780	1986	–	In service.
2008	EMD	GP38u	1968	34714	Ex-CR GP40 3250; Ex-PC; Built as NYC	1986	–	In service.
2401	EMD	E9A	1955	20494	Ex-AMTK 430; Built as UP 957	1981	1986	To WSOR 10A, 1992.
2402	EMD	E9A	1956	21605	Ex-AMTK 434; Ex-MILW 32A; Built as MILW 202A	1981	1986	To WSOR 10C, 1990.
2500	EMD	GP35	1964	29595	Acquired new	1964	1965	To ARR 2501, 1965.
2501	EMD	GP35	1964	29592	Ex-ARR 2500	1965	-	In service.
2502	EMD	GP35	1965	29870	Acquired new	1965	-	In service.
2503	EMD	GP35	1965	30055	Acquired new	1965	1976	Wrecked; to GP35u 3051, 1977.
2504	EMD	GP30u	1963	28171	Built as ARR GP30 2000	1974	-	In service.
2801	EMD	GP49	1983	837049-1	Acquired new	1983	-	In service.
2802	EMD	GP49	1983	837049-2	Acquired new	1983	-	In service.
2803	EMD	GP49	1983	837049-3	Acquired new	1983	-	In service.
2804	EMD	GP49	1983	837049-4	Acquired new	1983	-	In service.
2805	EMD	GP49	1985	847035-1	Acquired new	1983	-	In service.
2806	EMD	GP49	1985	847035-2	Acquired new	1983	-	In service.
2807	EMD	GP49	1985	847035-3	Acquired new	1983	-	In service.
2808	EMD	GP49	1985	847035-4	Acquired new	1983	-	In service.
2809	EMD	GP49	1985	847035-5	Acquired new	1983	-	In service.
3000	EMD	GP40-2	1975	74759-1	Acquired new	1975	1975	To ARR 3006, 1975.
3001	EMD	GP40-2	1975	74759-2	Acquired new	1975	-	In service.
3002	EMD	GP40-2	1975	74759-3	Acquired new	1975	-	In service.
3003	EMD	GP40-2	1975	74759-4	Acquired new	1975	-	In service.
3004	EMD	GP40-2	1975	74759-5	Acquired new	1975	-	In service.
3005	EMD	GP40-2	1975	74759-6	Acquired new	1975	-	In service.
3006	EMD	GP40-2	1975	74759-1	Built as ARR 3000	1975	-	In service.
3007	EMD	GP40-2	1976	757143-1	Acquired new	1976	-	In service.
3008	EMD	GP40-2	1976	757143-2	Acquired new	1976	-	In service.
3009	EMD	GP40-2	1976	757143-3	Acquired new	1976	-	In service.

Diesel Locomotive Roster (*continued*)

Road No.	Builder	Model	Date Built	C/N	History	Acq.	Ret.	Notes
3010	EMD	GP40-2	1976	757143-4	Acquired new	1976	–	In service.
3011	EMD	GP40-2	1976	757143-5	Acquired new	1976	–	In service.
3012	EMD	GP40-2	1978	777093-1	Acquired new	1978	–	In service.
3013	EMD	GP40-2	1978	777093-2	Acquired new	1978	–	In service.
3014	EMD	GP40-2	1978	777093-3	Acquired new	1978	–	In service.
3015	EMD	GP40-2	1978	777093-4	Acquired new	1978	–	In service.
3016	EMD	GP40u	1967	33492	Ex-CR 3081; Ex-PC 3081; Built as NYC 3081	1983	–	In service.
3017	EMD	GP40u	1967	33497	Ex-CR 3086; Ex-PC 3086; Built as NYC 3086	1983	–	In service.
3018	EMD	GP40u	1967	33509	Ex-CR 3098; Ex-PC 3098; Built as NYC 3098	1983	1996	Scrapped 1996.
3019	EMD	GP40u	1967	33510	Ex-CR 3099; Ex-PC 3099; Built as NYC 3099	1983	–	In service.
3020	EMD	GP40u	1967	33513	Ex-CR 3102; Ex-PC 3102; Built as NYC 3102	1983	–	In service.
3021	EMD	GP35u	1965	30055	Ex-ARR 3051; Built as ARR GP35 2503	1992	1995	Frame & shell to Forget-Me-Not Lodge, Fairbanks, AK.
3051	EMD	GP35u	1965	30055	Built as ARR GP35 2503	1977	1992	To ARR 3021.
7107	Alco	S-2	1943	70266	Ex-USA 7107 Built as Benecia Arsenal	1955	March 1964	Destroyed in earthquake.
7109	Alco	S-2	1943	70257	Ex-USA 7109 Built as Benecia Arsenal	1955	1972	Scrapped, 1973.
7112	Alco	S-2	1943	70081	Ex-USA 7112 Built as Tooele Ordnance Depot	1955	1972	Scrapped, 1973.
7123	Alco	S-2	1943	70190	Ex-USA 7123 Built as Benecia Arsenal	1955	1975	Sold for scrap, 1976.
7249	GE	45-ton	1942	15713	Ex-USA 7249 Built as Cornhusker Ordnance Plant (Ovina, NE)	1974	1983	Temporarily operated at Valdez. To CCPR; to Samuels Steel 4501.
7324	GE	45-ton	1942	15244	Ex-USA 7324 Built as Weldon Springs Ordnance Works	1974	1983	Temporarily operated at Valdez. To MATI.
7331	GE	45-ton	1941	12985	Ex-USA 7331 Built as Ravenna Ordnance Works 451	1974	1983	To CCPR, 006 To Kerr-McGee Chemical Co KM1L.
7356	GE	45-ton	1941	13139	Ex-USA 7356 Built as Plum Brook Ordnance Works 336	1974	1983	To CCPR; To Rabanco.

Notes: 4001–4016, EMD, SD70MAC, on order (delivery: 1999)
1019, 1020, 1022–1025, 1085, 1089 (may never have operated on ARR as RSD-1s)
1801–1809 rebuilt by ICG Paducah, KY shop in mid-1970s.
All MP-15s are DC type

Abbreviations:
B/D	Built Date
B/N	Builder's Number
Acq.	Year unit Acquired
Ret.	Year unit Retired
ADM/X	ADM Transportation (Archer-Daniels-Midland)
AMR	Alaska Metal Recycling
AMTK	Amtrak
ARR	Alaska Railroad
ASAB	Atlanta & St. Andrews Bay Railway
BAP	Butte, Anaconda & Pacific Railway
BDLX	
CCPR	Chelatchie Prairie Railroad
CR	ConRail
CRIP	Chicago, Rock Island & Pacific
DOT	Department of Transportation
DRGW	Denver & Rio Grande Western Railroad
FRA	Federal Railroad Administration
GN	Great Northern Railroad
KCNW	Kelley's Creek & Northwestern Railroad
LEF	Lake Erie, Franklin & Clarion Railroad
MATI	Museum of Alaska Transportation & Industry
MDT	Mountain Diesel Transportation (Dealer)
MILW	Chicago Milwaukee St. Paul & Pacific Railroad
NH	New York, New Haven & Hartford
NYC	New York Central
NYSW	New York, Susquehanna & Western Railroad
PC	Penn Central
RARW	Rarus Railway
SCRX	Santa Clarita Railway
SEPTA	Southeast Pennsylvania Transit Authority
SQVR	Sequatchie Valley Railroad
UP	Union Pacific
USA	U.S. Army
USN	U.S. Navy
USWD	U.S. War Department, Quartermasters Corps
VCRR	Verde Canyon
WSOR	Wisconsin & Southern Railroad
WYCO	Wyoming & Colorado Railroad
ALCO	American Locomotive Company (Alco Products), Schenectady, NY
BUDD	Budd Company, Philadelphia, PA
EMD	Electro-Motive Division of General Motors, LaGrange, IL
GE	General Electric, Erie, PA
PLYMOUTH	Plymouth Locomotive Works, Plymouth, OH
PORTER	H. K. Porter, Pittsburgh, PA (Davenport, IA)
WHITCOMB	Whitcomb Locomotive Works, Rochelle, IL
(x)	Dealer

ARR train 6, the northbound mixed with no freight, nearin Denali Park Station, May 4, 1985. The E9's were shortlined, from 1982–86. (Curt Fontenberry)

Evans Jones Coal Company

The Jones Company, one of the largest in the Matanuska Valley, also owned some equipment, the first of which was put into operation in August 1936. All were battery-powered mine-type locomotives. The equipment disposed of with the closing of the facilities is listed in the table below.

Battery Locomotives

Road No.	Bldr.	Const. #	Type	Built	Notes
1	General Electric	12126	4-wheel, 5-ton	August 1936	Purchased new.
2	General Electric	9976	4-wheel, 5-ton	1925	Purchased in 1936.
3	Westinghouse-Whitcomb	80217	4-wheel, 10-ton	April 1947	Originally built for U.S. Treasury as 60-cm–gauge, to EJC No. 3.
4	Mancha	2352	4-wheel, 3-½-ton		
5	General Electric	15830	4-wheel, 6-ton	June 1942	Originally Alaska Railroad, to EJC No. 5, to Klondike Cement Co.
6	General Electric	15829	4-wheel, 6-ton	June 1942	Originally Alaska Railroad, to EJC No. 6.
7			4-wheel		
8	Westinghouse-Whitcomb	80216	4-wheel, 10-ton	April 1947	Originally built for U.S. Treasury as 60-cm–gauge, to EJC No. 8, to Klondike Cement Co.
9	Westinghouse-Whitcomb	80219	4-wheel, 10-ton	April 1947	Originally built for U.S. Treasury as 60-cm–gauge, to EJC No. 9, to Klondike Cement Co.

Notes: Nos. 3, 8, and 9 were originally constructed for use in the USSR but were never shipped.

Alaska Railroad Railcars

Road No.	Builder	Model	Date Built	C/N	History	Acq.	Ret.	Notes
100	Ford/AEC	–	–	–	Ex-AEC 100	–	–	Wrecked in the late 1920s.
102	Ford/AEC	–	–	–	Ex-AEC 102	–	–	
104	Buick/AEC	–	–	–	Ex-AEC 104	–	–	
105	Edison-Beach	–	1912	–	Ex-Tanana Valley RR Ex-AEC 105	–	–	Narrow-gauge.
106	ARR	–	–	–		–	–	
107	Brill	75	1925	2285		–	–	Rebuilt into trailer No. 304, 1931, body to Evans-Jones coal mine, body to Alaska-Yukon Chapter NRHS, displayed, Anchorage, destroyed 1970s.

Road No.	Builder	Model	Date Built	C/N	History	Acq.	Ret.	Notes
108	McKeen	1910	July 1908	–	Ex-Yuma Valley RR	1926	–	Baggage section added, 1916, (Bureau of Reclamation), rebuilt with round nose, 1927 and repowered, rebuilt to unpowered combine No. 83, 1931, retired late 1940s, body privately owned, Anchorage, ex-San Diego, Cuyamaca & Eastern, sold 1912.
109	ARR	–	–	–		–	–	12-passenger.
110	ARR	–	–	–		–	–	12-passenger, narrow-gauge.
111	Kalamazoo	–	–	–		–	–	Renumbered No. 211.
112	ARR	–	–	–		–	–	12-passenger.
113	ARR	–	–	–		–	–	12-passenger.
114	Brill	250	1927	22539		–	–	Renumbered No. 214, 1947.
115 (2nd)	Brill	250	1927	22563	Ex-Lehigh Valley 5	1938	–	Renumbered No. 215, 1947.
116	ARR	–	1927	–		–	–	
116 (2nd)	Brill	–	1927	22544	Ex NYC M-400	1944	–	Renumbered No. 216, 1947.
201	Kalamazoo	–	–	–		–	–	4-wheel coach.
202	Kalamazoo	–	–	–		–	–	4-wheel baggage.
211	See 111							
212	Edwards	21	–	198	Ex-U.S. Navy	–	–	
213	ACF	–	1942	2514	Ex-U.S. Navy 19	–	–	
214	See 114							
215	See 115							
216	See 116							
301	ARR	–	–	–		–	–	Narrow-gauge coach trailer.
302	ARR	–	–	–		–	–	Narrow-gauge 4-wheel baggage trailer.
303	Brill	–	1927	22540		–	–	Coach trailer, one open platform.
304	See 107							
701	Budd	RDC-3	January 1953	5703	Ex-SEPTA 9171 Ex-PC 93 Built as NH 126	1986	–	In service.
702	Budd	RDC-3	May 1953	5819	Ex-SEPTA 9170 Ex-PC 96 Built as NH 129	1986	–	In service.
711	Budd	RDC-2	May 1952	5609	Ex-AMTRAK 36 Ex-PC 82 Built as NH 121	1987	–	In service.
712	Budd	RDC-2	July 1951	5420	Ex-AMTRAK 34 Ex-PC 80 Built as NYC M480	1987	–	In service.
721	Budd	RDC-1	March 1952	5802	Ex-AMTRAK 15 Ex-PC 44 Built as NH 44	1987	–	Used for parts, never run. Numbered for accounting purposes only.
1205		–	–	–	Ex-Sportman's Inn	1966	–	"Ice Worm," on display at Wasilla.

Notes:

B/D	Built Date
B/N	Builder's Number
Acq.	Year unit acquired
Ret.	Year unit retired
AEC	Alaskan Engineering Commission
AMTK	Amtrak
ARR	Alaska Railroad
NH	New York, New Haven & Hartford
NYC	New York Central
PC	Penn Central
SEPTA	Southeast Pennsylvania Transit Authority
ACF	American Car & Foundry, St. Charles, MO
Brill	J. G. Brill & Company, Philadelphia, PA
BUDD	Budd Company, Philadelphia, PA
Edison-Beech	Federal Storage Battery Car Company, New York, NY
Edwards	Edwards Railway Motor Car Company, Sanford, NC
Kalamazoo	Kalamazoo Manufacturing Company, Kalamazoo, MI
McKeen	McKeen Motor Car Company, Omaha, NB

Although still dressed in its ARR paint, 1718 is actually owned by the U. S. Air Force and stationed at Clear ARS, AK. 1718 is an EMD MRS-1. The unit is being replaced in 1999 by GE 80 tonners. (Curt Fortenberry)

The Denali, President Warren G. Harding's private car when he was in Alaska for the Golden Spike ceremony at Nenana on the Alaska Railroad in July 1923. The car is now on display at Alaskaland in Fairbanks. (Western Airlines)

Chapter 10

Tanana Mines Railway, Tanana Valley Railroad

Alaskan Engineering Commission (Nenana–Chatanika)
A Porter 0-4-0 wood-burning saddle-tank locomotive located in Fairbanks is one physical reminder of a 45-mile narrow-gauge railroad that operated in the Fairbanks area from 1905 to 1917 until it was taken over by the Alaskan Engineering Commission (AEC). It ultimately became part of the government-owned Alaska Railroad.

The Tanana Mines Railway was organized and incorporated in 1904 under the laws of the state of Washington by Falcon Joslin, an enterprising, Tennessee-born attorney who had been extremely successful in Dawson City and served as former president of the Dawson Electric Light and Power Company. He planned to build a railroad from a point on the Tanana River near the town of Chena to a point on the Yukon River near Circle City, with branch lines to Fairbanks and the mines in the Fairbanks District.

Financed by the Close Brothers firm (whose investments included the White Pass and Yukon), the Tanana Mines Railway (TMR), which became the Tanana Valley Railroad (TVR) in 1907, was part of an overall plan to expand a route to Circle City and Dawson City, with a 600-mile link to Nome.

This little Porter, which saw service for more than a quarter-century on several different railroads, has earned a well-deserved retirement. It carried No. 1 on the Tanana Mines Railway, the Tanana Valley Railroad, and the U.S. Government Railroad (Alaskan Engineering Commission). Now being restored by the Friends of the Tanana Valley Railroad in Fairbanks, the narrow-gauge engine was built in 1899. (H. Clifford)

Gold was in its heyday in the area when the narrow-gauge Tanana Mines Railway started operating from Chena to Fairbanks. This photograph shows the July 17, 1905, ceremony in which the golden spike was driven, marking the completion of the first portion of the line. (University of Alaska Archives, Terry Cole Collection)

Another line was planned up the Tanana Valley across the Yukon boundary and south down the Chilkat River to a point on Lynn Canal near Haines. This route would pass through 800 miles of what was believed to be rich gold and copper country.

The railroad was built in two stages. In 1905, the road was put in from Chena to Gilmore on Pedro Creek, with a spur of 4.7 miles to Fairbanks, which started operating in September 1905. The next year, this 26-mile section of line was considerably improved. In 1907, the six-month working season brought an extension of the line, now called the Tanana Valley Railroad, to Chatanika.

The obstacles overcome by Joslin and his associates were considerable.

This Porter 0-4-0 acquired by the Tanana Mines Railway from the Coal Creek Coal Company near Dawson City (another Joslin interest) prepares to depart from a station in the Fairbanks area with its train of one passenger car. The little narrow-gauge locomotive was the TMR No. 1. The locomotive is now being restored. (Clifford Collection)

Land near Chena was low and subject to periodic flooding. Trestles up to 600 feet in length had to be built over creeks. Spruce was available in suitable quantity and quality for ties and trestles, but the 30-pound rails and equipment had to be transported as much as 6,000 miles and handled as many as 11 times. There were other transportation nightmares. Six flatcars intended for the TMR wound up at the bottom of the Yukon River. Laborers were paid $7.50 a day—considered extraordinary for the time but necessary to keep workers from the lure of the nearby gold fields—and as many as 200 workers were employed at times during the construction.

Offices and shops for the line were located at Chena, where the tracks ran down Front Street for ⅔-mile alongside warehouses and docks. There were terminal grounds at Chena Junction, Fairbanks (Garden Island), and Gilmore. The amount of money spent on surveys, preliminary work, actual construction, and equipment amounted to $815,969.05. When the TMR was completed from Chena to Fairbanks in the summer of 1905, a gold spike ceremony took place. Federal District Judge James Wickersham made the principal speech of the day. The road was built without any government subsidy except for a five-year dispensation from the federal tax of $100 a year for each mile of track.

During the riverboat months, usually lasting from the end of May to early October, the Tanana Valley Railroad moved people and goods out of the port of Chena, located on the Tanana River. For the rest of the year, trains picked up express and passengers arriving in Fairbanks over a sledge stage route from Valdez on Prince William Sound.

As Chena started to decline, Fairbanks became the dominant city in the interior of Alaska, and operations were transferred to Garden Island in Fairbanks in 1915.

Early equipment consisted of four locomotives, four passenger coaches, and 30 freight cars. Included was the Porter 0-4-0 saddle-tanker, which had been obtained from the Coal Creek Coal Company near Dawson City and barged down the river to Fairbanks, arriving in early July 1905.

The second locomotive, a Baldwin 4-4-0 built in 1878, was obtained from the White Pass & Yukon Railroad in 1905. A Brooks 2-6-0 was also obtained from the White Pass & Yukon (No. 65) in 1906 and became the TMR No. 51. The TMR also obtained a Baldwin 2-6-0 built in May 1890 from the Alberta Railway & Coal Company (No. 12), which became the Tanana No. 52. All these locomotives were subsequently acquired by the Alaskan Engineering Commission (Government Railroad) and later scrapped.

Like other early day railroads, the TMR/TVR had its problems. In the spring, Goldstream Creek, one of many creeks in

---

Tanana Valley R.R.

TIME CARD

Effective Sept. 16th, 1912.

Leave Fairbanks .... 8:30 am.
" Ester Siding .... 8:45 am.
" McNeer .... 9:20 am.
" Carlson .... 9:30 am.
" Fox .... 10:05 am.
" Gilmore .... 10:30 am.
" Ridgetop .... 11:30 am.
" Olnes .... 12:05 pm.
" Little Eldorado .... 12:25 pm.
Arrive Chatanika .... 12:40 pm.

Returning.

Leave Chatanika .... 1:20 pm.
" Little Eldorado .... 1:30 pm.
" Olnes .... 1:45 pm.
" Ridgetop .... 2:15 pm.
" Gilmore .... 3:05 pm.
" Fox .... 3:30 pm.
" Carlson .... 3:40 pm.
" McNeer .... 3:50 pm.
" Ester Siding .... 4:15 pm.
Arrive Fairbanks .... 4:35 pm.

CHENA TRAIN.

Leave Fairbanks .... 5:05 pm.
Arrive Chena .... 5:40 pm.

Returning.

Leave Chena   7:00 pm.
Arrive Fairbanks .... 7:35 pm.

Motor car leaves Fairbanks for Gilmore at 10:30 am. and 4:05 pm.

Returning leaves Gilmore at 7:55 am. and 12:05pm.

Parker's Auto connects with trains and electric car at Ester Siding for Ester City.

McLean's Stage connects with trains at Gilmore for Fairbanks Creek on Mondays, Wednesdays, and Friday.

Stage connects at Chatanika for Cleary City.

C. W. Joynt,
General Manager

A Tanana Valley Railroad time card for September 16, 1912, as published in a Fairbanks newspaper of the period. The schedule listed daily service between Fairbanks and Chatanika, as well as Fairbanks and Chena. There was also twice-daily motor car service between Fairbanks and Gilmore. Stage connections with the various trains are also listed. (Clifford Collection) the area, overflowed its banks and the railroad tracks as well. With several feet of water on the Goldstream Flats, the brakemen had to don hip boots, climb out on the locomotive pilot or leading flatcar with a pike pole, and then wade through the water, checking to feel that the tracks were not displaced or that they had fallen down the embankment. Sometimes the force of the water running across the tracks floated the ties and rails out of position so that the train couldn't progress.

Another problem was complying with Interstate Commerce Commission regulations regarding the transportation of explosives. The ICC rules required a 10-car spacing between the car carrying dynamite and the car carrying the explosive caps. Sometimes this was a problem, since there were often not enough cars in the consist. Such a situation might have caused some railroads trouble, but not the Tanana Valley. The workers loaded the dynamite in the last car and then handed the caps to one of the passengers with instructions that when the train stopped at the station where the dynamite was to be unloaded, the passenger should hand the package to the conductor for delivery. Technically, the railroad had not "loaded" the caps on the train and was not in violation of ICC regulations.

Trains traveling in the winter also often became stranded in the drifting snow on the north side of Ridgetop. In one instance, a dog team was sent out to rescue passen-

A Tanana Valley Railroad Baldwin 4-4-0 with snowplow attached serves as a work train locomotive at a gravel pit near Fairbanks. The Baldwin was built in 1878 for the Olympia and Tenino Railway and served with several other railroads, including the White Pass & Yukon, before being acquired by the TVR. The narrow-gauge was later acquired by the Alaskan Engineering Commission and was scrapped in 1930. (Clifford Collection)

gers and crew from a stranded train. The train itself did not make it back to Fairbanks for more than two weeks.

At the height of its operation, the TVR ran twice-daily service in both directions between Fairbanks and Chena. In addition, a motor-car operated twice daily between Fairbanks and Fox or Gilmore. Passenger and freight totals depended on mining activity, with a maximum of passengers in the mid-and high-50 thousands in 1909 and 1910 and as low as the mid-20 thousands in 1914. In 1900 approximately 16,000 tons of freight was carried, which had dropped by more than a third by 1914. Passenger revenue was 13¢ per passenger mile, and freight was 58¢ per ton mile, compared with $3 for teams prior to inauguration of service by the railroad.

Shortly after the line was extended into Fairbanks, plans were made to extend the line to the Sourdough mining district along what is now the Richardson Highway, but a pole trestle built across the Chena River during the winter of 1906–7 was washed out in the spring and the tracks never went farther than the Weeks Field area. These tracks did not go to waste, however. They were used to haul firewood from Weeks Field storage area for Northern Commercial Company's power plant and supplies for the machine shop on Third and Barnette Streets. The only passengers this line carried were company employees who rode the train to the annual Fourth of July picnic held in the log storage area, which was empty at that time of year following a winter's use of logs. Motive power on this disconnected piece of railroad was supplied by draft animals. This service was discontinued in 1924 when the steam plant converted to coal.

Tanana Valley Railroad Timetable No. 13 as published in a Fairbanks newspaper. The schedule was effective May 10, 1909, and listed three trains daily in each direction between Fairbanks, Gilmore, and Chatanika. Below the Tanana Valley schedule is a notice of service on the White Pass & Yukon Route for those contemplating a trip outside—to the "South 46." (Clifford Collection)

By this time, Fairbanks was reporting steady growth, and in five years, what had been a tent city now had 5,000 inhabitants and the usual amenities of community life. Services included a bookstore, two hospitals (St. Joseph's and St. Matthew's), a greenhouse, and two fortune tellers (Mlles. Melbourne and Zelpha). A reader of Fairbanks papers in 1908 could learn that the Tanana Valley Railroad would handle livestock by special arrangement only, but that empty beer kegs and soda bottles would be carried free of charge; that ice and roller rinks and moving pictures were advertised; and that "not a single good location can be found for rent and there is a lively demand among those desiring to buy cabins." For the musically inclined, Sunday concerts featured such original compositions as "Toast to the Brides of Fairbanks" and "St. Fairbanks Tickle." Feature stories described an increase in the use of cigarettes and "How It Feels to Fly an Aeroplane."

A TMR excursion train makes its way over a trestle at Noyes Slough in the Fairbanks area. The locomotive is believed to be the former White Pass & Yukon Baldwin Nos. 4 and 54, which were acquired by the TMR in 1905. (University of Alaska Archives, Erskine Collection)

A Tanana Valley train makes its way over Ridgetop during the winter with the assistance of a helper locomotive in the rear. Trains in this area were often stranded in heavy snow, and crews and passengers had to be rescued by dog team. (University of Washington Historical Library, Northwest Collection)

In 1909, the railroad ordered an Edison-Beech storage battery car to serve dwindling passenger demand. The car had a range of about 100 miles between charges and was ideally suited to a one-man crew. The four-wheel, trolley-like vehicle served the line well, performing its assigned chores into the late 'teens.

From an investor standpoint, the Tanana Valley never proved a financial success, though it was able to meet expenses and pay interest on its debts of $660,000. Operating expenses were about 62 percent of gross earnings. It must not be overlooked that, although not a moneymaker, the Tanana Valley's service to the gold creeks was important. On weekdays, the railroad brought passengers, fuel, and supplies. Sometimes on Sundays and holidays excursions were offered at bargain rates to sightseers.

The Alaskan Engineering Commission brought changes to the Tanana Valley Railroad. In 1917 the line was first leased and then sold to the government. Considering the poor state of the roadbed and the age of the equipment, the sale price of $300,000 seemed fair to all concerned. Under government operation, the roadbed was improved and a temporary narrow-gauge line was built to Nenana. Pending construction of a bridge across the river, freight was brought across by ferry in the summer and by sledge and narrow-gauge tracks that had been laid on the ice for trains in the winter. Upon completion of the Alaska Railroad and the construction of a bridge across the river in 1923, the Nenana-Fairbanks section was converted to standard gauge.

Two Tanana Valley Railroad locomotives are snowed in on the north side of the notorious Ridgetop. Dog teams sometimes had to be sent out to rescue passengers from the stranded cars, and occasionally trains were not able to free themselves from the snow for weeks. (Clifford Collection)

In 1922, the Edison-Beech car was rebuilt into a gas-electric, and service was started to the Alaska Agricultural College and the School of Mines, which had just opened. In 1931 the College-Fairbanks narrow-gauge track was ripped out, and the ex-TVR car was replaced by larger Brill gas-electric cars. These cars resembled present-day railroad coaches rather than the trolley-like Edison-Beech vehicle.

Five years later, commuter service by rail was discontinued between College and Fairbanks, and the Brill cars were sent to the Matanuska Valley near Palmer and used for transportation between Palmer and Anchorage until the 1950s. Track from College was extended to the Eielson Airforce base for military cargo use. It continues to be used today.

In August 1930, the remaining portion of the narrow-gauge operation to Chatanika was discontinued, and the rails were removed. Little remains today to indicate where the line once ran, but its contribution to the development of mining in the Fairbanks area and its role in the eventual rail connection between Fairbanks and the coast cannot be forgotten.

This Porter 0-4-0 saddle-tanker, the first locomotive on the Tanana Mines Railway, is shown at Chena Junction, on the leg of the wye to Fairbanks. The little No. 1 locomotive is now being restored in Fairbanks. (University of Alaska Archives, Charles Bunnell Collection)

Tanana Mines Railway/Tanana Valley Railroad
Locomotive Roster

Road No.	Wheel Arr.	Builder	C/N	Year	Cylinders	Drivers	Notes
1	0-4-0T	Porter	1972	1899	6x10	24"	Built for North American Transportation & Trading Company No. 1, sold in 1903; to Coal Creek Coal Company No. 1, sold in June 1905; to Tanana Mines Railway No. 1, sold in January 1907; to Tanana Valley Railroad No. 1, sold in December 1917; to Alaskan Engineering Commission No. 1, transferred in 1923; to Alaska Railroad No. 1, retired before 1929, on display in 1930, to Friends of the Tanana Valley Railroad, preserved.
50	4-4-0	Baldwin	4294	March 1878	12x16	42"	Built for Olympia & Chehalis Valley No. 1 "E. H. Quimette," sold in May 1891 to Columbia & Puget Sound No. 10, sold in 1898; to WP&Y No. 4, renumbered 54, sold in 1905; to Tanana Mines Railway No. 50, sold in January 1907; to Tanana Valley Railroad No. 50, sold in December 1917; to Alaskan Engineering Commission No. 50, transferred in 1923; to Alaska Railroad No. 50, retired before 1924, scrapped in 1930.

On the Tanana Valley Railroad, two trains meet at one of the junctions of the Tanana Valley Railroad near Fairbanks. This narrow-gauge railroad later became part of the Alaska Railroad. (Clifford Collection)

Locomotive Roster *(continued)*

Road No.	Wheel Arr.	Builder	C/N	Year	Cylinders	Drivers	Notes
51	2-6-0	Brooks	578	1881	14x18	42"	Built for Kansas Central Railway No. 8 (UP No. 103, 1885), sold 1890,[1] to Trail Creek Tramway No. 3, sold in April 1896; to Columbia & Western Railway No. 3, sold in 1898; to Canadian Pacific Railway, sold in August 1900; to WP&Y No. 65, sold in September 1906; to Tanana Mines Railway No. 51, sold in January 1907; to Tanana Valley Railroad No. 51, sold in December 1917; to Alaska Engineering Commission No. 51, transferred in 1923; to Alaska Railroad No. 51, retired before 1924, scrapped in 1930.
52	2-6-0	Baldwin	10880	March 1890	11x18	38"	Built for Alberta Rwy. & Coal Co. No. 12, sold in 1906; to Tanana Mines Railway No. 52, sold in January 1907; to Tanana Valley Railroad No. 52, sold in December 1917; to Alaskan Engineering Commission No. 52, transferred in 1923; to Alaska Railroad No. 52, scrapped in 1930.

[1] Initial owner and construction specifications are unconfirmed.

The Tanana Mines Railway No. 50, a Baldwin 4-4-0 locomotive in construction service near Gilmore, the terminus of the TMR. The locomotive was built for the Olympia and Tenino and later saw service on the White Pass & Yukon before purchase by the TMR in 1905. The flatcars still bear the lettering of their previous owner, the Klondike Mines Railway. (University of Alaska Archives, Bunnell Collection)

Chapter 11

Yakutat & Southern Railroad

One of the few railroads in the world that operated on a tide table as well as a timetable was the Yakutat & Southern, which served the Yakutat area for more than 60 years. This unusual railroad was conceived in 1903 when F. S. Stimson of Seattle and associates incorporated the Stimson Lumber Company and the Yakutat & Southern Railroad, with the announced intention of operating a salmon cannery, a sawmill, a railroad, and a general store.

They did all four, but the railroad and sawmill came first—the railroad to haul timber and the sawmill to produce lumber to build the rest of the facilities. The sawmill had a capacity of 36,000 board feet a day, and an adjacent planing mill could turn out 5,000 board feet a day. When the cannery began operating in 1904, the sawmill turned out shook for the wooden cases in which the cans were packed.

Yakutat is a fishing village located on Yakutat Bay at the extreme northwest corner of the Alaska Panhandle, about 350 miles southeast of Anchorage. Most of the inhabitants have Tlingit Indian ancestry. Russian explorers established a colony on Yakutat Bay in 1795, but it was wiped out by Native Americans a few years later. Settlers finally returned, but until World War II Yakutat was one of the most isolated areas in the territory, accessible only by boat. The war brought the construction of a paved airport runway, and now Yakutat receives regular air service. A road connecting the community with the Alaska Highway, about 60 miles away, is planned, but it has not yet been constructed.

Some placer mining occurred in the Yakutat area in the 1880s. In 1888, the Swedish Mission Convenance established a mission there, and soon afterward a couple of salteries were built to pack both salmon and herring. The first real industrial development began in 1903 when the Stimson group started the lumber mill and the railroad.

The original Stimson company carried on the operation for a number of years, after which it was taken over by Gorman & Company, which had a number of salmon canneries in Southeast Alaska. In 1913, the operation was sold to Libby, McNeill, and Libby, and in 1951 the Bellingham Canning Company took over.

The Yakutat & Southern trackage, which started on the cannery wharf and ended 11 miles away in the brush on an uninhabited riverbank (Situk), was standard gauge with 40-pound rails. The tide table became necessary when operations began hauling fish rather than wood products, since it was only when the tide was high that fishing vessels could unload their boats and fish scows could be brought alongside the track to load fish for the cannery.

Passengers and their baggage were carried free of charge. There were no tickets—one just got aboard a wooden, open-platform Hollingsworth-built combination car, provided the passenger had the nerve to ride.

The line originally had a branch along Lost River, but this was abandoned when an automobile road took its place. Early on, there was talk of extending the railroad southeast about 35 miles on the coastal plain to the mouth of the Alsek River at Dry Bay—crossing the Situk, the Ahrnklin, the Dangerous, the Itallo, the Akwe, and the Ustay Rivers on the way—but nothing came of it. Some say that the formidable number of bridges required for the trackage to traverse such a route was the main deterrent.

A 2-6-2 Lima Prairie locomotive built in 1907 was acquired from the Lima Works in 1913. It was retired in 1949 following World War II because it was too expensive to operate—it used two tons of coal to complete one round trip to the Situk River.

The Lima was supplemented by a diesel, constructed from the running gear of the old Heisler. The bell from the Lima went to one of the Alaska Steamship Company's freighters that served the Yakutat area. Other rolling stock included flatcars, some gondolas, and a pair of Plymouth locomotives—with an unknown history. At one time, a Packard sedan with flanged-wheels was used. Later the line's rolling stock consisted of a Chevrolet truck with flanged wheels and a homemade gondola. A handcar was also available for use by berry pickers and picnic parties.

This well-traveled 28-ton Heisler became the 2nd No. 1 of the Yakutat and Southern. Prior to its sale to the Y&S, it had seen service on four logging lines in the South 48. In 1940, the locomotive was converted to internal combustion (diesel) and became the primary motive power on the line. Its remains can still be seen in Yakutat. (Steve Hauff collection)

Chapter 11: Yakutat & Southern Railroad   157

This Lima locomotive, built in 1907 and acquired in 1913, was the second locomotive to see service on the Yakutat & Southern. The engine was retired in 1949 after heavy service. It is stored at Yakutat. (University of Alaska Archives, McCracken Collection)

Since operations ceased in the mid-1960s, the Lima locomotive has belonged—twice by gift and once by purchase—to the Alaska-Yukon chapter of the National Railway Historical Society. But failure to move the 26-ton locomotive from cannery properties has entangled it in various legal problems because the cannery was sold numerous times and in 1972 was involved in bankruptcy court in Seattle.

Plans have been mooted for the reconstruction of some of the trackage and the restoration of the Lima as a tourist attraction in the area.

When it became uneconomical to operate steam locomotives on the Yakutat & Southern, they were replaced with a truck with flanged wheels. This truck is shown pulling a fish car between the cannery and the loading area on the Situk River. The trains hauled fish from the river landing to the cannery and personnel and supplies from the cannery area to the fish boats along the river. (University of Alaska Archives, McCracken Collection)

Yakutat and Southern Railroad

Locomotive Roster

Road No.	Wheel Arr.	Builder	C/N	Year	Cylinders	Drivers	Notes
1	0-4-2T	Porter					From unconfirmed photo.
1 (2nd)	2-truck	Heisler	1092	August 1906	12-½x12	33	23-ton, rebuilt to diesel 1940 by Skagit Steel & Iron Works. Originally A. H. Kneeland. To Minard & Company (Elma Lbr. Co.). To Vance Lumber Company. To Buffelen Lumber & Mfg. Company. To Libby, McNeil & Libby (Yakutat & Southern RR).
2	2-6-2	Lima	1057	1907	10x16	36	To Libby, McNeil & Libby (Yakutat & Southern RR) in 1913. To National Railway Historical Society (Alaska-Yukon Chapter). On display at Yakutat.

Note: Two Plymouth gas locomotives were used on the railroad: a 1930 Packard sedan with flanged wheels and a 1949 Chevrolet truck with flanged wheels.

Chapter 12

Valdez and the Keystone Canyon Caper

The late 1800s and early 1900s brought a rush of proposed railroad builders to the open ports and harbors of Prince William Sound. These builders believed they could attain instant wealth if they could bring together the rich copper deposits that had been discovered in the Copper River Valley, the coal at Bering River, and a variety of other minerals in the Tanana and Yukon River Valleys. But this section of Alaska had few feasible rights-of-way because of its precipitous grades over rocky mountain passes that were blanketed with deep snow fully half of the year.

At about this same time, the 55th Congress came to the aid of those attempting to construct railroads by passing the Transportation Act on May 14, 1898. This act agreed, with stipulations, to grant franchises only to "railroads, duly organized, under law." Land for rights-of-way and terminals, and timber and stone for construction, were made available. After a construction grace period of four years, a tax of $100 per year for each operating mile was levied against the railroads.

More than a dozen speculative railroads were proposed from Valdez, and from nearby Port Valdez on Valdez Arm, up the Lowe River Valley, through the narrow confines of Keystone Canyon, over to the Copper River Valley, and then on to the interior. This inundation of proposals resulted in a great deal of confusion since records and reports were not diligently kept in those days.

There were only two practical routes a railroad line could take into the interior from the Valdez area. The routes were identical for a distance of about 27 miles, extending up the Lowe River Valley as far as Heiden Canyon.

From there one route led through Marshall Pass, at an elevation of 1,700 feet, and down the Tusnuna River to its junction with the Copper River, 54 miles from Valdez. From there the route continued into the interior. The other route crossed Thompson Pass at an elevation of 2,550 feet, climbed a minor summit at Ernestine Pass, and reached the Copper River Valley about 100 miles from Valdez.

Of the many roads proposed over these routes, only four builders did any significant construction (besides preliminary surveys). They were the Valdez, Copper River, and Tanana Railroad Company, the Copper River & Northwestern Railway Company, the Valdez-Yukon Railroad Company, and the Alaska Home Railroad Company.

Among those who did little more than try to raise money by selling stock was the Alaska Central Railroad Company of Arizona (not to be confused with the Alaska Central, which started construction at Seward and later became the Alaska Northern and eventually the present-day Alaska Railroad), which planned to build from Prince William Sound to the Yukon River near the boundary between Alaska and British North

America, a distance of 330 miles. The papers were filed with the government land office in May 1898.

In 1899 a group of Iowa business developers founded the Copper River & Yukon Railroad Company to build a railroad and telegraph line from Valdez to the Klondike, with a branch line from a point east of Mantasta Pass, thence along an undefined stream to the Yukon River on or near the Canadian border. This group sought 50-year rights and a government subsidy of $16,000 per mile through an application made in Congress by Representative Curtis of Iowa.

In February 1900, the Akron, Sterling, and Northern Railroad Company of Colorado filed to build from Valdez Bay via Marshall Pass to Eagle City, a distance of 409.42 miles. This group proposed certain branches that would reach into the coal, copper, and other mineral fields.

The great Trans-Alaska Railroad Company (one of three companies carrying this or similar names), made news in 1901 with plans for a land route directly to the door of Siberia. The southern terminus, as planned by Captain John Healy, well known for his Klondike activities, was to be at Valdez. The line would pierce the valley of the Copper and Tanana Rivers, continue west at the junction of the Tanana and the Yukon to the Bering Strait, and then proceed via Norton Sound to Port Clarence and the Nome country. The total distance was approximately 1,200 miles, with the proposal that the route tap the Canadian border at locations desirable to development and mining interests. The proposal was for English capital to pay for the all-American route, in the same way that the White Pass & Yukon was financed.

This is how McKinley Street in Valdez looked shortly after the turn of the century when such railroads as the Copper River & Northwestern, the Valdez-Yukon, and the Alaska Home centered their activities here. Today, despite never having a successful railroad, Valdez is a thriving seaport community and the southern terminus of the trans-Alaska oil pipeline. (University of Washington Library, Northwest Collection)

The Trans-Alaska never advanced past the planning stage because it ran into financial difficulties. The plan for the line was revised in 1903, and it was renamed the Valdez and Copper River Railroad. The new proposal was much less ambitious, but it also ran into fundraising problems and fell by the wayside.

Another railroad that came closer to being built than many of the others was the Valdez-Eagle (City) Railroad. This line was headed by Captain J. R. DeLamar of New York, who had acquired a large number of mining properties along the proposed route. He announced that he had obtained the services of Michael J. Heney, the White Pass & Yukon builder. The Valdez-Eagle was to run from Valdez through central Alaska to Eagle City, with a proposed extension from Eagle City to the Klondike. This course would make it a predominantly all-American route to Dawson City. Financing was to be provided by London Loan, Mortgage, and Trust Company, with capitalization at $15 million. One of the major promoters of this railroad company was Frank Bradshaw of Los Angeles.

Grading and track-laying on the Valdez-Yukon Railroad. Work on the right-of-way started in August 1906 and extended several miles up the Lowe River to Keystone Canyon. The Valdez-Yukon was the last of the railroad companies to withdraw construction activities from the Valdez area. (Clifford Collection)

One of the more ambitious projects was that of the Alaska, Copper River, and Yukon Railroad Company, which not only planned a rail link between a point on Prince William Sound and the Yukon River in the vicinity of Eagle City but also proposed to operate a steamship line between Seattle and Prince William Sound. In addition, it planned to operate smelters and refineries and set up a general mining business in Alaska.

Capitalization was $25 million, and the railroad system alone would cost in the neighborhood of $10 million. The entire amount was to be provided by eastern U.S. and European financiers. Articles of incorporation were filed in Washington State in 1902 by F. D. Bannister, Alfred B. Iles, and C. L. Parker. From the terminal on Prince William Sound, the line would run through Mantasta Pass and touch the Yukon River somewhere near Eagle.

Early in 1902, an Alaska land grant right-of-way was filed with the U.S. Congress for the

The first and only locomotive for the Valdez-Yukon Railroad was this Rogers 4-6-0 purchased from the Southern Pacific Railroad. The engine was never delivered to the V-Y—the end of the railroad occurring before the locomotive could be shipped north. (Clifford Collection)

Alaska Gulf and Yukon Railway Company by Representative Jenkins of Wisconsin to build a railroad to Eagle City. The land grant would consist of alternate sections 10 miles in width on each side of the track. Mineral rights were to be available to the company upon completion of the railroad. In the late summer of 1902, the Valdez, Copper River, and Yukon Railroad Company was incorporated with capitalization of $23 million to operate a railroad through the Copper River Valley and central Alaska from Valdez to Eagle City and Dawson on the Yukon River. The road was to be 380 to 400 miles in length. At the same time the Anglo-American Construction Company was formed and capitalized at $3 million to handle the construction of the railroad. Both organizations were incorporated under the laws of New Jersey. F. C. Jelm was the manager of construction and one of the prime movers on the project. Plans called for the construction of 40 miles the first year and completion of the entire route in two and a half years.

At about this time, promotional work was being done on the Pacific and Yukon Railroad Company by D. A. McKenzie. Like so many others, the project never actually came into being and soon dropped from sight.

In mid-summer 1903, the Valdez and Copper River Railway Company (V&CRR) announced that it had secured financing and that contracts for construction had been let to contractors James F. McDonald and John Hays Hammond. The contract called for the road to be built in 14 months, and the promoters provided $1 million in funds to the construction firm. The project attracted some attention since McDonald had a reputation as a railroad builder in Columbia and other South American countries and Hammond was a mining engineer and promoter of South African projects. Like so many others, however, the V&CRR died on the vine.

In April 1904, papers were filed with the government land office by the Valdez, Marshall Pass, and Northern Railroad Company of New Jersey (formerly the Valdez and Northern Railroad Company) to build a railroad from Valdez to Eagle City; the route and distance were not listed on the proposal. The project never made it past the proposal stage.

On January 31, 1905, a bill was introduced in Congress creating the Alaska Railroad (not to be confused with the Alaska Railroad as it exists today). The bill authorized the company to lay out, locate, construct, furnish, maintain, and enjoy continuous railroad, telegraph, and telephone lines from a point on the Gulf of Alaska northward to a point on the Yukon River near Eagle. Preliminary surveys of the various routes had been made by Judge D. A. McKenzie and a party of surveyors, who packed in to the Copper River Valley and then went down the river to its mouth and on to Valdez and other points on Valdez Bay in search of a terminal location.

More active, but not any more successful, was the Valdez, Copper River, and Tanana Railroad Company, which proposed a steel highway from Valdez to the American Yukon River by way of the Tanana diggings early in 1903. This road was promoted by A. B. Iles (who had been active in the Alaska, Copper River, and Yukon Railroad Company, a company from Portland, OR). It also was the first to attempt to raise local Valdez money to support construction and was successful in getting a pledged contribution of $75,000. In May 1903, Iles secured a permit from the town council to allow construction along Front Street, and the company completed a dock and a 1,300-foot long connecting trestle. Under the supervision of George F. Baldwin, the company's chief engineer, the preliminary survey of the first 35 miles of the route was completed.

The Valdez, Copper River, and Tanana Railroad was also the first to announce that a locomotive and two rail cars were being brought to Valdez. There is, however, no record that the equipment actually arrived. The firm also let a contract for the construction of the first 5 miles of road, which apparently was never completed.

First proposed in 1905, the construction of the Valdez-Yukon Railroad actually started under the direction of Colonel A. W. Swartz. The first spike was driven on August 16, 1906, at the railroad's terminal site about a mile west of Valdez. Grading was completed for a distance of several miles up the Lowe River to the mouth of Keystone Canyon. The Valdez-Yukon also bought a locomotive, a Rogers 4-6-0 manufacturer's #2858, built in 1881 for the Southern Pacific. The engine bore several SP numbers, including Nos. 187, 1665, and 2098. The Valdez-Yukon was the last of the early companies to leave the Valdez area.

Early references to the Copper River and Northwestern Railway Company (CR&NW) are a bit confusing because official records show that the company was chartered on May 16, 1905, under the laws of Nevada. The Sitka Alaskan of July 8, 1905, carried news of the incorporation of the Copper River & Northwestern Railway Company in Washington State by Monty Thomsen, formerly of Spokane; John Rosene, an Indianapolis barber who hit it rich at Dawson City; and others. Capital stock was shown at $250,000, of which $5,000 was reported subscribed. The story also stated that the railroad's principal place of business would be Seattle but that the chief office would be in Carson City, Nevada, where the State Agent and Transfer Syndicate, Inc., was named as agent.

In 1905, the Copper River & Northwestern applied for the right-of-way under the 1898 Railway Act of Congress. The company was financed by the Guggenheim family, which was active in Alaska and the Yukon mining circles and already had been accused of high-handed treatment of smaller railroad and mining interests.

In compliance with the Act, the CR&NW filed a description of the tracts of land needed to build a railroad from a point west of Valdez to and through Keystone Canyon to the interior of Alaska. On January 17, 1906, the application was approved by the secretary of the interior.

The original Copper River route survey had been made by George C. Hazelette, who had come to Alaska with a survey party to find a feasible railroad route from tidewater to Eagle on the Yukon. This party made two surveys, one up the Copper River Valley, the other from Valdez by way of the military trail over the range. Joining at what is now Willow Creek, these two routes became identical and continued north to the Tanana through the richest mineral belt in the territory.

Because of the obviously great engineering difficulties involved in navigating the Copper River Valley, the Valdez route was determined to be the most practical and was the one recorded by the company. Work was started on schedule under the direction of Hazelette, with John Rosene also active in the program.

During the time the CR&NW was active in the Valdez area, it completed about one third of the grading necessary between Port Valdez and Valdez, and then nothing else in the area until it reached Keystone Canyon. About 25 percent of the necessary grading was completed through Keystone Canyon, including 200 feet of tunnel, at a cost of $85,000. However, no work was undertaken beyond the canyon. It was obvious that the Copper River intended to stake its claim to the route through its work in the narrow canyon. The company, however, had failed to comply with the Railway Act, which specified that 20 miles of roadbed must be constructed within one year. Meanwhile, Mike Heney had contacted the Guggenheims in New York with the intention of selling them on the railroad construction that was already completed through the Copper River Valley.

It was also during this period that the Alaska Syndicate was formed as a partnership by the Guggenheims and J. P. Morgan & Company, along with the Havemeyer financial interests and Kuhn, Loeb, & Company. The agreement was signed in July 1906, and one of the first changes brought about by the pact was the ordering of another survey of the Copper River route as a result of Mike Heney's prodding. One of the most promising and respected railroad engineers in the east, M. K. Rogers, was called upon to make the survey. He made a casual survey of the Valdez and Copper River routes, and then proceeded on his own to Katalla in the coal district. Rogers's report to the New York interests was enthusiastically in favor of Katalla as a base of construction. His report was adopted, and the combined Guggenheim-Morgan interests advanced $1 million for construction from this point.

In early August, Rogers announced in Valdez that the CR&NW proposed to move its operations to Katalla, much to the disappointment of the Valdez residents. Depression and gloom settled over the city. By 1907 Valdez had lost out, although the Copper River & Northwestern maintained a skeleton staff at Keystone Canyon to prevent its use by competing railroads and to preserve the Valdez option while the feasibility of the Katalla and Cordova sites was being sorted out.

Local citizens took pride in volunteering to work with picks and shovels in grading the first mile of roadway for H. D. Reynolds's Alaska Home Railroad on August 13, 1907. Headquarters for the project were set up in the church building. (Clifton Valdez Museum)

In this bleak hour, Henry Derr Reynolds appeared with a hopeful proposition for Valdez citizens. Reynolds presented plans for the Home Railroad Company, also known as the Alaska Home Railroad, to Valdez citizens on August 9, 1907. Ex-Governor John C. Brady chaired a town meeting the following evening in McKinley Hall, where the proposal was discussed. Both Reynolds and Brady were well known to the residents of Valdez from previous business dealings, and when the meeting was over Reynolds had raised $106,000 in contributions ranging from 10¢ to $10,000 from the citizens of the community. Thus began one of the most bizarre episodes in Alaskan history, an effort made up of bold planning, visionary dreams, stirring adventure, possibly some larceny, and most surely tragedy. It was an episode that would have political impact on the territory for many years to come.

The Copper River & Northwestern Railway cut in Keystone Canyon where Alaska Home Railroad employees battled with Guggenheim employees. This alignment was the only route to the interior through the canyon. The tent that served as headquarters for Deputy Marshall Edward Hasey is seen in the background. The "battle" resulted in a least one death (though arguably because of poor medical treatment), and several people were wounded. (Clifford Collection)

Reynolds's plan called for the building of a railroad to the summit of the coast range in 90 days, a distance of 34 miles, from which passengers and materials would be transferred to the government trail for transportation to the interior. The road would be a narrow-gauge line, constructed with 30-pound rails. Power would be provided by electricity generated at nearby waterfalls. The project would be capitalized at $10,000 per mile of completed road. Shares would be sold at $1 per share. There would be no construction profits, no graft, and no incompetence. There would be no free passes for travelers and no rebates; no promotional shares would be issued; no bonds; and no other indebtedness. The railroad would be constructed and operated in the people's interest, of Alaska, by Alaska, and for Alaska.

Headquarters were established in an old church that had been donated to the railroad. A survey was made for the Valdez terminals. Warehouses, a wharf, and a sawmill were acquired, and on August 12 engineers began the actual survey of the route. At the same time, the company received a 99-year franchise from the Valdez City Council, giving the Alaska Home Railroad exclusive use of the city's streets and alleys. The first shovelful of earth was turned by Ex-Governor Brady on August 13, and the citizens of the town graded the first mile of right-of-way. Antonelle and Nelson of Seattle were named contractors for the project.

Meanwhile, other events were taking place. On August 19, a branch of the Reynolds Bank was established in Valdez to facilitate the financing of the road. The next day, Reynolds acquired a major interest in many of the business establishments in the town, including the Valdez Prospector, the newspaper. Stock subscriptions were increased, and in late August Reynolds arrived in Seattle, set up headquarters, and acquired additional properties, including the Boulder-Alaska Copper Company, the

This tunnel, 200 feet in length, was the center of the gun battle between Guggenheim employees protecting Copper River & Northwestern Railway property and workers on the Alaska Home Railway. Today a historic marker along the highway marks the spot and gives a brief description of the melee that took place on September 27, 1907. (Clifford Collection)

Local citizens gathered at the railroad's terminal site in Valdez for the ceremonial driving of the first spike of the Valdez-Yukon Railroad on August 16, 1906. Colonel A. W. Swartz, well known in railroad circles, was in charge of construction for the Valdez-Yukon and drove the first spike. (Clifford Collection)

LaTouch-Alaska Copper Company, the Reynolds-Alaska Coal Company, the Alaska Coast Copper Company, and the Alaska Coast Steamship Company. The foundation of this early day conglomerate was the Alaska Development Company, capitalized at $3,000,000, with H. D. Reynolds serving as president.

On August 29, the railroad established offices in New York and was incorporated in the state of Washington for $10,000,000. The company filed with the office of land management in early September for a permit to build from Valdez through Keystone Canyon. Meanwhile, on September 14 the first railroad equipment, including the Home Railroad's locomotive, cars, and rails, arrived in Valdez on the steamer Jeannie. As the week progressed, it became necessary for Alaska Home survey crews to enter Keystone Canyon, where the CR&NW crews continued to occupy the right-of-way. Warnings were issued against the Alaska Home crews about trespassing, and a confrontation was in the offing.

It has been suggested by many that this inevitable conflict with the CR&NW was one of the keys to Reynolds's plan for the railroad (in addition to his stock-selling efforts). The ace up his financial sleeve was that he had planned his survey along the original Guggenheim-Morgan route, in a location where there was room for only one railroad. His plan was that someday the wealthy Syndicate would pay him a substantial sum to abandon the location in the Keystone Canyon rather than institute legal proceedings with the ensuing costly delays for the CR&NW. He would then set off for a life of luxury in Boston, his old home.

However, Reynolds's scheme was conceived too late, and his offer met with a flat refusal from the Guggenheim interests. The CR&NW had already become deeply involved in the Katalla operation and for all practical purposes had given up on Valdez. In a last desperate attempt, Reynolds sent his construction gangs into the disputed territory.

Thus the scene was set for the Battle of Keystone Canyon. On September 25, Reynolds's workers forced the issue. A work party of 150 to 200 men set out from Valdez to establish construction camps in and beyond the canyon. Two Deputy U.S. marshals, Ed C. Hasey and Duncan Dixon, both purported to be on the Syndicate's payroll, were stationed in the canyon to safeguard the threatened Guggenheim camp. A barricade had been erected halfway across the grade. A white tent had also been pitched by the barrier to serve as headquarters for the marshals.

The Home Railroad crew approached the barrier carrying work tools; no one carried arms. At first, there was some good-natured bantering between the two work forces, as friend recognized friend across the line. General foreman William Koch, who was riding a stallion, headed up the Home forces, and William O'Neill was in charge of the CR&NW group. O'Neill is reported to have come forward from behind the barrier and been seized by some of the advancing men. Ed Hasey, who was known to be quick tempered and who recently had been transferred to Valdez from Ketchikan where he had been found innocent of killing a man who had resisted arrest, fired shots into the air and demanded O'Neill's release. There was no response from the men. The Home forces were egged on by the railroad counsel, Charles E. Ingersoll from Juneau, who told them that the CR&NW no longer had any right to Keystone Canyon because its right-of-way permit had expired. This confused the Home workers, who had been told that there would be no violence, that Dixon and Hasey were Deputy U.S. marshalls whose duty it was to keep the peace. It was unthinkable to them that those across the line would fire on their unarmed friends, but they were mistaken. Perhaps it was the shots reverberating off the cliffs above that caused Hasey to believe that the Home forces were returning fire; William Quitsch, newly hired by the Syndicate to assist as watchman, testified to that effect when he gave detailed information on the incident.

The advancing workers still thought that perhaps the shots were only a warning, but when some of their companions collapsed, they knew that they were under fire. Their immediate reaction was to flee. They turned and stormed down the narrow canyon. The shots continued—five to seven in all. Five struck flesh. As the wounded fell, some of their friends stopped to help them; others fled down the grade.

The town of Valdez erupted in rage when the wounded were carried in. Chris Olsen had a bullet hole near his heart. Others were hit in the limbs. Threats of reprisals swept through Valdez, but the U.S. marshall and a few troops from nearby Fort Liscum restored order. Fred Reinhardt died from a thigh wound, and Olsen, apparently the most seriously wounded of the five, disappeared from Valdez, never to be seen again. Hasey was indicted on five counts of intent to kill. Because feelings ran so high in Valdez, a change of venue to Juneau was granted and the

It was a big day in Valdez when Mrs. Blamey Stevens, wife of the chief engineer of the Alaska Home Railroad, took the throttle to start this little saddle-tanker over the first mile of rails on October 4, 1907. Little Valdez Cameron, the first non-native child born in Valdez, was at the whistle. It was the Alaska Home Railroad's day of glory. (Clifton Museum)

Enthusiasm ran so high that citizens brought their own picks and shovels to start work on the grading of the right-of-way for the Alaska Home Railroad in Valdez. Despite the enthusiastic sendoff, the project soon came to a tragic end and scores of Valdez citizens lost their life's savings. (Clifton Valdez Museum)

trial was set for sometime in March 1903.

Charges and counter-charges of bribery, threats, and tampering flew during Hasey's trial. He was acquitted of the initial charges involving Reinhardt and Olsen, but the government charged him with wounding two other men. He was found guilty and eventually served 18 months in prison.

Meanwhile, work on the Home Railroad continued with renewed vigor. Reynolds stated from Seattle that Alaska Home had complied with the law in every respect and that it had been the policy of the company not to antagonize the Guggenheims. He characterized the shooting of unarmed citizens as the work of common assassins.

Mayor T. C. Quinn took over the throttle from Mrs. Blamey Stevens as the first locomotive carried its first passengers on the Alaska Home Railroad on October 4, 1907. Approximately 1 mile of track had been laid by this time. (University of Alaska Archives, Valdez Cameron Henry Collection)

The first rails were laid in early October 1907 by Alaska Home crews, and the first train ran on October 4. Mrs. Blamey Stevens, wife of the chief engineer for the railroad, was at the throttle, and little Valdez Cameron was on the whistle cord. This was the railroad's day of glory.

The Alaska Home Railroad collapsed later in October. All work had ceased on October 10, and hundreds of penniless workers began walking the streets, carrying worthless time checks. The city of Valdez provided emergency food and housing until a ship could remove the workers—some to other railroad jobs in Katalla. Governor William B. Hoggatt ordered all saloons closed, and the Reynolds bank closed its doors. The collapse of the railroad was blamed on its inability to sell stock.

The workers were owed about $30,000, local merchants another $20,000, and liabilities in Seattle were estimated at $75,000. The bank had liabilities of some $85,000. Everything belonging to Reynolds was attached or liened, although he was able to sell the Alaska Coast Transportation Company to Tacoma interests before its assets were frozen.

Shortly thereafter, Reynolds was seen boarding a train in Tacoma headed east. The law caught up with him the next spring, and he was tried and convicted of fraud and sent to prison.

In the meantime, an English syndicate obtained an option on the Valdez-Yukon Railroad and on a couple of copper properties, but soon thereafter work on the V-YR ceased and the equipment went to the Copper River & Northwestern Railway.

It was not until the advent of the trans-Alaska oil pipeline that Valdez again became a major transportation center. During pipeline construction, Valdez had a short railroad consisting of two ex-Alaska Railroad 45-tonners, No. 7324 and No. 7249, that worked on the dock.

Chapter 13

Katalla, Where the Rails Meet the Sails

Promoted as the "Coming Metropolis of Alaska, Where the Rails Meet The Sails," Katalla became the center of Prince William Sound railroad construction activity following the demise of Valdez as the key point.

Katalla was a boomtown built on energy—literally. Since the mid-1890s, locals were aware of the presence of oil. Large seeps oozed from the ground in the area. Residents used the sticky material to start their fires, and as early as 1897 a trio of entrepreneurs tried to market the resource. By 1902, the first gusher was brought in, and 1,600 barrels a day began to flow from the well. The well showed the presence of oil at 250 feet and a large flow of oil at 360 feet. It was Alaska's first producing well. Because of the issuance of a federal ban on oil claims in 1910 that lasted until the passage of the Leasing Act of 1920, Katalla was Alaska's only patented oil field. Again, however, shipping was a big problem.

Oil activity at Katalla was revived, the field was overhauled in 1924, and a regular marketing station was established in Cordova. But the Chilkat Oil Company that operated at Katalla shut down its operations in December 1933 when the boiler house for the refinery burned down.

Katalla was also the gateway to the Bering River coal fields. The region was blessed with gigantic, high-grade copper deposits. If the Bering River coal could have been brought together—economically—with the rich copper ore from the interior, there would have been millions of dollars to be made.

As such, Katalla became a typical boomtown in which saloons, dance halls, and gambling dens sprang up practically overnight. Five to ten thousand residents crowded

Construction crews along the waterfront had built a causeway to one of the outer islands in the Katalla region, but winter storms washed out all such work and left the area in shambles. It was soon deserted as far as railroad construction was concerned. (University of Washington Library, Northwest Collection)

the town by 1907, lured by the promise of jobs or riches in the oil fields, in the coal mines, or with the fledgling railroads being built to serve the energy industry.

In the years following the turn of the century, almost as many railroad companies that had shown an interest in Valdez joined in the rush to follow the two leaders, the Alaska-Pacific Railway and Terminal Company (APR&T) and the Copper River and Northwestern Railway Company (CR&NW), in trying to reach the rich copper and coal fields from Katalla. As was the case at Valdez, competing railroads of questionable intentions and financial backing sprang up, willing to sell their locations, surveys, or rights-of-way at any time for a substantial sum.

Workers for the Katalla Company, builders of the ill-fated Copper River & Northwestern Railway project at Katalla, are seen at Bruner Crossing as they take a break from their duties to pose for the photographer on July 14, 1909. The Katalla Company was one of several firms engaged in railroad building in the Katalla area. (Alaska Historical Library)

The Copper River and Northwestern Railway Company moved its operations from Valdez at a cost of thousands when the Guggenheim-Morgan interests (the Alaska Syndicate), tired of slow progress, physical hardship, and legal entanglements, decided against investing more money without additional feasibility studies. The Syndicate had sent M. K. Rogers to look the area over, including Mike Heney's survey from Eyak (Cordova), but Rogers made a decision favoring the Katalla locality as the proper terminus for the project.

Copper River construction was handled by the Katalla Company, headed by Rogers. The next 12 months saw the most spectacular spending orgy in the early history of Alaska. More than $2 million was spent in a futile attempt to show the construction virtues of the route selection, a widely known impossibility to all well-informed Alaskans. Rogers, as well as Katalla, with its treacherous harbor and its well-known gift of kicking up a real 100 percent storm in short order, both began making history for themselves.

Vessels from the States, heavily loaded with supplies and materials of all kinds, stopped, looked, and listened at the entrance to this temperamental body of water before taking the chance of becoming shipwrecked. It was a case of "get in and get out" just as quickly as possible, if possible. Many a ship in the process of unloading had to weigh anchor and head for open water as a violent storm, typical of the area, hit with unbelievable suddenness and violence. Others left their anchors buried in the bottom of the harbor when their anchor chains were detached by the heavy poundings of a hurricane-like storm.

Lighters were used to get goods to shore, but with little success and much expense. On one occasion, and perhaps one that was destined to contribute heavily to the decision to eventually abandon Katalla as a terminus for the railroads, was the loss of the winter supply of whiskey, beer, and potatoes aboard a barge being towed to shore. Many ships were lost, including the old gold ship Portland, which had escaped many such storms in the past. Others escaped by the narrowest of margins.

The CR&NW attempted to construct a high-tide rubblestone jetty built from a pile trestle, which advanced into the open seas by use of a pile driver at the head of the trestle. The proposed jetty had a shore arm extending 4,000 feet into the sea in a generally southern direction, and from that point 2,000 feet farther in a direction bearing about 30 degrees northeast. Most of the construction took place in depths exceeding 30 feet, and a considerable part in depths up to 50 feet and lower.

At the same time, the company built 8 miles of standard-gauge track toward the Bering coal fields and did some construction work in the direction of the Copper River.

Survey crews had been sent out as far as Chitina, a distance of 220 miles, in the heart of bear country. In one bear encounter, a worker sat down to eat a pot of beans, and a bear approached. He quickly abandoned the beans to climb a tree, and the bear followed him but then returned to devour the beans. The man was reportedly so frightened and so well hidden that it took rescue teams more than six hours to find him. On another occasion, a man camped out with a couple of blankets was chased by a brown bear. He dropped the blankets and rushed to the top of a hill, from where he observed the bear making himself comfortable for the night on the blankets. The man maintained a lonely vigil on top of the hill until morning.

The Alaska-Pacific Railway and Terminal Company was organized and incorporated in Washington State to build from Martin Island in Controller Bay to the Yukon River near Eagle City, with additional branch lines. The proposal was filed with the Land Office of the territory of Alaska on January 23, 1906. The APR&T was headed by Dr. M. W. Bruner, and his operation was often referred to as the Bruner Road. The Keystone Construction Company was hired to do the construction.

The APR&T also proposed the creation of an artificial harbor. It planned the construction of a breakwater on the west side of the Martin Islands. The plan was to build a double trestle connecting Whale and Fox Islands by a breakwater and to anchor another breakwater on Outer Island. This structure would extend 2,150 feet in a northerly direction. The breakwater between the two islands was to be 1,600 feet long in water not exceeding 30 feet in depth. The APR&T also constructed a sawmill to supply ties and timbers, but this was soon put out of operation by winter storms that flooded the mill.

Both artificial harbors left a considerable section unprotected against the winds, and both were subject to rapid filling in the event of littoral sand drift.

There was a great rivalry between the two outfits, and on one occasion the Alaska-Pacific workers dynamited a trestle and equipment owned by the Guggenheim-Morgan syndicate and took over the property. An armed counter attack led by Tony de Pascal was successful, and he was presented with a $1,000 cash bonus. On another occasion, the Guggenheim forces were trying to lay track over a right-of-way disputed by the APR&T, which had constructed a "go-devil" of railroad rails to protect the right-of-way. The go-devil was swung back and forth over the disputed property by armed men behind fortifications, its railroad rail quills spelling death or destruction for anyone or anything unfortunate enough to contact it.

A similar $1,000 bonus was offered by the Guggenheims, and this time an Alaskan pioneer worker, Jack McCord, led an armed band of laborers in laying track over the disputed right-of-way—with bullets whizzing over their heads. One worker was killed, and 10 were seriously wounded. A shipload of soldiers soon restored order. The Syndicate forces also tangled with Mike Heney—but with less success. He had taken control of the desirable railroad location in the narrow Abercrombie Canyon on the Copper River and was accomplishing construction work there for his railroad from Cordova. Heney's workers had mined the area with dynamite and were successful in turning back the invaders without bloodshed. Control of this area ultimately resulted in the Guggenheim-Morgans later purchasing his right-of-way and hiring him to construct the railroad up the Copper River for them.

The distance to the copper mines would be approximately the same for both the Alaska-Pacific and Copper River and Northwestern railroads from Katalla. Both lines would follow the Katalla River Valley, go over a low divide to Bering Lake for coal, around the coastal headlands, and along the western boundary of the Copper River delta plain. There would be practically no grades—the most difficult being 0.87 percent and the longest about 2 miles in length.

After a lengthy and expensive battle with the elements, the Guggenheim-Morgan forces called Rogers to New York for a conference. They also summoned E. C. Hawkins, who had been called in to do another survey, and Mike Heney, who had started work on the Copper River Railroad out of Cordova. Following the conference, it was announced in the fall of 1907 that the Copper River & Northwestern Railway Company would make its temporary headquarters in Cordova until a breakwater was built at Katalla. The Katalla Company office personnel were moved to Seattle.

By the end of 1907, checks issued by the Alaska Pacific Railway and Terminal Company were returned from the banks, spelling the end of that operation also. Following a further announcement by Hawkins that "work on the Copper River line from Katalla had been suspended, one of the reasons being the financial stringency in the States," the CR&NW locomotives at Katalla were moved to Cordova.

Other railroad companies began to enter the competition. The Catalla and Carbon Mountain Railroad Company of Washington filed in November 1907 to build from the mouth of the Bering River at Controller Bay and up the river 21.87 miles to the coal fields. Three surveys were filed in Juneau, one on October 2, 1909; another on August 21, 1909; and the third on December 20, 1907. The company was organized by Clark Davis and reverted to the old spelling of Catalla. Plans called for the building of a 3.5-mile trestle over the flats to a dockside location on a deeper channel. The road would run from the far end of the coal fields to the water.

The Kush-Ta-Ka Southern Railroad Company was another competitor. It filed a survey on February 15, 1909, to connect the Copper River and Northwestern to the coal fields. The firm was headed by Charles F. Munday and was surveyed by J. L. McPherson to run to the claims of Mike Heney and his brother Patrick A. Heney (known as the "English Group" because of their ties to the Close brothers). The Kush-Ta-Ka route included a trestle to Kanak Island for its dock site. The line was projected to Lake Kush-Ta-Ka, and it progressed up the west side of the lake.

The Bering River Railroad Company of Washington filed in March 1908 to build from Kayak Island across Controller Bay and up the Bering River to Clear Creek, a distance of 27.2 miles. Surveys were also filed on March 12, 1909, and on March 25, 1909. The proposed Bering River route was similar to that of the Kush-Ta-Ka line, but upon reaching the lake went to the east side rather than to the west. C. J. Smith was president of the Bering River Railroad, and H. L. Hawkins was the locating engineer.

One railroad, the Katalla Coal Company Railroad—also known as the Goose City Railroad—did reach the coal fields and operated for several years from Goose City and up past Katalla to a point 9 miles inland. The line operated from the early 1900s until it was closed down when the government withdrew entry to the coal fields following the Ballinger-Pinchot controversy. The company also encountered difficulties in shipping coal and other materials from Katalla. The firm had proposed building a smelter for copper at Katalla, and the CR&NW was to build a spur line from Mile 39 on the main line to the smelter location.

At about this time, the Pacific Coal and Oil Company, headed by Falcon Joslin (who was involved in the Tanana Mines Railway at Fairbanks) and George Hazelette (who started the original Copper River railroad project at Valdez), announced plans to build its own railroad. This line would travel from Katalla to the coal fields in the

The aftermath of a winter storm in the Katalla area left wreckage such as this. One of the saddle-tank locomotives (No. 5) used in construction is mired in the mud. The trackage it rested on has almost totally disappeared. (Alaska Historical Library)

Just about every high tide brought floodwaters into Katalla during the height of the winter storm season. Stumps and other debris floated through the center of town. The frequency of violent storms and the lack of a suitable harbor soon ended attempts to build a railroad from the coast to the interior from this location. (Alaska Historical Library)

Bering Lake area and would handle coal and oil shipments. Known as the "English Company," the firm stated that there were good harbor possibilities at nearby Chilkat and that they planned to build a dock there to ship their products.

The Katalla Company obtained additional financing, moved its staff back to Katalla, and resurveyed a line to the coal fields. This line was about 25 feet above the original survey along the waterfront, which the company hoped would reduce exposure to the high water disasters that had plagued the railroad before. The Alaska-

Pacific Railroad obtained new financing and was granted a one-year extension to complete the necessary franchise work. A condition of the extension required the company to complete 20 miles of roadbed prior to March 18, 1908.

Another firm in the field was the Controller Bay and Navigation Company, incorporated under the laws of New Jersey to build from Controller Bay to the coal fields. Filings were submitted on December 10, 1910, with a capitalization of $500,000. However, this firm, along with the Katalla Company and the Alaska Pacific, failed to get major construction projects started.

A latecomer, and one that gave every indication of being a successful operation, was the Alaska Anthracite Coal and Railway Company, which was organized in Seattle on April 19, 1909, to build from tidewater on Controller Bay to the Bering River coal fields. It was not until late in 1915, however, that actual work began on the project. A construction camp was set up on the east bank of the Bering River where there was a good landing for barges. A sawmill was erected and bunkhouses and shops built. This line too was located at what was known as Goose City, and its planned route closely followed the line surveyed by the Catalla and Carbon Mountain Railroad Company.

Actual construction began in 1916 and continued in 1917, and 17 miles of standard-gauge track was laid. Three 40-ton flatcars were brought in, along with a 16-ton 0-4-0 locomotive.

The track ran from Goose City across the flat and swampy ground as far as the coal land holdings of the Alaska Petroleum and Coal Company. Some $2 million was spent in construction, and though about 80 percent of the line had been completed, the difficult parts remained to be built—a 6.5-mile branch line to the Alaska Coke and Coal Company and the 9 miles of road from the Goose City site to Controller Bay, where a deep water wharf was needed.

In 1921, the company was reorganized by Seattle interests, with John A. Campbell serving as president, and was renamed the Alaska Anthracite Railroad. Twenty-year bonds, bearing an interest rate of 6 percent, were authorized in the amount of $1.5 million, but these failed to sell. A couple of years later, the firm went into receivership. Companies involved in the Alaska Anthracite project included the Alaska Petroleum and Gas Company of Seattle, the Alaska Coke and Coal Company of Portland, OR, and the Alaska–Pacific Coast Company, a Washington and New York firm.

On July 15, 1925, a new organization led by N. W. Quigg of Los Angeles took over the project and made plans to raise $1.5 million to complete the railroad, wharf, and other facilities. Unfortunately, nothing came of this scheme, and no further work was done on the Alaska Anthracite Railroad. The remains of Goose City and the line across the flats and through the grass—along with some equipment that is currently sinking in the marsh—are still there.

The Alaska Development Company, under the direction of T. A. Hamilton, had surveyed for a railroad from the coal oil springs and coal beds to the Yukon River. The coal oil springs were located near the shore of Bering Haven Bay between Cape Suckling and Cape Martin, near the mouth of the Copper River. Surveyors reported that the proposed railroad route was feasible from the deposits up to the Copper River where the Chitina empties into it, across to where the Delta River empties into the Tanana, and then across the Tanana and on to the junction of Minook Creek and the Yukon River. This route never developed.

For all intents and purposes, railroading in Katalla was dead. Oil well construction, however, kept a limited amount of activity in the area, and a total of 44 wells were eventually drilled. Katalla had its moment of glory—which lasted more than a quarter of a century—but despite its resource riches, and its grand dreams of becoming a transportation center, it is now only a forgotten boomtown.

Chapter 14

Copper River & Northwestern Railway

Just as it was gold that inspired the building of the White Pass and Yukon Railroad, it was copper in the Wrangell Mountains and coal in the Bering River that brought about the construction of the Copper River & Northwestern Railway.

Michael J. Heney, who had successfully conquered the White Pass in the construction of the railroad considered "impossible to build" from Skagway to Whitehorse, was living a life of leisure in the East—much against his style and better judgment. With interest, he watched the development of Alaska, its growth, its transition to a territory, and finally the discovery of rich copper deposits in the Wrangell Mountains, plus oil and coal in the Katalla region. These developments, and the announcement of plans for the building of a dozen or so railroads to bring these rich resources together and to the United States proper, together with the urging of White Pass & Yukon (WP&Y) President Samuel H. Graves, brought the Irish Prince into action once again.

In 1904, Heney made his first move. He journeyed to London and secured the financial backing of his previous partners, the Close Brothers. He studied the routes from Valdez to the copper discoveries and determined that they were not conducive to railroad construction. He visited Katalla and decided that the harbor would not accommodate the steamships that would be required to bring in supplies and take out oil, coal, and copper.

Heney and his engineers, Sam Murchison and H. L. Hawkins, studied the Copper River route from the Wrangells to Prince William Sound and decided that a water-level route would be the most feasible. There were problems with this route, such as the blocking of the Copper River by the Miles and Childs Glaciers some 50 miles from the coast. Another difficulty would be building a roadbed through Abercrombie Canyon, where the stone walls rose almost straight up toward the sky and where the water currents were strong and dangerous enough to kill anyone unfortunate enough to fall in. There were also the treacherous mud flats at the mouth of the river to be crossed.

Other engineers determined that these obstacles were impossible to overcome. Heney thought otherwise. He filed his survey and started to prepare for his assault on the Copper River.

Mike Heney (right), builder of the Copper River & Northwestern and the White Pass & Yukon railroads, with one of the backers of the Copper River project. This photo was taken during the height of construction on the CR&NW. (Clifford Collection)

> The Alaska Syndicate had acquired a majority of the copper claims in the Kennecott and Bonanza regions, and it was determined to build a railroad to bring the ore out. The Syndicate had been established in 1906 by J. P. Morgan and Company, Guggenheim and Sons, and others for the development of mining holdings. The Syndicate soon purchased interests in the Bonanza Copper Mines and also signed an option (in 1907) that anticipated the development of coal claims that Clarence Cunningham and his associates were pushing to patent. Stock in the Beatson copper mines was added to the combined holdings of the Syndicate in 1910.
>
> The Syndicate also purchased the Northwestern Commercial Company and became involved in various subsidiary interests. Northwestern Commercial owned the Northwest Steamship Company—a prime property to provide transportation to and from Alaska—and Northwest Fisheries, a company that owned 12 of the 40 canneries operating in Alaska, and which put up an eighth of the fish pack. The fisheries interests were subsequently disposed of to the Booth Company. The Northwestern Railroad Company was another of the early Syndicate purchases. After six years of experimentation with routes from Valdez and Katalla, it became known as the Copper River & Northwestern.
>
> The steamship interest was merged with the formerly independent Alaska Steamship Company and became the strongest of the few public and private lines operating in northern waters.

Because of its extensive interests, the Alaska Syndicate also sent engineers into the area to survey the various available routes. One of these engineers was George Cheever Hazelette, who was sent to find a feasible route from tidewater to Eagle on the Yukon. His party made two surveys—one up the Copper River Valley, the other from Valdez by way of the military trail over the range. Joining at what is now Willow Creek, the two routes became identical and continued north to the Tanana River, through the richest mineral belt in the area.

Because the surveyors believed it impossible to overcome the engineering difficulties of the lower Copper River Route, the Valdez Trail was determined the most practical route and was recommended when the two surveys were sent east. The Valdez route was duly recorded and filed with the proper departments in Washington, and the Copper River survey was tucked away in an obscure office in New York and promptly forgotten.

Construction and logistical difficulties developed in the Valdez area, and once again the Syndicate sent an engineer to Alaska to survey a route. This time it was M. R. Rogers, acknowledged as one of the nation's top railroad engineers. He surveyed both the Copper River and Valdez routes and then proceeded to Katalla on the coast, just a few miles away from the newly discovered Bering River coal fields. Rogers's report to New York was highly in favor of building from Katalla to the copper fields and at the same time tapping the rich coal deposits. His report was accepted, and he was put in charge of the construction of a railroad from Katalla.

This construction plan proved disastrous since Katalla was located on a wild and unprotected coast, open to the full sweep of terrible winter storms. The first big winter storm destroyed the newly-constructed wharf and artificial breakwater, which were essential to the project. A wire to New York informed the backers of the problems, and another conference was called at which J. P. Morgan is reported to have slammed the table with his fist and declared, "Whatever the route, we've got to bring the copper and the coal together!"

Meanwhile, at the site he christened Cordova, Mike Heney began planning the construction of the Copper River Railroad on April 1, 1906. The site Heney had chosen had everything essential to the building and operation of a railroad—an abundance of level ground, a rare occurrence on this rocky shoreline, together with an excellent land-locked deep-water harbor. Nothing else was needed but workers and money, and he had both.

Heney had purchased this unique piece of land, along with its substantial and commodious buildings—the property of an abandoned cannery with a large dock—through a middleman, a close personal friend, for a moderate sum. Had it been known that this was to be the terminal of a $20 million plus railroad, the price would have soared considerably.

The natives and Swedish fishermen were greatly surprised one day in the early spring of 1906 when a large ocean-going steamer arrived at Eyak and unloaded scores of workers with their equipment and bed rolls, hundreds of tons of building materials, railroad equipment, and horses.

Heney's plan called for a standard-gauge line with a slight overall grade from Eyak (Cordova) up the Copper River with a branch line to the much-discussed Bering River coal field at Mile 32. The line would then proceed 100 miles farther up into the mountains to the Bonanza mine, some 200 miles from the terminus of the railroad at saltwater, and then on to the interior to tap the vast bodies of coal in the Matanuska Valley.

On August 8, 1906, the first spike was driven on the curved causeway leading away from the waterfront. A steamer pulled alongside the dock on September 5 and

This is Eyak in 1906 when Mike Heney purchased the town to build the Copper River Railroad. The fish cannery tramway, used by the Alaska Packers Association, which owned the town before Heney's purchase, runs down the street at the left. This part of the town became known as "Old Town" when the community grew in size and was renamed Cordova. (University of Washington Historical Library, Northwest Collection)

unloaded the first locomotive. No sooner had Heney's workers driven the first spike than the Guggenheim-Morgan group became very interested. If an engineer of Heney's reputation thought that the river could be bridged, and he was able to build the railroad, the coal and copper could be brought together with one rail line up the Copper River.

Another engineer, E. C. Hawkins, who had been chief engineer for the White Pass construction, was called in by the Syndicate to make a survey. He concurred that if copper and coal were to be brought together, the route up the Copper River was the most logical one.

The Guggenheim-Morgan field crew was determined to lay out its own route up the river. The survey party was met in the narrow confines of Abercrombie Canyon by Heney's men, who warned them that the entire canyon was loaded with dynamite in preparation for blasting and that they would be entering the canyon at their own risk.

The Copper River & Northwestern Railway rails extend out onto the ocean dock at Cordova where steamers load and unload at the water terminus of the railroad. Cordova was near the former village of Eyak, which Mike Heney purchased to serve as a base of operations for the construction of the Copper River Railroad, and later the CR&NW. (University of Alaska Archives)

Heney was well known for not bluffing. He fully intended to hold Abercrombie Canyon against any and all comers. The Syndicate knew the game was up and initiated negotiations to buy the route.

Heney was called to New York to discuss the deal and turned the field operations over to Sam Murchison, his chief assistant. Construction labor was limited in Alaska in those days, and pirating from other operations was a way of business. Only a faked case of small pox developed by a trusted employee of Heney's, who used a liberal application of Oleum Tiglit, commonly known as Croton Oil, prevented the pirating of much needed laborers from the Copper River operation. The "small pox" case resulted in the town being quarantined, which prohibited an expected steamer from landing and prevented those workers, who had quit the Copper River operation, from leaving town. After idleness ran into days and even weeks, the workers returned to their jobs with the CR&NW and the labor pirate begged for a passport to leave and return to his home base at Seward. Instead, he was offered a job on one of the work gangs, but he promptly refused. Eventually, he made his way out of town, never to return.

Heney's trip was successful, resulting in his sale of the Copper River Railroad—which by this time had reached some 5 miles out of town—to the Alaska Syndicate at a handsome profit for both himself and his backers, the Close Brothers. Work was suspended on rail construction as the Syndicate continued to focus its efforts on the Katalla project, and Heney spent the summer relaxing and cruising on the Yukon River.

Things went from bad to worse at Katalla, however, and the harsh winter weather became a factor in the Syndicate's decision to give up on the project. Pivotal in the decision was a report that Captain "Dynamite Johnny" O'Brien, one of the most capable and best known of the captains in Alaska service, made to the Syndicate. O'Brien battled high seas and a severe winter storm at anchorage for 11 days, trying to get inside the Katalla breakwater to unload his ship, the Seward. After losing two anchors and endangering the ship, which was heavily laden with construction materials, O'Brien headed for the sheltered harbor at Cordova and unloaded his cargo without incident.

The Guggenheims had wasted five years and millions of dollars and were no closer to tapping their mineral riches than the first day they came to Alaska. To get a successful rail project underway, Heney was given the contract for the construction of his projected railroad up the Copper River. E. C. Hawkins was named chief engineer. This pair had combined their skills to successfully construct the White Pass & Yukon against tremendous odds.

Others on the Copper River staff included Alfred Williams, assistant chief engineer; H. L. Hawkins, one of the original surveyors with Heney, and F. A. Hansen, J. C. Surrey, and C. E. Wingate, locating engineers. J. R. Van Cleve was superintendent of the operating department; M. E. Smith served as chief surgeon; and A. C. O'Neill was superintendent of bridge construction—which proved to be one of the most important tasks in the entire operation. Heney's assistants were Sam Murchison, superintendent; A. W. Shields, storekeeper; and Dr. F. S. Whiting, surgeon.

Michael Heney, with his brother Pat, formed a partnership with the Seattle Sand and Gravel Company to ensure an uninterrupted flow of supplies for the building of the railroad. Pat remained in Seattle handling that end of the project, while Michael supervised the construction at Cordova.

Time was essential. Under their permits from the government, the Syndicate had five years to complete the railroad, and it had lost much time at the abortive projects in Valdez and Katalla. In places, track was laid on ice and snow over frozen ground—grading could follow later. Any and all time-saving measures were employed, and the only requirement was that work trains be carried safely over the line.

The first obstacle was the tremendous Copper River flats, with miles of quicksand and mud and the prohibitive cost of constructing trestles. Heney let Mother Nature do

Most of the work on the Copper River & Northwestern Railway, as well as other construction projects of the period, was performed by hand labor. Wherever possible, steam power such as this rail-mounted shovel was used. The steam shovel is clearing the right-of-way at Camp 6, Mile 22. (Seattle Historical Society)

her part by freezing the immense bog into a solid foundation, and then he built a roadbed fortified by thousands of carloads of heavy ballast, which withstood the spring thaw and remained as a permanent support, thus avoiding the great cost of piling.

The single-line track was laid on ties of native timber to standard gauge with 70-pound steel from Cordova to Chitina and 60-pound rails from Chitina to Kennecott.

Heney's smooth-running organization was

Trestle building on the Copper River flats in August 1908. This was the quick way to get across the flats. Later, after rails had been laid, trainloads of gravel were dumped along the right-of-way as ballast. (Clifford Collection)

soon functioning automatically, and tremendous progress followed. Workers were strung along the grade for miles, where at varying intervals miniature cities of tents sprang up like mushrooms. Alaska's virgin soil was now receiving a very wholesome baptism of dynamite, and heavy detonations disturbed the stillness both night and day. Machine shops and roundhouses soon appeared at headquarters, and miles of steel rails crept farther and farther into the wilderness, where giant locomotives creaked and labored at the heads of long, heavily laden construction trains.

As construction work proceeded up the Copper River, the chief of one of the Indian tribes threatened to bring suit against the company. He claimed that the noise and whistles of the engines scared the game from the forest and the fish from the river, and that his tribe would be in danger of starving. The suit was never filed.

A roadbed had to be blasted into the sides of precipitous bluffs in Abercrombie Canyon, where the cost of building the railroad ran as high as $200,000 per mile. Similar conditions were also met farther up the line, where the faces of mountains and canyons were literally torn away by tremendous dynamite blasts in which one charge alone consisted of 1,000 kegs of black powder and 35 cases of dynamite.

At the peak of construction, about 6,000 men were working on the project. Approximately a total of 8 of the 196 miles of track was laid on bridges or trestles. There were 129 bridges in the 131 miles between Cordova and Chitina, including five major steel bridges, which were built using 20 million pounds of steel.

The first major bridge at Mile 27 was 1,300 feet long, and the second a mile farther on was 560 feet in length. These two bridges were completed in the summer of 1909 at a cost of $560,000. Next came the "hot cake" bridge at Mile 34; it was 525 feet in length. At Mile 47 stood the most famous of them all—the Miles Glacier cantilever bridge that was to become known as the "Million Dollar Bridge," although it actually cost about $1.5 million. Some 18,000 cubic yards of concrete went into its two abutments and three caissons, and 5 million pounds of steel were required for its 1,550 feet of length. Construction was not simple. Since Heney was busy with the actual construction of the railroad and wooden trestles, the three largest steel bridges were constructed with A. C. O'Neill, stellar American bridge-building engineer, in charge.

The bridges had to be able to withstand the impact of 1000-ton icebergs, floodwaters, and debris, so the task of construction was complicated. O'Neill had introduced the novel feature of armoring the piers for the bridge at Sheridan Glacier with sharp steel faces, which were designed to catch and shatter the ice before it could strike the concrete.

When construction reached the Miles Glacier bridge site, Heney had to devise ways to work around it since the bridge would not be completed for two years. Ferries, barges, runabouts, and a small stern-wheeler operated on the river in the summer. In winter, ingenious sledges were devised. In fall and spring, a few supplies could cross the river by cable trolley. To work the glacier area, a steamship (the Chittyna) was

The first locomotive, No. 50, on the Copper River & Northwestern Railway is seen here with a work train on the flats outside Cordova. Construction crews built trestles and then filled them in with gravel to maintain a roadbed across the flats. Dump cars such as these were a valuable construction asset for the period. (Seattle Historical Society)

Falsework holding the No. 3 span of the Miles Glacier Bridge in place. The spring breakup on the Copper River came only minutes after the bridge span had been safely and securely placed on the piers—thus averting a disaster that would have cost the builders of the Copper River & Northwestern Railway a year's work and hundreds of thousands of dollars. (Washington State Historical Society)

freighted piecemeal from Valdez and assembled on the upper river. Heney was everywhere, seeing to the thousands of minute details, distributing supplies, handling workers and mules, and always spurring the work on.

Construction of the bridge at the meeting of the Miles and Childs Glaciers saw a Chevaux-de-frise of concrete and steel set a short distance upstream from each pier. Three concrete piers and two bulkheads were required to construct the foundation for the great steel structure, which spanned the river at a height far enough above the surface to allow ample space underneath for passing icebergs. Caissons were sunk 50 to

The Miles Glacier Bridge, looking upstream toward Childs Glacier, as it appeared upon completion in 1910. The bridge was one of the most important links in the building of the Copper River & Northwestern Railway, with span No. 3 lowered into place on the concrete piers just minutes before the ice carried away the construction falsework holding the structure in place. (Washington State Historical Society)

60 feet from riverbed to bedrock to construct the piers.

The three piers were completed late in the fall of 1909 after more than a year of construction. The steel work was to be put in place during the middle of winter while the river ice was solidly frozen. Obviously, no falsework could withstand the battery of

The Miles Glacier "Million Dollar Bridge" as it looked when it was part of the Copper River & Northwestern Railway. The bridge construction was a masterpiece of the time. It withstood the pressure of thousands of tons of ice calving off the nearby Miles and Childs Glaciers, only to see the earthquake of 1964 cause one span to drop into the river. The "Million Dollar Bridge" crossing the Copper River and separating the Miles and Childs Glaciers was made famous in Rex Beach's "Iron Trail." Metro-Goldwyn-Mayer filmed part of the "Trail of '98" at Mile 52 just above the bridge and lost three men in Abercrombie Rapids—more than were lost in the actual construction of the bridge or the blasting of the right-of-way in the mile-high rock cliffs on each side of the canyon. (Anchorage Historical and Fine Arts Museum)

breakup, so piles were driven through the 7 feet of motionless ice and into the bed of the river 40 feet below.

Difficulties in the eastern mills and winter storms delayed the delivery of the bridge steel for two months. The first of it did not leave Seattle until March 17, 1910. Another two months would certainly find the ice moving in the river—and the possible loss of a million dollars worth of work, which would flow downstream with it. Up until March 23, it looked as if a delay of a whole year was inevitable. On April 5, however, the last piece for the first two spans was on the ground and checked. Even a single piece found missing later would have spelled ruin. With less than six weeks to complete the job, only enough bridge workers available to make a single shift, and abominable weather conditions, the work of putting together more than 1,100 feet of heavy steel bridge began.

The Miles Glacier Bridge after the March 24, 1964, earthquake. One span of the bridge, which had become an important link in the Copper River Highway, dropped into the river. Repairs and improvements on the bridge were held up by conservation groups. (Alaska Department of Highways)

Despite rain, sleet, storms that raged about half of the time, and alternating bitter cold and rapid thaws, the first two spans were put into place without too many problems. The first span of 400 feet was completed on April 16 in 10.5 days; the second span of 300 feet went up in six days and was completed by April 24. Work on the third span was started on May 6. The construction of this span was fraught with many problems and was completed just minutes before the potential destruction of the entire structure. The pocket diary of E. C. Hawkins, under the date of May 14, 1910, carries the following entry: "The falsework under the third span of the bridge was moved out fifteen inches by the ice and had to be put back." That was all. However, it set the groundwork for one of the most spine-tingling construction efforts ever.

The third span of the Miles Glacier Bridge was 450 feet long. The falsework consisted of 1,000 or more piles, driven deep into the bottom of the Copper River, 40 feet below the surface. The ice was a solid sheet 7 feet thick and covered a 12-knot current. The forest of piles was solidly frozen into it. When the rising water suddenly began to lift the ice and with it the 450 feet of falsework on which the third span was being put together, there was a preliminary emergency. It might easily have been only an hour or two's work for the river to wreck the whole span that way. The crisis had to be handled, as scores of others had been handled before.

Steam from every available engine was driven into small feed pipes, and everyone in camp was put to work steam-melting or chopping the 7 feet of ice to clear the piles.

The holes were kept open during a day and night of bitter cold, and hundreds of crosspieces were unbolted and shifted while the river rose 21 feet. Then the ice began its movement downstream. At first, it was only an inch a day; then it was 3 or 4 inches. The melting and chopping went on almost unceasingly, and then the ice made its heaviest charge. A construction line was established. The falsework was 15 inches out of line.

Heavy anchorages were hastily built into the ice above the bridges. Block and tackle were rigged to them, and while a gang thawed and chopped the ice around the piles in the maddest of races, the entire bridge was dragged inch-by-inch back into position.

The rest of the span placement was an even more furious race with the ice, for it was moving each day more freely. The last bolt of the span was sent home at midnight. One shift worked an 18-hour day, blocks were knocked out, and the third span settled on its concrete bed. At 1 A.M., the whole 450 feet of falsework was a chaotic wreck. The river had won its fight, but the bridge was placed with less than an hour to spare. That hour meant a year saved, and that year represented a fortune.

One of the little saddle-tankers used in the construction of the Copper River & Northwestern Railway (No. 3) is pictured alongside one of the newly arrived 2-8-0s upon its arrival at Cordova. No. 20 was one of four such engines acquired by the Copper River in 1907. (Seattle Historical Society)

The copper mill at Kennecott Mines with a flatcar on the rail spur in the foreground. The rich Kennecott mines were the main reason for the construction of the Copper River & Northwestern Railway—to bring the rich ore to the port of Cordova for shipment to Tacoma and other copper refining centers. (Seattle Historical Society)

The now famous Miles Glacier Bridge had become a reality—the weakest link of the entire chain had become the strongest—and it remained so until the 1964 earthquake plunged one end of a single span into the river.

Hawkins gave credit to his workers as follows: "They were on the job at seven in the morning, no matter what the weather. They worked without ceasing till the noon whistle blew, then raced each other to the mess tent. A few minutes later they were flying back like an army of squirrels. And there they stayed until eleven or twelve at night, or until flesh and blood could stand no more. It was the most amazing exhibition of loyalty, efficiency and endurance I have ever known." Hawkins later cited an example of the workers' desire to complete the job. On one occasion, a man had broken several of his toes and was ordered to the hospital. He stayed there fretting for one day, and the next morning was discovered missing. When the seven o'clock whistle blew, he was found on the highest steel work, and neither orders nor threats could budge him from his job.

After the ice went out and the floodwaters subsided, it was not difficult to construct the fourth span of the bridge, since the river channel was free of ice once more. The span No. 4 falsework was completed, and work on the span itself was started on June 10 and completed on June 19, when daily trains began operating across the bridge.

If bridging the Copper River wasn't difficult enough, other problems were encountered at Baird Glacier when the track was laid over the glacial moraine, a few hundred feet back from the glacier itself, which moved forward with the ice about a foot a day. Gravel was dumped on the ice by the carload, shoveled under the ties, and tamped, but for years the track had to be moved inch by inch against the glacier until it was in alignment again.

The highest bridge of all was the Kuskulana River Bridge, 283 feet above the floor of its gorge and 550 feet long. This construction was carried out during the dead of winter. There were days of terrific blizzards, when workers could not even stand upright, much less work. Temperatures at times dropped to 60 degrees below zero, and the heavy chains used in construction had to be heated to keep them from breaking in the extreme cold. The work was done, however, and the span across the Kuskulana gorge was completed on Christmas Day, 1910.

Officials of the Copper River & Northwestern Railway are pictured at Miles Glacier on October 5, 1908, where the "Million Dollar Bridge" was to be constructed. Building the bridge took two years, but in the meantime workers and materials had to be transported beyond that point. Pictured left to right are: W. C. Robinson, transportation master who held the same position on the White Pass & Yukon construction project; Dan Hedican, walking boss; Mike Heney, builder and contractor for the Copper River as well as the White Pass & Yukon; J. R. Van Cleve, superintendent of motive power, Katalla Company; Archie Shields, supply; W. L. M. McCune, assistant auditor, Katalla Company; James English, track superintendent; Sam Murchison, superintendent of construction and Heney's assistant; Dr. F. B. Whiting, chief surgeon, who also handled medical chores on the White Pass & Yukon; Pat O'Brien, bridge superintendent; E. C. Hawkins, chief engineer and another White Passer; and H. R. "Bill" Simpson, steamshovel and snow king. (Seattle Historical Society)

The wooden Gilahina River Bridge, 880 feet long and 80 to 90 feet high, was built in eight days during January 1911. The bridge contained almost 500,000 board feet of timber. The longest bridge crossed the Copper River near Chitina at Mile 132. It was 2,790 feet long and had to be rebuilt every year when ice would destroy it during the spring thaw.

Work above Abercrombie Rapids was assisted considerably by powerful riverboats that moved food and material

A roadbed begins to appear on the steep walls of Abercrombie Canyon as workers literally blast their way through. Despite the danger and the treacherous rapids below, a legendary terror, no lives were lost during the construction. (Washington State Historical Society)

through high water and low, struggling up and down the shifting bars of Wood Canyon. Supplying the upline camps was one of the major problems during the winter months. On one occasion, there was a desperate need for coal and other supplies at the Tiekel River camp, 50 miles above Glacier Crossing, over which the track had not been kept open during the winter. When the rotary snowplow was started on this stretch under the able direction of "Rotary Bill" Simpson, who had been the hero of many such occasions during the construction of the White Pass & Yukon as well as the Copper River Route, extraordinary conditions were discovered. The rains had penetrated the deep snow and become packed down and frozen so that the entire 50 miles of track was covered with from 6 inches to 2 feet of solid ice.

The rotary was driven into this combination of ice and snow. It would stick its nose in, sending the snow flying, for about 15 feet or more. Then it would climb up on top of the ice cap. The next procedure would be to pull back the rotary, but when it landed the wheels would be on the ties instead of on the rails. While one part of the crew replaced the heavy plow on the track, another group would chop out the exposed ice, and the entire operation would be repeated. It took 31 days of constant work to reach the Tiekel with the rescue train, making an average speed of a mile and a half every 24 hours. E. C. Hawkins stated that the plow went off the track in this way no less than 1,500 times.

The winter of 1910–11 saw the road driven far up into the Chitina basin. By the end of September 1910, the railroad had reached Chitina at Mile 131. The line had a first-class roadbed, water grade, and slight curvature. From Chitina, a 62-mile-long branch was constructed to Kennecott, which was completed on March 29, 1911.

Sadly, Mike Heney, leader and driver behind this superhuman effort, would not see the completion of the project that was so dear to his heart and for which he had gambled his own fortune—with success. Perhaps the imminent decline of his health

Workers blast their way through some of the solid rock in the construction of the Copper River & Northwestern Railway. Work was slow and dangerous. (Washington State Historical Society)

began with the event that took place while he was returning from one of his numerous trips "outside." Heney was two days out of Seattle aboard the S.S. Ohio when the vessel struck a submerged rock in Hickish Narrows during the night. He was on the bridge with the captain at the time, and although the captain believed they could make the sandy beach nearby in Carter Bay, passengers were awakened and took to the lifeboats. Heney did not think of himself, but rather of the 20 head of horses he was having transported to Cordova for work on the railroad. He made every effort to free the animals from the deck below and allow them to swim to the nearby shore. His efforts were unsuccessful, however, and he was aboard the vessel when it slowly went under during a calm and moonlit night. He was able to free himself and make his way to a group of lifeboats standing by in the distance. Although badly overloaded, one of the boats came back for him, and though unable to take him aboard, towed him to the

(Facing page) Bridge builders still argue about which of the two major steel bridges on the Copper River & Northwestern Railway was the most difficult to construct. The Miles Glacier span was a battle against time and ice. The span over the Kuskulana River Gorge was a battle against the winter elements, with blizzards and temperatures of 50 to 60 degrees below zero. Acetylene lights had to be used continuously, since construction took place during the dark winter months when there was little daylight in that part of the world. On New Year's Day, 1911, after a two-month battle against the elements, the work on the 525-foot cantilever bridge over the 238-foot deep chasm was completed. (Washington State Historical Society)

beach where other survivors and nearby natives and fishermen had built fires to warm their bones. After the rescue, Heney did what he could to alleviate distress among the survivors; buying clothes and gear lost in the shipwreck and paying for funerals and for passage home in some cases.

Though Heney made it to Cordova and worked alongside his men in preparation for the last big push to finish the railroad, his health began to fail and he returned to the States. As the winter and next summer passed, his condition worsened.

Breaking camp and moving on to a new location was a hectic time for workers on the Copper River & Northwestern Railway. This photo was taken as workers loaded equipment and materials at Camp Mile 52 to move to another location. (Seattle Historical Society)

Back in Alaska, Heney's faithful crews continued work under the leadership of Sam Murchison with all of the efficiency he had built into his organization. Meanwhile, Heney's health failed steadily, and in October 1910 he developed pneumonia and died—six months before the railroad was completed. The wreck of the Ohio had left its mark, and Alaska had lost its Napoleon. Although his workers grieved when word of his death reached them, it drove them to complete the Copper River & Northwestern Railway by March 29, 1911.

Sam Murchison and E. C. Hawkins alternately swung the sledges to drive the beautiful hand-wrought copper spike, fashioned from native Alaska copper by a blacksmith on the crew. It was presented to S. W. Eccles, president of the CR&NW, and sent to New York. While the spike was being driven, Heney's own little engine, the one he had brought to Cordova in the spring of 1906, which was affectionately known as "Old No. 50," stood puffing and spewing steam and smoke. Attached to the front of the engine hung a picture of Heney—the man who had made it all possible.

Heney didn't forget Captain Johnny O'Brien, who had carried him back and forth many times on various ships and who played an important role in the Syndicate's decision to move its operations from Katalla to Cordova. Heney left Captain O'Brien $150 a month for life in his will and gave most of the rest of his fortune to charities.

The construction completed, the railroad began conducting business on April 23, 1911. Cordova celebrated "Copper Day" when the first train of copper ore, carrying approximately 1,200 tons, arrived from the mines and was poured into the holds of the steamship Northwestern, bound for the smelter in Tacoma, Washington.

Riverboats played an important role in the construction of the Copper River & Northwestern Railway because there was no other way to get workers and materials upriver to the advance surveying and construction camps. One of the steamers was the Chittyna, a 70-ton vessel, which was moved from Valdez and reassembled on the shores of the Tasnuna. The single heaviest piece was the boiler, which weighed 5,700 pounds. (Clifford Collection)

As with many infant railroads, maintenance of the new line was expensive and demanded a virtual reconstruction of the whole line. Grades had to be raised and relined, bridges built, and some bridges removed. The freshly blasted rock frequently slid into the roadbed and had to be removed. Snowsheds were built so that the trains could operate in comparative safety during the winter months.

Branch lines were planned to the rich Bering River coal fields at Katalla, and also from Chitina to the Matanuska Valley and from Chitina to the Yukon River near Fairbanks. These routes, however, were never constructed—partially due to the withdrawal of the coal, oil, and timber by the federal government.

The CR&NW Route became one of the prime tourist attractions in Alaska, and thousands of visitors marveled at the Miles and Childs Glaciers and others. The snow-capped peaks of Mount Sanford, Mount Regal, Mount Wrangell, and Mount Blackburn reared their heads from 14,000 to 16,000 feet above the level of the river route. One of the most popular of the scenic tours was known as the Golden Belt Tour. Tourists left the steamer at either Cordova, northbound, or on arrival at Seward. Those leaving the ship at Cordova made the trip from the coast to Fairbanks in the interior, over the Copper River & Northwestern Railway via Childs Glacier, Copper River Canyon, Chitina, and then over the Richardson Trail by automobile to Fairbanks. Tourists returned to the coast over the Alaska Railroad (ARR) to Seward, where they caught a connection with the following steamer to Seattle. Those leaving the steamer at Seward made the trip in reverse. Two other popular tours were the Circle and Keystone Canyon trips.

During the CR&NW's 28 years of operation, millions of tons of ore came down over the tracks and over the Cordova docks, which made this one of the most successful and profitable railroads in Alaska. Near the beginning of its operation, the Copper River and Northwestern had 15 locomotives, 8 passenger cars, 256 freight cars, 4 steam shovels, 2 rotary plows, and 1 wrecking crane. Chitina, a division point on the railroad, was also a transfer point for freight from the railroad to the interior.

In May 1939, the mines closed, and the railroad was abandoned with ICC approval. The CR&NW had been the second longest railroad in Alaska, constructed at a cost of

With a picture of the late Michael Heney looking down from a position just below the locomotive headlamp, E. C. Hawkins, chief engineer, and Sam Murchison, superintendent of construction, who took over after Heney's death, alternately drove the copper spike that marked the completion of the Copper River & Northwestern Railway on March 29, 1911. The locomotive is the CR&NW's No. 50, the railroad's first and reputed to be Mike Heney's favorite. (University of Alaska Archives, Raymond McKeown Collection)

$23,500,000, of which $8,500,000 was spent for labor. The steel for the four magnificent bridges erected in the building of the railroad weighed 20,300,000 pounds and cost approximately $2,500,000; the Miles and Childs Glacier Bridge alone accounted for $1,500,000. An army of 6,000 laborers worked for three years constructing the railroad.

In 1940, the company sold three locomotives and 30 freight cars to the Alaska Railroad. A 13-mile section from Cordova was used by the army during World War II. Until 1947, light tram cars operated over the rusty rails from Chitina to McCarthy, near Kennecott—a distance of 60 miles.

Copper River & Northwestern Railway locomotive No. 20. An American Locomotive Company 2-8-0 Rhode Island built in 1907 was one of four such engines operated by the railroad. (Washington State Historical Society)

In 1964, a Washington salvage firm pulled the last rails from the right-of-way, which had been turned back over to the federal government. In recent years, work on turning the route into a highway has been undertaken. The 1964 earthquake saw one section of the Miles Glacier bridge fall into the Copper River,

Remnants of the railroad still litter the Copper River landscape, but only ghost whistles are heard echoing off the walls of Abercrombie Canyon. Some of the riches of the Kennecott country still remain, as do the Bering River coal deposits, but they will never again be tapped by the rails of the Copper River & Northwestern.

Copper River & Northwestern Railway

Steam Locomotive Roster

Road No.	Wheel Arr.	Builder	C/N	Year	Cylinders	Drivers	Notes
1	0-4-0T	Dickson	41749	January 1907	14x22	44"	Delivered to Katalla. Transferred to Cordova, to Aloha Lumber Co. No. 1
2	0-4-0T	Dickson	41750	January 1907	14x22	44"	Delivered to Katalla. Transferred to Cordova, to Willapa Harbor Lumber Mills No. 5, to Port of Grays Harbor No. 5
3	0-4-0T	Dickson	41751	January 1907	14x22	44"	Delivered to Katalla. Transferred to Cordova, to Alaska Anthracite RR, abandoned at Bering River. May be moved to Cordova for display.

Steam Locomotive Roster *(continued)*

Road No.	Wheel Arr.	Builder	C/N	Year	Cylinders	Drivers	Notes
4	0-4-0T	Dickson	41753	January 1907	14x22	44"	Delivered to Katalla. Transferred to Cordova, to U.S. Army, No. 4, Cordova.
5	0-4-0T	Dickson	42765	April 1907	14x22	44"	Delivered to Katalla. Transferred to Cordova.
6	0-4-0T	Dickson	42767	May 1907	14x22	44"	Delivered to Katalla. Transferred to Cordova.
20	2-8-0	Alco-RI	44597	November 1907	20x26	56"	Used as boiler at Cordova, early 1940s, scrapped post-WWII.
21	2-8-0	Alco-RI	44598	November 1907	20x26	56"	Scrapped post-WWII.
22	2-8-0	Alco-RI	44599	November 1907	20x26	56"	Scrapped post-WWII.
23	2-8-0	Alco-RI	44600	November 1907	20x26	56"	To U.S. Army, No. 23, Cordova. To Alaska Railroad No. 101, 1945–6, scrapped 1947.
50	4-6-0	Baldwin	11265	October 1890	17x24	54"	Originally Port Townsend Southern No. 4, sold in 1897, to Columbia & Puget Sound No. 4, sold in 1906, to Copper River Railway No. 50, sold in 1907, to Copper River & Northwestern No. 50, gone by 1942.
51	4-6-0						Original owner unknown, to Alaska Central No. 3, sold in 1907, to Copper River & Northwestern No. 51.
70	2-8-2	Alco-Brooks	55490	November 1915	20x28	48"	To Midland Terminal No. 62, to Mexican Northwestern No. 200, to Chihuahua Pacific No. 200.
71	2-8-2	Alco-Brooks	55491	November 1915	20x28	48"	Retired in 1936, to Alaska Railroad after WWII, not used.
72	2-8-2	Alco-Brooks	55492	November 1915	20x28	48"	To McCloud River Railroad No. 26 in 1938, scrapped in 1956.
73	2-8-2	Alco-Brooks	57291	April 1917	20x28	48"	To McCloud River Railroad No. 27 in 1938, scrapped in 1953.
74	2-8-2	Alco-Brooks	58164	August 1917	20x28	48"	To Midland Terminal No. 63, to Mexican Northwestern No. 201, to Chihuahua Pacific No. 201.
100	2-6-0	Baldwin	9030	January 1898	19x24	51"	Originally Buffalo, Rochester & Pittsburg No. 82, to Copper River & Northwestern No. 100, to U.S. Army No. 6990, Ft. Richardson, to Elmendorf AFB.
101	2-6-0	Alco-Brooks	46183	May 1909	19x26	57"	To U.S. Army No. 101, Cordova, to Elmendorf AFB.
102	2-6-0	Alco-Brooks	46184	May 1909	19x26	57"	To U.S. Army No. 102, Cordova, to Elmendorf AFB.

Chapter 14: Copper River & Northwestern Railway

A relief map of the Copper River country shows the various railroad routes from Prince William Sound to the rich interior. The Copper River & Northwestern Railway is at the right, while the routes from Seward used by the Alaska Central, the Alaska Northern, and eventually the Alaska Railroad are at the left. (Seattle Historical Society)

An excursion train on the Copper River & Northwestern Railway at the Miles Glacier Bridge. Such excursions were the highlights of a trip to Alaska in the early 1900s. Tourists would begin such an excursion by steamer to Seward or Cordova, continue on the Alaska Railroad or the Copper River & Northwestern and the Richardson Highway to Fairbanks, and return to the coast via either the CR&NW or the ARR, depending on which had been taken northbound. (Seattle Historical Society)

An ore train outside Cordova on the Copper River & Northwestern Railway. The locomotive No. 23 was an American Locomotive Company Rhode Island 2-8-0 built in 1907. It was one of four owned by the CR&NW. (Seattle Historical Society)

Chapter 15

Wild Goose, Geese, or Gooses?

To say that railroad history in Alaska and the Yukon is at times confusing is to put it mildly, what with the lack of records, no building or construction permits, frequently questionable promotional schemes, and so on.

One of those confusing situations, at least to those not knowledgeable about northern geography, is that of the Wild Goose Railroad—or to be more exact, railroads. There were two, and they both operated on Alaska's Seward Peninsula, within about 60 miles of one another. Both were built by the same man, at about the same time, and to make matters worse, they shared some of the same equipment. One ran from Nome to Anvil Creek and the other from Council City to No. 15 Ophir Creek.

To build such a railroad—or railroads—over the unstable arctic terrain without proper ballast is the kind of impossible dream today's construction industry, with all its engineering know-how, might attempt. But almost a century ago, only dreamers attempted such a task. These lines were located slightly more than 100 miles south of the Arctic Circle, some 2,500 miles northwest of Seattle, the nearest supply base, and

Reaching Council City, where rich gold strikes had been made, was the goal of the Council City & Solomon River Railroad in the early 1900s. The gold petered out, however, before the CC&SR reached Council City, although the Golofin Bay Railway operated in the area in 1902–3. This is First Street in Council City as it looked at that time. (University of Alaska Archives, Seppala Collection)

in an area where ocean transportation was available for about four months of the year at most.

Gold was discovered in the Nome area in September 1898 when a party from the Swedish Mission at Golovin Bay was driven ashore by a summer storm. Erik O. Lindbloom, John Bryntesen, and Jefet Lindeborg staked claims at "Discovery" in the Anvil Creek area, and on October 18 these three and some other newcomers saw the necessity of forming a mining district, which they called Cape Nome.

In less than two years, a train rolled into Anvil City, the actual site of the famous strike, something even these daring first gold miners never would have dreamed possible. By this time, prospectors were everywhere—on claims along the miles of beach stretching east and west of Nome, and on the streams whose headwaters lie in the peninsula's rugged interior.

The miners needed supplies, and moving materials over the soggy, spongy tundra was expensive—$200 to $300 a ton—and time consuming. One of those forced to pay these exorbitant prices was Charles D. Lane, a prominent Nome resident and president of the Wild Goose Mining and Trading Company, which owned profitable operations in

Laying track across the spongy tundra was a real problem in the building of railroads in the Arctic. A construction crew is laying rails on the Golofin Bay Railway during the summer of 1902. (University of Washington Historical Library, Northwest Collection)

the Anvil Creek area. Lane, who had become wealthy from mining enterprises in the California, Idaho, and Nevada gold fields, convinced his firm's directors that the building and operation of a railroad to the Anvil Creek area would be a good investment.

Upon receiving approval, Lane lost little time in carrying out his plans. He shifted into high gear in short order: he bought an ocean-going steamer and renamed it Charles D. Lane; and he loaded the entire cull stock of a Northwest lumber mill; a Class A, Climax, narrow-gauge, geared locomotive; rails; a dozen 8-wheel flatcars; and other necessary supplies onto the ship.

No time was lost. As soon as the ship anchored in the Nome harbor, work started on the railroad. Crews, under the direction of Major William V. Monroe, a former Civil War veteran who had worked on the construction of both the Union Pacific and Southern Pacific lines, started laying cull lumber for a roadbed across the soft tundra. These first crews were followed by rail workers. The Wild Goose construction gangs moved foot by foot on the soggy landscape. By July 1900, 4 miles of road had been completed to Discovery on Lower Anvil Creek. Crews worked late into the season, and an

Parades were the thing in boomtown Nome during the height of the gold rush. Members of the Yukon Order of Pioneers head this 1901 Fourth of July parade through the business section of town. It was at this time that railroads such as the Wild Goose had their most prosperous years. (University of Washington Historical Library, Northwest Collection)

additional 2.5 miles of track was laid to Anvil Station, on the western slope of Anvil Mountain.

Anvil Creek was highly profitable for the Wild Goose Company, since the area alone produced $21 million in gold and most of the claims were held by the Wild Goose. The little narrow-gauge, operated under Superintendent Frank Shaw, proved profitable too. The fare from Nome to Discovery was 50¢ each way. To travel round-trip to the end of the line cost $2. The line generated close to $200,000 in revenue in its first season.

Freight cost 2¢ a pound. The cost of construction had been $5,000 per mile, but by the end of the first summer income was more than nine times the cost of construction and equipment.

Trains closed down in November for the winter, but the locomotives kept busy during the summer. Passengers rode anywhere they were lucky enough to find space. Sightseers during 1901 and 1902 arrived in Anvil City, the name tacked on the community at the mining site, and found several saloons, a restaurant or two, the mining company mess house, and the Wild Goose Railroad station, plus hundreds of tents belonging to prospectors and miners.

Despite an 8-mile-per-hour speed limit, fully half of the train's crew time was spent jacking either the engine or the train of flatcars back onto the tracks because the roadbed had the habit of continually sinking into the marshy tundra in various

Climax locomotive No. 212 used by the Wild Goose Railroad is seen here as the crew pumps water from the river to replenish the water tank. The Wild Goose used four Climax narrow-gauge locomotives during its short life in the early 1900s. (Yukon Archives)

The first train on the original Wild Goose Railroad. It was a foggy day when the first train left Anvil for Nome on the Wild Goose Railroad on July 19, 1900. Passengers, mostly construction workers or miners, sat where they could on the open flatcars. (University of Washington Historical Library)

spots, causing a roller coaster effect. A train ride on this line was enough to give "a timid man a feeling of seasickness."

Whenever one of the ladies from the stockade made a strike in the creeks by grub-staking a miner, she invariably chartered the Paystreak Express to convey her guests to the party that she would throw at one of the roadhouses outside Nome. The singing, whooping gang would start out merrily enough, but it would not be long before the men would be out trying to put the train back on the tracks, with plenty of encouragement from the ladies. If the train reached its destination without several such derailments it was a miracle, but no one cared. It was all part of the fun.

Business thrived sufficiently to require the purchase of a third Climax by 1902. It too was a Class A with a box cab to enclose the crew from the weather. A fourth Class A Climax was added later.

The line originally began on the sandspit at the mouth of the Snake River, near the beach and opposite the center of Nome. Later a line was built into Nome itself, and two branches were built out at right angles along the old beach line.

As the Wild Goose Mining and Trading company sought new operations in the Ophir Creek district near Council City, Lane planned the construction of a second Wild Goose Railroad, formally known as the Golofin Bay Railway Company, to run between Council City and No. 15 Ophir Creek, a distance of about 8 miles.

Construction on the railroad started in late June 1902 and was finished by July 21. Lane moved equipment, rails, and supplies to his new operation. Motive power on the second road was the No. 313 Climax brought in on July 26, 1902.

The first excursion train over this narrow-gauge route was enjoyed by 150 people, who turned out on August 17 to enjoy the ride on the Golofin Bay Railway. Planks

One of the engines used on the Wild Goose–Nome Arctic–Curly Q Railroad in later years was the Fordson tractor with flanged wheels. This type of equipment was also used on some Seward Peninsula Railroad trackage and possibly on the Golofin Bay Railway trackage. The tractor is located near a Nome playfield, where it is gradually being destroyed by vandals and bad weather. (H. Clifford)

were laid on boxes on open flatcars to accommodate the merry crowd on its Sunday outing to the mines at Ophir Creek.

For a time, the Golofin Bay Railway proved prosperous too, as long as gold was plentiful. But the railroad folded in 1906 or thereabouts, as did the Council City and Solomon Railroad, when gold in the area petered out. In the meantime, the Wild Goose continued—under a variety of names and operators.

In 1903, Charles Lane started disposing of some of his interests in the mining company and the Wild Goose Railroad. The railroad was reorganized as the Nome-Arctic Railroad.

J. Lindeborg, who acquired some of Lane's interests, later teamed up with Lane to play an important role in the efforts to thwart the nefarious McKenzie-Noyes conspiracy. Judge Arthur J. Noyes would appoint Alex McKenzie as court receiver while the rights to some of the early discoverers were being argued in court. As Judge Noyes set legal blocks whenever possible to stall and delay the trial, McKenzie would be working the disputed claims for all they were worth, and the miners would be robbed of whatever prize they sought. In time, the judge and McKenzie were exposed and convicted, but they had stolen millions in the meantime. (Rex Beach's novel, *The Spoilers,* was based largely on this affair.)

At about this time, the plan to bring the railroad into town was revived with a terminal on Second Street, from which a spur was run to the beach. The line ran along Fourth Street, behind St. Joseph's Church, across Stedman Avenue, and then south to Second. Another branch line was built from Anvil Road to about ¼-mile beyond the Wild Goose Company's plant on the Snake River.

Work was suspended on the Nome-Arctic Railroad in the fall of 1905, according to the *Nome Nugget*. Major W. N. Monroe, manager of the company, cited the government tax of $100 per mile and the Nome city assessment of $20,000 as the reason for the suspension. There were also troubles with longshoremen, and the road had operated only four months during 1905, its final year of operation.

Chapter 15: Wild Geese, Goose, or Gooses?

A pair of Climax locomotives—one on each end—handle an excursion train loaded with passengers riding on flatcars out of Nome on the Wild Goose Railroad. Generally such excursions were run on holidays such as the Fourth of July. (University of Washington Historical Library, Northwest Collection)

The terminus of the Wild Goose Railroad was Anvil Creek, where a small community known as Banner Station developed. Passengers and cargo rode predominantly on open cars, sometimes a rather tricky ride since the rails were very uneven from the melting permafrost and cars often tipped at precarious angles. (University of Washington Historical Library, Northwest Collection)

Wild Goose Railroad
Nome, Alaska

Steam Locomotive Roster

Road No.	Wheel Arr.	Builder	C/N	Year	Cylinders	Drivers	Notes
212	Class A	Climax	212	April 1900	7x7	26"	Sold 1903 to Nome Arctic RR, sold 1906 to Seward Peninsula RR 15 ton, used as rip-rap in Nome seawall.
315	Class A	Climax	315	April 1902	7-1/2x7	28"	Sold 1903 to Nome Arctic RR, sold 1906 to Seward Peninsula RR 18 ton, used as rip-rap in Nome seawall.
399	Class A	Climax	399	1903	7x7	26"	Sold 1903 to Nome Arctic RR, sold 1906 to Seward Peninsula RR 15 ton, converted to internal combustion.

Wild Goose Railroad (Golofin Bay Railway)
Council City, Alaska

Road No.	Wheel Arr.	Builder	C/N	Year	Cylinders	Drivers	Notes
313	Class A	Climax	313	April 1902	7-1/2x7	28"	Last used ca. 1910, to Charles Reader, Nome AK, sold 1979 to Keith Christenson, Eagle River, AK, under restoration, 15 ton.

Nome Arctic Railroad

Steam Locomotive Roster

Road No.	Wheel Arr.	Builder	C/N	Year	Cylinders	Drivers	Notes
212	Class A	Climax	212	April 1900	7x7	26"	Originally Wild Goose RR, sold to Nome Arctic RR 1903, sold 1906 to Seward Peninsula RR 15 ton, used as rip-rap in Nome seawall.
315	Class A	Climax	315	April 1902	7-1/2x7	28"	Originally Wild Goose RR, sold to Nome Arctic RR 1903, sold 1906 to Seward Peninsula RR 18 ton, used as rip-rap in Nome seawall.
399	Class A	Climax	399	1903	7x7	26"	Originally Wild Goose RR, sold to Nome Arctic RR 1903, sold 1906 to Seward Peninsula RR 15 ton, converted to internal combustion.

Chapter 16

Council City & Solomon River Railroad

Little remains today of a railroad that at one time showed promise of becoming one of the most prosperous in Alaska. It was the Council City & Solomon River Railroad, also known as the North Star Line. Despite its name, the railroad never actually reached Council City, and perhaps that fact begins to tell the story.

The Council City & Solomon River Railroad was chartered on March 27, 1902, under the laws of New Jersey. Incorporators included President Edward A. Olds of New York; Vice President J. Warren Dickson, who also served as general manager; Treasurer Ernest S. Emanuel; and Secretary A. Dwight Keep. Among the directors were J. H. Emanuel Jr. of J. P. Morgan and Company, a financial institution also active in the construction of the Copper River & Northwestern Railway at Cordova.

In September 1902, Herman Heinze, a U.S. deputy surveyor, revealed that he had completed a survey from the coast near the mouth of the Solomon River to Council City. Although he did not announce whether the road would be a wagon trail or a railroad, he did say that the route was a good one with easy grades. On May 3, 1903, the *Nome Nugget* reported that the Western Alaska Construction Company of Chicago had been granted a right-of-way by the government to build the Council City & Solomon River Railroad, which was authorized to issue up to $1,000,000 in common stock. The railroad would "connect all the principal producing areas and centers of population known at present throughout the Solomon River, Council City, Ophir Creek, Bluestone, York, and Nome regions with tidewater and vessel transportation at Solomon River, Grantley Harbor, Port Clarence, and Good Hope Bay, thus grid-ironing the peninsula."

This impressive building (for the time and location) was the general office building for the Council City & Solomon River Railroad at Dickson. The railroad shops and freight yard are in the background. The building also served as headquarters for the Western Alaska Construction Company, which was in charge of building the railroad. (University of Alaska Archives, Charles Bunnell Collection)

This was one of the richest and most promising mining districts in Alaska, and despite "impossible" transportation costs across the muck and mire of the tundra between the area and the closest major port, Nome, it was a prosperous one. By 1906, the mines at Ophir Creek had produced about $4,500,000 in gold. The Discovery Mining District was inland and its claims not as accessible to miners as those at and near Nome, but Council City grew and thrived despite the excessive expense and inconvenience of freighting supplies from Nome at a cost of up to more than $55 per ton.

The boom following the start of work on the Council City & Solomon River Railroad in 1903 saw the town of Solomon grow by leaps and bounds. In no time at all, there were half a dozen restaurants and almost as many saloons, and word was sent back to Nome that a town marshall was needed to keep order. Solomon was located across the Solomon River from Dickson, the southern terminus of the railroad. (University of Alaska Archives, Cliff N. Allyn Collection)

Preliminary work started on June 19, 1903, and a couple of weeks later the steamer Aztec arrived with 4,000 tons of cargo, including a pile driver and hoisting engine, two locomotives, boxcars, and flatcars. Workers were to be paid $3 a day with room and board, and an initial payroll of $30,000 a month supported 160 laborers who worked 10 to 15 hours a day. J. Warren Dickson of Seattle, the firm's vice president, shortly thereafter forever imprinted his name on the maps of Alaska by naming the southern terminal of the railroad Dickson—just east across the Solomon River from the mining town of Solomon.

Major activity was centered around Dickson with docks, a bridge over the lagoon, offices, waiting rooms, and machine shops under construction. The headquarters complex consisted of a large two-and-a-half-story building with 12 rooms, which served as the residence of company officials, a 45-by-90-foot machine shop, a 16-by-48-foot, two-story office building, and a 10,000-gallon water tank to supply the area.

In no time at all, Solomon had six restaurants and five saloons, which were open day and night, and word shifted back to Nome that a town marshall or commissioner was needed to keep order, since "dance hall girls and brawls" were becoming common.

As mid-summer rolled around, additional employees were hired. Soon 450 workers were on the job, and the payroll rose to $76,000 a month. The Aztec arrived with an additional 5,000 tons of supplies. Cargo landed at Dickson that first summer totaled more than 4 million board feet of lumber, 165,000 ties, 50 miles of rails, the locomotives and freight cars previously mentioned, and 104 miles of copper wire, plus a number of "Bell telephones," since the railroad had become the exclusive licensee of the Bell Telephone Company on the Seward Peninsula.

By August 19, 7 miles of track had been completed. By September 2, 10 miles had been laid, and service was inaugurated over that portion of the railroad to about 1.5 miles below Big Hurrah. A passenger fare of $1 was advertised, and service began. However, despite statements that "50 miles of track would be completed before the snow flys (sic)," that was the extent of progress during that first season of construction.

During the summer of 1904, several new businesses were attracted to Dickson, including the Northwestern Commercial Company and the Tanner and Clark Lumberyard and warehouse. A 10-bed hospital was opened under the direction of Dr. William

Hopper, and plans were announced for the Hotel Dickson—the second largest on the Seward Peninsula. The railroad officials completed arrangements with the Alaska Pacific Express Company so that miners could send money orders from Dickson and various points along the line to anywhere in the world.

Actual construction on the railroad, however, was slow. Only 1,000 feet of track had been added by July 1, 1904, and the company instead opened a stage service from Right Branch Station on the railroad to Council City. That was it for the season. Dickson resigned from the company to pursue other ventures, and some time he later announced plans for the construction of a railroad from Nome to the Kougarok region.

The year 1905 again saw many promises of new construction, but there was little action. The only addition to the line was a 927-foot bridge across the Solomon River and the laying of track to and across the bridge, bringing the overall total length of

Members of a work crew, along with locomotive No. 1 of the Council City & Solomon River Railroad, at Rock Creek as they construct the roadbed over the tundra. The photo was taken September 25, 1903. All of the CC&SR locomotives were formerly New York Elevated Railroad engines. (University of Alaska Archives, Charles Bunnell Collection)

trackage to 13 miles. The company was reorganized, and a new contractor and general manager, Hugh F. Magee, arrived to take charge of the operation.

In the meantime, Major Wilds P. Richardson, president of the Alaska Road Commission, visited Council City and stated that a road was needed and that it would be one of the first projects of the 1906 season. Transportation, however, seemed to go from bad to worse, and freight rates to the Council area from Nome rose to $66 a ton, 10 times the cost of shipping from Seattle to Nome.

By April 1906, the Nome Nugget was predicting that construction of the Council City & Solomon River Railroad would be abandoned, but this prognostication appeared to be premature by about a year. The railroad, however, did sell rails and quantities of fishplates, ties, and other construction materials to the Seward Peninsula Railroad of Nome. Perhaps Magee needed cash. Shortly after the transaction, he was replaced by Theodore Knowlton, who took over the job in June 1906 and pushed construction work through Cheyenne Creek, bridged Coal Creek, and by August had added 10 miles of finished track. By September 19, the trackage had reached Penelope Creek, bringing the total length of mainline to 35 miles. Construction stopped there because the supply of track materials ran out.

Knowlton admitted, however, that the prospects for further construction were somewhat gloomy, and the railroad's future depended upon his report to the board of directors in New York. He added that business in 1906 had not equaled that of 1905, and he foresaw further declines. He pointed out that it would cost about a quarter of a million dollars to extend the trackage to Council City. Total rolling stock at the time consisted of three locomotives, two passenger cars (constructed from flatcars), and 17 freight cars.

Locomotive No. 1 on the Council City & Solomon River Railroad was a former New York Elevated Railroad engine built in 1886. Remains of this 0-4-4T locomotive, along with the other CC&SR engines, can still be seen on the flats near the ghost town of Dickson on the Solomon River east of Nome. (University of Alaska Archives, Charles Bunnel Collection)

The railroad operated during at least part of the 1907 season, with the advertised schedule effective July 15, 1907, calling for trips to East Fork on Mondays, Wednesdays, Thursdays, Saturdays, and Sundays only, and to Penelope Creek on Tuesdays and Fridays. Running time to East Fork was one hour and to Penelope three hours. In October 1907, Jerome D. Gedney of East Orange, NJ, was appointed receiver by the Court of Chancery of New Jersey. Of the $1,000,000 in authorized stock at $10 a share, $895,460 was outstanding, along with a funded debt of $347,000 secured by a first mortgage at 6 percent. Three-year gold bonds, due May 1, 1908, with interest payable May 1 and November 1 each year, were also outstanding with no payment having been made and no money available for payment. At this point, the railroad and

Although the train was standing still, high winds make it appear as if this Council City & Solomon River train was heading out under a full head of steam. The passenger car was built up from one of the railroad's flatcars. The locomotive originally served the New York Elevated Railroad. The photo was taken in the early 1900s. (Clifford Collection)

equipment had cost the company $1,231,034.

Thus came the end of the Council City & Solomon River Railroad. Some trackage, collapsed buildings, and the rusty remains of three locomotives and a few flatcars are all that remain of the dream. The Nome Nugget of April 28, 1906, commenting on the CC&SR, blamed the failure of the project on a "well planned but miserably executed enterprise. The original promoter's ideas were alright but his judgment wanting. The road started on a too elaborate scale and much money [was] spent uselessly and needlessly. Had sound judgment coupled with practical experience prevailed, Solomon and Council would have been connected by rail.

"And now this seems far distant. Mr. Dickson was a sanguine. He did not consider carefully. He announced his intention to move Nome to Solomon (or Dickson) within two years—and now his road is to be abandoned. Had he been less optimistic and more practical, the result might have been much different.

"The failure of an enterprise like the building of the Council City road is a detriment to the development of the country. And yet it is not the country's fault, but it is rather due to the short-sightedness of the promoters."

The official demise of the railroad did not occur until nine years later when, in February 1916, the remaining officers of the company officially notified Poor's Manual that the railroad was no longer in business.

Council City & Solomon River Railroad

Steam Locomotive Roster

Road No.	Wheel Arr.	Builder	C/N	Year	Cylinders	Drivers	Notes
1	0-4-4T	New York	137	June 1886	11x16	42"	Originally New York Elevated 2nd 21 (Manhattan Railway); rebuilt 10/19/94; sold 4/28/03 to Western Alaska Construction Co. (CC&SR); abandoned at Dickson, AK.
2	0-4-4T	New York	149	August 1886	11x16	42"	Originally New York Elevated 159 (Manhattan Railway); rebuilt 6/30/94; sold 4/28/03 to Western Alaska Construction Co. (CC&SR); abandoned at Dickson, AK.
3	0-4-4T	Baldwin	5622	May 1881	11x16	42"	Originally New York Elevated 303 (Manhattan Railway); rebuilt 5/10/94; sold 8/13/04 to Western Alaska Construction Co. (CC&SR); abandoned at Dickson, AK.

All that remains of the Council City & Solomon River Railroad are the rusting hulks of these locomotives and a few flatcars, deserted on the tundra near the ghost town of Dickson. These locomotives saw service on the New York Elevated Railroad before being shipped to Alaska. At the time of its construction, the CC&SR had the distinction of being North America's farthest north and farthest west standard-gauge railroad. (Bruce Campbell)

Chapter 17

Seward Peninsula

As *activity on the Nome-Arctic and the Council City & Solomon River Railroads (CC&SR) began to diminish, plans for construction of a railroad from Nome to the Kougarok mining area began to be discussed.*

In June 1905, J. Warren Dickson, who had resigned as vice president and general manager of the CC&SR, announced plans for the Seward Peninsula Railroad Company, financed by New York money. The SPR would run from Nome to Kougarok.

The *Nome Nugget* of April 26, 1906, carried comments on an earlier article about the organization of a company in New York by John Rosene and Major L. H. French called the Northwestern Development Company. Organized with a capital of $2 million under the leadership of John Rosene, the company intended to build a railroad into the Kougarok country and to develop extensive mineral holdings that the company had acquired in that region. The road was to be built from Nome, and construction was to start with the opening of navigation and push forward as rapidly as possible.

Major French had previously obtained an option to purchase the Nome-Arctic Railroad, and he eventually exercised this option through the new firm. Construction of the railroad was part of Rosene's optimistic plan to connect the Seward Peninsula with Valdez. He had been active in the project to build the Copper River & Northwestern Railway from Valdez to the rich copper fields at the head of the Tanana River.

Actual officers of the developing company turned out to be H. C. Davis, president, Eugene Small, and Cable Whitehead and George Henderson, vice presidents. Headquarters were located in the Hanover Bank Building in Manhattan. Whitehead was also president of the Alaska Bank and Trust Company and later had the distinction of being the only officer of an Alaskan railroad to lose his life on the line. An engine he was riding flipped over near Salmon Lake, 42 miles from Nome, and he was killed.

Meanwhile, on April 27, 1906, the Seward Peninsula Railroad (Peninsula and Peninsular were used interchangeably in the railroad's title) was incorporated in Nevada to operate the road that was to be built by the Northwestern Development Company. E. A. Mathews served as president and T. A. Davis vice president. The company was headquartered in the Mutual Life Building in Seattle. In 1910, Davis became president, and a new slate of vice presidents was named. Such was the organization and promotion of railroads in Alaska in those days.

During the 1906 construction season, the railroad reached Lane's Landing, or Shelton, on the Kuzitrim River, a distance of some 85 miles, the farthest point reached during its operation. Shelton was the supply point for the Kougarok country, and it served as the road's terminus.

The first few miles of the line were very inexpensive to construct, costing about $5,000 per mile. Later trackage, through the Pilgrim River and Nome Valley, cost more because the road required 128 bridges and trestles. A trestle that crossed over the

Kuzitrim River and was about 1,000 feet in length was destroyed by ice during the winter of 1907. Thereafter, it was removed each winter and reinstalled in the spring.

As was the case with the Wild Goose Railroad, the thawing tundra presented many operational problems—the soggy mud created a roadbed with the stability of a wet sponge, and derailments were a normal consequence of operation.

The extension of the railroad to Shelton and subsequent increased business required additional locomotives. The Seward Peninsula had taken over the three remaining class A Climax locomotives from the Wild Goose Railroad (Nome-Arctic)—the fourth having gone to the Golofin Bay Railway and been abandoned there.

The first of the "new" equipment was the road's first rod engine, already a museum piece, a Porter 0-6-0 that had been built in January 1878. It was built for the Walla Walla & Columbia River Railroad in Washington State, where it had been named "Blue Mountain." The engine had seen service on the Oregon Railway & Navigation Railroad at The

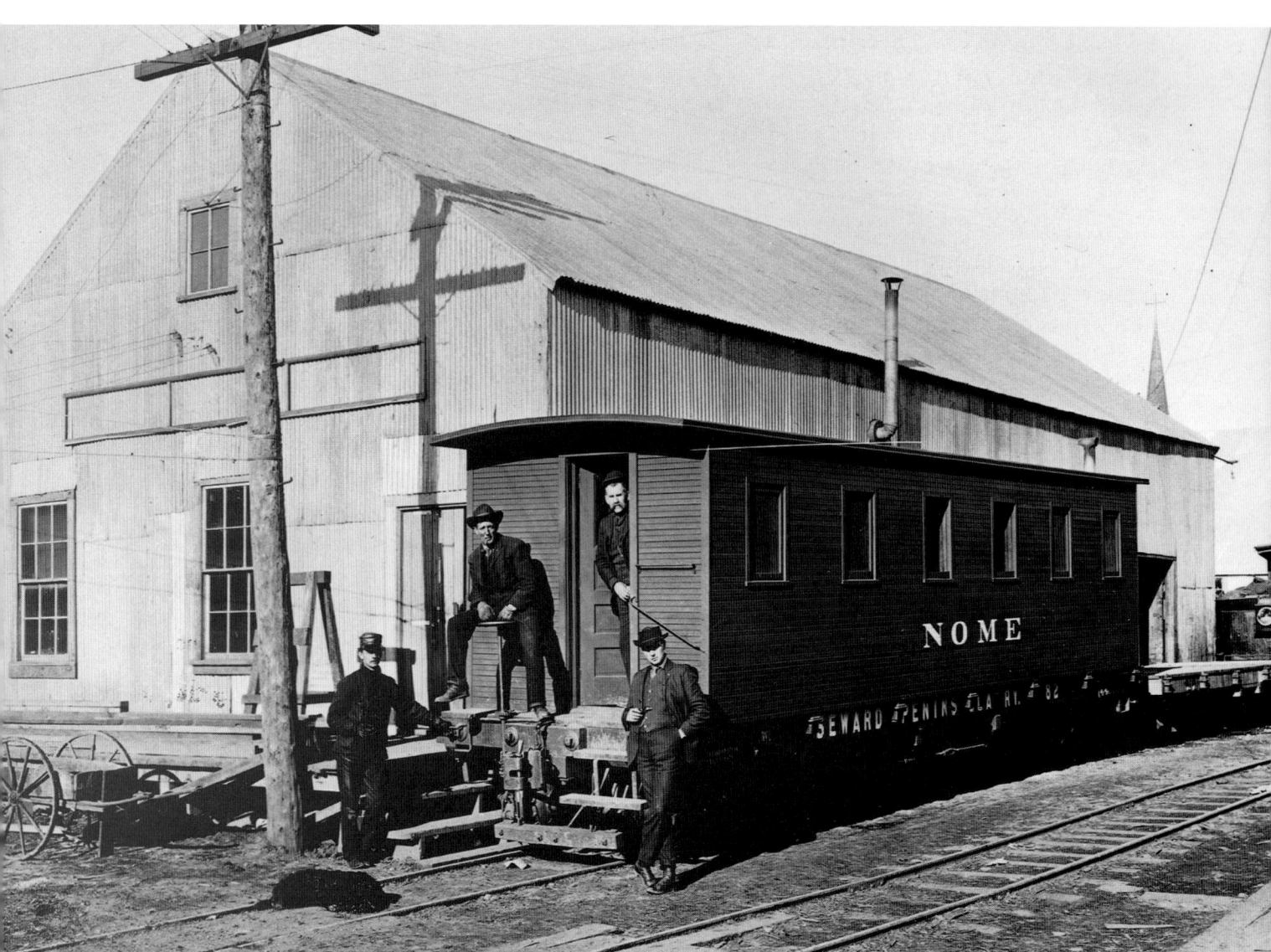

This is Warehouse No. 5 and the "Cannon Ball Express" of the Seward Peninsula Railroad in Nome. The express is composed of a caboose, a flatcar, and a locomotive. The photo was taken October 1, 1906. (University of Washington Historical Library—Northwest Collection)

Dalles after which it went to work on the former Mill Creek Flume & Manufacturing Company line at Walla Walla. It was eventually purchased by the Northern Pacific. In 1906, the engine was obtained by the Seward Peninsula. The little Porter was the most popular locomotive owned by the company. It was "low slung and powerful," and the crews could make good time with it. Most of the other engines had to be handled with great care on the curves and poor roadbed.

The line also purchased three new larger Climaxes in 1908. These were Class "B" engines, No. 5, No. 6, and No. 7. They were in service only one season, proving to be too heavy and cumbersome for the unstable trackage of the Seward Peninsula. They were shipped back to the States for use on logging lines in Washington and Oregon.

In 1906, another 0-6-0 was acquired and numbered No. 5. It was larger and newer than the little Porter—a Baldwin (c/n 10882) turned out in 1890 for the Alberta Railway and Coal Company and used in the Lethbridge area as No. 1 for years before being declared surplus.

"End of Track" was the ultimate in 1906 rail excursions in the Nome area. But nobody knew where that would be from day to day. A timetable was published in the Nome Gold Digger, announcing that trains left daily at 8 a.m. and 2 p.m. for Little Creek, Discovery, Banner, Summit, Dexter, Ex, and End of Track. On the return, however, a departure time was not given for End of Track, but only a warning that trains would leave Ex at 10:15 a.m. and 4:15 p.m.

Freight trains with a light load made the run from Nome to Lane's Landing in about 10 or 12 hours, but if many cars were added the time could be extended to 16, 18, or even 20 hours. For a return trip, the cars would usually be empty and would bounce along into Nome in a matter of only 6 or 8 hours.

Soon after the tracks finally reached Lane's Landing, business on the Seward Peninsula began to decline. By the close of the first decade of the century, the train schedule had been cut to two or three trips a week. In the fall of 1910 as gold mining declined, railroading on any real commercial scale came to an end on the Seward Peninsula.

Nomeites were inconvenienced by the lack of service, and the still-operating mines were in need of supplies. In 1911, the Seward Peninsula started changing hands, with the Maine Northwestern Development Company gaining possession for $1,074, although there were probably other considerations. The Nome court records show a quit claim deed from the Seward Peninsula Railroad to the Maine company on May 28, 1913, for the consideration of $1.

On that date, Jefet Lindeborg, operator of the Pioneer Mining and Ditch Company, apparently leased the railroad. On August 10, 1920, he purchased it at a U.S. marshall's sale for $10,100 as a result of a judgment of $52,947.50 by the State Street Trust Company of Boston against the Maine Northwestern Development Company.

During the period of Lindeborg's operation, the line was used intermittently for the transportation of light freight, a few passengers, and the mail. It was during this period that a wide assortment of picturesque conveyances were used for travel over the tracks, including carts pulled by dogs—known as pupmobiles.

Shortly after Lindeborg's purchase, the Territory of Alaska Legislature passed a bill that was approved by the governor on May 5, 1921. The bill provided for the purchase of the road and all equipment at a price not to exceed $30,000, and further provided that "it shall be put in good operating condition and operated as a public tram and highway."

One of the several locomotives used by the Seward Peninsula Railroad, along with its tender. This locomotive is the 0-6-0 Baldwin built in 1890 for the Alberta Railway and Coal Company as No. 1. The Seward Peninsula purchased it in 1906. (University of Alaska Archives—Henderson Collection)

Later that same year, Lindeborg transferred the property to the Pioneer Mining and Ditch Company, of which he was a principal. The bill of sale was dated November 18, 1921, but no amount was mentioned. A month later, the property was deeded to the Territory of Alaska by Pioneer Mining in consideration of $30,000. The sale included, besides the roadbed and certain real estate in Nome, five locomotives, Nos. 1, 2, 3, 4, and 5; a coach, No. 92; a boxcar, No. 1; a cook car, No. 97; a bunk car, No. 109; twelve flatcars; and two rolltop desks.

On October 13, 1922, the Alaska Road Commission, a federal agency that handled road and trail construction, took over the road for the Territory at a purchase

A favorite way of getting around in the Nome area following the demise of the Seward Peninsula Railroad was by "pupmobile." Residents used dog teams and a flanged-wheel cart on the tracks of the old SPRR rather than try to cross the mushy tundra in the summer months. This photo shows a team in action in 1914. (University of Alaska Archives)

price listed as $24,000 and noted that repair of the "87-mile tram" was of "great public interest."

During the summer of 1924, the portion of the line between Little Creek and Nugget Roadhouse was rehabilitated at a cost of between $20,000 and $25,000. By the end of the year, the Alaska Road Commission had spent $32,653.85 and 42 miles of line had been put in good operating condition for light loads.

Again, arrangements were made for draft animals and so on to use the right-of-way, and planks were placed between the rails on bridges and trestles. A light gasoline locomotive was purchased by the commission for use over the road. Regulations were put into effect. A powered vehicle was required to have a siren, suitable brakes, a sander, and if pulling a loaded car, a "hired employee." Each locomotive was to be numbered, and if one planned to wander beyond the Nome River area, a "travel plan" was to be filed giving destination and time of departure.

Dog-powered rigs, however, proved to be the most practical since they could be derailed and launched again upon meeting an oncomer. In such cases, the vehicle with the heavier load had the right-of-way, with the vehicle being derailed went to the high side of the track so that the owner/operator could put it back on the rails.

Such operations continued until the war years, with everything imaginable that had wheels being used on the track at one time or another.

During World War II, the military made some repairs, controlled traffic, and brought a couple of LeRoy-powered Plymouth locomotives for use on the trackage as far north as Little Creek.

In the postwar years, the line returned to the Territory, and maintenance and repair again became top priority. The trackage, however, was used only occasionally. In 1953, Charles M. Reader dubbed the line the "Curly Q" and operated a small gasoline rail bus as far as Salmon Lake, carrying tourists each summer. He sold out to Thomas Martin a few years later, but by 1955 people had stopped using the tramway and the Highway Commission converted some of the roadway into highway use.

In 1963, August Krutzsch purchased some 70 miles of trackage for $6,501, along with the remains of the little No. 4 locomotive, which in the meantime had been used as part of the Nome seawall before finally being rescued by history-minded Nomeites. Plans for restoring the engine never came about, and the Porter was shipped south to Washington.

Seward Peninsula(r) Railroad

Steam Locomotive Roster

Road No.	Wheel Arr.	Builder	C/N	Year	Cylinders	Drivers	Notes
212 (1)	Class A	Climax	212	4/1900	7x7	26"	Originally Wild Goose RR, sold in 1903 to Nome Arctic RR, sold in 1906 to Seward Peninsula RR, 15 ton, used as rip-rap in Nome seawall.
315 (2)	Class A	Climax	315	4/1902	7-½x7	28"	Originally Wild Goose RR, sold in 1903 to Nome Arctic RR, sold in 1906 to Seward Peninsula RR, 18 ton, used as rip-rap in Nome seawall.

Steam Locomotive Roster *(continued)*

Road No.	Wheel Arr.	Builder	C/N	Year	Cylinders	Drivers	Notes
399 (3)	Class A	Climax	399	1903	7x7	26"	Originally Wild Goose RR, sold in 1903 to Nome Arctic RR, sold in 1906 to Seward Peninsula RR, 15 ton, converted to internal combustion.
4	0-6-0	Porter	283	January 1878	10x16		Originally Walla Walla & Columbia River RR, "Blue Mountain" No. 4, sold in July 1879, to Oregon Rwy & Navigation Co., No. 4, sold in 1883, to Cascade Portage RR, No. 283, No. 3 (1883-1894) (OR&N), to Mill Creek Flume RR (1894-1903) (OR&N), to Mill Creek RR (1903-1905) (NP), in 1906 to Seward Peninsula, No. 4, retired in 1910. Used as rip-rap in Nome seawall. To Herb Engstrom in 1967, to Washington State Railroad Historical Society, Pasco, WA, 1992 for restoration.
5	Class B	Climax	670	1906	9x12	28"	Sold to J. A. Veness Lumber Co. (standard gauge), sold to Chehalis River Lbr. Co., sold to Wind River Lbr. Co.
5 (2nd)	0-6-0	Baldwin	10882	1890			Orig. Alberta Rwy. & Coal Co., No. 1., sold 1906 to Seward Peninsula, No. 5. Used as rip-rap in Nome seawall.
6	Class B	Climax	672	1906	9x12	28"	Sold to Adna Mill Co. (standard gauge), sold to Ninemire & Morgan Lbr. Co., sold to Union Machinery & Supply Co., sold to Sidney Burnett (Tenina Lbr. Co.), sold to Crown Timber Co.
7	Class B	Climax	682	1906	11x12	30"	Sold to Hofius Steel & Equipment Co., sold to Wisconsin Lbr. Co. (standard gauge), sold to H. Syverson & Hill. Sold to Hill Logging Co., sold to Nehalem Valley Lbr. Co., sold to Neness & Shives

Chapter 18

Minor Railroads in Alaska and the Yukon

Atlin Consolidated Mining Company
During the years from 1906 to 1909, a short, narrow-gauge electric railroad operated at Pine Creek in the Atlin District of the Yukon. The railroad had three 5-ton locomotives and 40, 4-wheel side dump cars, and it moved gold-bearing ore from an excavation area to a sluice box. Excavation was accomplished with a large (standard-gauge) rail-mounted Bucyrus steam shovel on a short length of track, which was moved as the working face advanced. The locomotives were equipped with an offset trolley pole, which drew 400 volts from a wire strung to the side of the track. After the operation ceased, the shovel and locomotives disappeared, but the remains of several of the cars can still be seen at Lake Atlin.

Alaska's first railroad operated between Seward City on Lynn Canal and the Berners Bay Gold Manufacturing Company's gold mine. Constructed in early 1894, the railroad used a little 0-4-0T narrow-gauge saddle-tanker, the first steam locomotive in the territory. The line tied the mine to the waterfront, a distance of about 3.5 miles. (Clifford Collection)

Berners Bay Gold Manufacturing Company

Written records of the name of Alaska's earliest railroad have been lost, but a photograph taken on May 15, 1894, shows a Porter 0-4-0T narrow-gauge locomotive pushing a flatcar loaded with passengers. This locomotive, the first in Alaska, operated over 3.5 miles of track between Seward City and the Berners Bay Gold Manufacturing Company's mine. The trains carried workers to and from the mine and ore back to the waterfront on Lynn Canal.

Alaska-Juneau Gold Mine Railroad

Several mining railroads operated in the Juneau-Douglas area during the height of the Southeast Alaska gold rush. One of the largest was the Alaska-Juneau Gold Mine Railroad, which operated over about 7 miles of track (not including sidings) that traveled to the waste dump and to various nearby shops and warehouses.

One of several Baldwin-Westinghouse locomotives used in the Alaska-Juneau Gold Mine at Juneau. These units pulled ore trains and carried workers to the far reaches of the mine. The mine is located above Juneau. (H. Clifford)

During 1911, the company drilled a tunnel through Mount Juneau from a location on the hillside above Juneau—adjacent to the milling plant overlooking Gastineau Channel—to Silverbow Basin. Trackage through the tunnel was initially 50-pound rails but was later upgraded to 72-pound, set at 30-inch gauge. The company's electric locomotives drew power from an overhead wire carrying 600 volts, D.C. Two-unit hauling motors, operating as cow and calf units, were used to haul personnel and ore throughout the mine area.

The mine was closed in April 1944. Most of the trackage and equipment were sold as junk and hauled out in 1964–65. The equipment that remained was used for a tour train that operated in the mine for several years. This train used four rebuilt personnel cars pulled by a battery-operated locomotive (brought in from the Lower 48).

Alaska-Gastineau Mining Company Railroad

Another mining railroad in the Juneau area was operated by the Alaska-Gastineau Mining Company of New York. In January 1913, the Alaska-Gastineau Mining Company took over the properties at Sheep Creek (Thane), which had been formerly operated by the Howell Company. It also took over the Perseverance Mine and other properties, which had been established in the area as early as 1896.

In April 1914, the firm built a 2-mile tunnel through the mountains from Sheep Creek to the Perseverance properties and constructed a 3-foot narrow-gauge mining railroad through the tunnel. The company obtained two 18-ton Baldwin-Westinghouse 4-wheel mining-type electric locomotives, which ran on 600-volt D.C. power supplied by an overhead trolley wire. Twelve-ton capacity four-wheel ore cars were used over the 5 miles of track.

By 1921, operating costs had increased. The mining properties became unprofitable, and they finally closed down. In 1923, the locomotives and other equipment were sold to the Pacific Cement & Aggregate Company, part of the Lone Star Cement Company, located in Davenport, CA.

Salmon Creek Dam Railroad

In 1913, the Alaska-Gastineau Mining Company built a construction railroad that originated at a point 2.5 miles north of Juneau on the Gastineau Channel and followed Salmon Creek upstream for a distance of 2.6 miles. Here the firm built a concrete dam 170 feet high with a crest 648 feet long. Two hydroelectric power plants, one near the dam and the other on the beach, used water from the reservoir to supply electricity for the city of Juneau and the Alaska-Juneau Gold Mining Company.

The Salmon Creek Railroad was 36" narrow gauge and used a 2-truck Shay during construction. This was the only known Shay to have operated in Alaska. At least two 0-4-0 locomotives were also used for switching, one at the beach and another at the upper end of the railroad, near the dam. The first 500 feet of railroad ran up a grade of about 20 degrees, and the cars were pulled up with a cable. At the top of the incline, the locomotive would handle a couple of cars to the upper powerhouse, a distance of about 2 miles.

Treadwell Mine Railroad

A 2-foot narrow-gauge railroad connected the various mines just south of the city of Douglas on Douglas Island, including the Treadwell, the 700, the Mexican, and the Ready Bullion Mines.

These mines began operating around the turn of the century, and the Treadwell continued operation under Gastineau Channel until a cave-in shut it down in April 1917. Most of the others ceased operating shortly thereafter, and the Ready Bullion was the last to close down in December 1922. Nearly $70 million in gold was extracted from operations in this area.

Rush and Brown Copper Mine Railroad

One of several mining railroads in Southeast Alaska that operated just after the turn of the century was the Rush and Brown Copper Mine Railroad on the Kasaan Peninsula on Prince of Wales Island. About 3 miles of narrow-gauge track, plus tramways, were operated by the firm for the Jumbo, the Mamie, and other mines to move their copper ore to the Hadley Smelter.

This narrow-gauge Porter 0-4-2T was recovered from the Rush and Brown copper mine on Prince of Wales Island in Southeastern Alaska. It has since been moved to Nevada. The locomotive hauled low-grade copper ore over a few miles of narrow-gauge track to the bunkers for transshipment. Copper was discovered in the area in 1865 by Russian inhabitants. Rush and Brown production started in 1905 and was closed down by 1908. (Clifford Collection)

Some of the equipment used in this operation still remains in the bush on Prince of Wales Island. One of the narrow-gauge locomotives, an H. K. Porter 0-4-0T, was moved from the island to Ketchikan and then shipped to Fallon, Nevada, where it is being restored for display.

Copper was first discovered on the Kasaan Peninsula by Russians in 1865. Production at the mines began in 1905, and by 1906 the Hadley Smelter was put into operation. Mining began to taper off in 1908 due to a lack of ore, and the operations closed down shortly thereafter.

Alaska Marble Company Tramway

A 3,200-foot gravity tramway operated by the Alaska Marble Company at Calder on Prince of Wales Island served in another mining operation in Southeast Alaska. The tram was used to move marble from a quarry on the mountainside 75 feet above the beach. A loaded car served as a counterbalance to bring up the empty cars. The quarry operated in the early 1900s and supplied pure white, blue-veined marble and light blue marble with a mottled background. The stone was not equal to the top-quality Italian marble, but it was said to be better than most American grades.

Ketchikan Pulp Company

For more than four decades, from 1954 to 1997, the Ketchikan Pulp Company ran a rail/barge operation to service its mill at Ward cove, just north of Ketchikan. Over the years, three locomotives that were owned and several that were leased switched the barges and mill. The railcars brought chemicals to the mill and took finished pulp out. Faced with the loss of a federal timber cutting contract and significant environmental upgrade requirements, the mill closed in early 1997.

Ketchikan and Northern Terminal Company

About 2,000 feet of track at Ketchikan and Northern Terminal Company was used in the loading and unloading of rail barges at this facility. Motive power was provided by a front-end loader with a coupler on the rear. If conditions warranted, the loader bucket could also be replaced with a coupler.

Alaska Lumber and Pulp Company

Two locomotives operated the railroad at the Sitka plant of the Alaska Lumber and Pulp Company. The operation was set up strictly to service the mill, and when the plant was shut down in 1993, the rail operation was eliminated.

Cook Inlet Coal Field Company Railroad

A 42-inch narrow-gauge railroad was constructed in 1899 on the Kenai Peninsula from the bluffs west of Homer to the end of the Homer Spit. The railroad was set up as a noncommon carrier and eventually operated over more than 7 miles of track.

A Porter 0-4-0T coal-burning locomotive was put into operation hauling the wooden coal cars that delivered coal to the dock for shipment to the boomtowns of Hope and Sunrise on Turnagain Arm. The operation ceased in 1902 due to a lack of market for the coal. In 1913, a bankruptcy sale was held and the railroad and equipment sold to the Miller Machinery Company of Seattle, which removed the railroad by December of that year.

Apollo Consolidated Mining Company

The westernmost railroad in North America was the Apollo Consolidated Mining Company railroad on Umga Island, located south of Cold Bay near the western tip of the Alaska Peninsula. The mining operation, consisting of numerous substantial buildings, tramways, tunnels, and shafts, started operating in 1886. The operation yielded low-grade gold quartz. The properties continued to prosper, and in 1897 a 0-6-0T Baldwin narrow-gauge locomotive was put into operation.

As the supply of gold ore diminished, the mine was gradually phased out, but the remains of the track, and some of the buildings, can still be seen in the area.

Crooked Creek and Whiskey Island Railroad

The Crooked Creek and Whiskey Island Railroad is a unique little venture that operates as a tourist attraction during the summer months at Alaskaland, the former Alaska Centennial site at Fairbanks. The 3-foot narrow-gauge scenic train runs around the 40-acre site. The locomotive is a gasoline-powered 0-4-0 built by C. M. Lovsted, Inc., of Seattle. The small engine moves its four cars at a leisurely pace that allows tourists to view the many displays.

Also on display at Alaskaland is the observation car Denali, which was used by President Warren G. Harding to travel over the Alaska Railroad to Nenana for the Golden Spike ceremony in 1923.

The Tanana Valley Railroad No. 1 locomotive, a 0-4-0T built H. K. Porter (c/n 1972, 1899) and currently under restoration, is also on display on the grounds.

Minor Lines

Maps and early reports show mining railroads of various types and lengths in the following areas, although very little other information is available:

- Goulding Railroad, serving Goulding Harbor on the west side of Chicago Island.
- Eagle Harbor to Eagle Glacier, serving the Eagle River Gold Mine, the Alice Gold Mine, and the Amalga Gold Mine.

Alaska-Gastineau Mining Company

36"-Gauge Electric Locomotives

Builder	C/N	Type	Acq.	Ret.	Notes
Baldwin-Westinghouse	41328	18-ton Trolley	1914	1923	Sold to Pacific Cement & Aggregate Company, to California State RR Museum.
Baldwin-Westinghouse	41329	18-ton Trolley	1914	1923	Sold to Pacific Cement & Aggregate Company, to California State RR Museum.

Note: The company also operated some 24"-gauge battery locomotives.

Alaska-Juneau Mining Company

Electric Locomotives

Builder	C/N	Type	Acq.	Ret.	Notes
Baldwin-Westinghouse	41326	4-ton, Battery	1914	1944	Scrapped 1964–1965.
Baldwin-Westinghouse	42593	4-ton, Battery	1915	1944	Scrapped 1964–1965.
Baldwin-Westinghouse	42629	4-ton, Battery	1915	1944	Scrapped 1964–1965.
Baldwin-Westinghouse	43942	4-ton, Battery	1916	1944	Scrapped 1964–1965.
Baldwin-Westinghouse		18-ton, Trolley		1944	Scrapped 1964–1965, 5 locomotives in this class.
Jeffrey	4118	10-ton, Trolley		1944	Scrapped 1964–1965
General Electric		6-ton, Trolley		1944	Scrapped 1964–1965, 5 locomotives in this class.
General Electric		9-ton, Trolley		1944	Scrapped 1964–1965, 3 locomotives in this class.

Salmon Creek Dam Railroad

Locomotive Roster

Road No.	Wheel Arr.	Builder	C/N	Year	Cylinders	Drivers	Notes
1	0-4-0T	Porter	1421	November 1892	7x12		Originally Berners Bay Mining & Milling Company, sold 1912, to Salmon Creek Dam RR, sold 1913, to Annex Creek, retired 1915, abandoned until 1976, to Jim Walsh, restored (No. 2, "Seward").
	22-truck	Lima	2190	1909	8x12	26-½"	Originally Northern Light Power & Coal Company, sold 1913, to Alaska-Gastineau Mining Company, No. 2 (Salmon Creek Dam Railroad), sold March 1921, to Puget Sound Machinery Depot, sold 1921, to Biles-Coleman Lumber Company, No. 2, No. 101, scrapped 1940.

Rush and Brown Copper Mine

Locomotive Roster

Road No.	Wheel Arr.	Builder	C/N	Year	Cylinders	Drivers	Notes
	0-4-2T	Porter	1392	July 1892	6x10		Originally Albany Street Rwy., No. 3 (Steam Dummy). Rebuilt as conventional locomotive, to Rush & Brown Mine, to Jim Walsh, under restoration.

Apollo Consolidated Mining Company

30"-Gauge, Steam Locomotive Roster

Road No.	Wheel Arr.	Builder	C/N	Year	Cylinders	Drivers	Notes
1	0-6-0T	Baldwin	15273	April 1897	9x14	30"	To Keith Christenson.

Currently in the South 48 for restoration.

Cook Inlet Coal Fields Company

42"-Gauge Locomotive Roster

Road No.	Wheel Arr.	Builder	C/N	Year	Cylinders	Drivers	Notes
	0-4-0T	Porter	2037	August 1899	8x14	26"(?)	To Mr. Williams, 1906, to Mr. Caldwill, to Mr. Ross, to Miller Machinery Company, 1913.

Note: The 1906 Marshal's sale showed a second locomotive. No details are known.

Alaska Lumber & Pulp Company

Diesel Locomotives

Road No.	Builder	Model	Date built	C/N	History	Acq.	Ret.	Notes
	Porter	65 ton						Unknown original owner. Gone by 8/1974.
	GE	65 ton	June 1943	1	7881			Originally NAD Puget Sound, No. 65-00056, to Alaska Lbr & Pulp 1965-6, to General Electric, Cleveland, OH, to RTA, No. 033, Chicago, IL.

Alaska Lumber & Pulp Company (continued)

Road No.	Builder	Model	Date built	C/N	History	Acq.	Ret.	Notes
9012	GE	70 ton	December 1946	28509				Originally Mississippi Export, No. 46, to Southwest Portland Cement, No. 7, No. 407, to Ventura County, No. 4, to dealer. Painted and lettered AL&P No. 9012, never sent to Alaska, to Modesto & Empire Traction (parts only).
1837	EMD	SW-9	April 1953	17817				Originally Union Pacific, No. 1837. Leased to AL&P, 1979. Rebuilt to UP SW-10, No. 1259, 12/1983

Ketchikan Pulp Company

Diesel Locomotives

Road No.	Builder	Model	Date built	C/N	History	Acq.	Ret.	Notes
(5300)	Whitcomb	50 ton	February 1953	61279	Built as KP	February 1953	199?	No evidence of actually carrying #5300.
5321	Baldwin	S-12	November 1952	75780	built as SP	1972	1991	Rebuilt by GE, Kent, WA 1974, to T&NO 121, to SP 2124, to Chrome Crankshaft, to KP 5321, to LP, to NRHS Portland, OR.
6600	EMD	SW 1200	January 1955	20117	Built as SOO 2125	November 1889	June 1897	To NRE, to LP 6600, to CEECO, to Port of Longview 157.

Leased Locomotives:

Road No.	Builder	Model	Date built	C/N	History	Acq.	Ret.	Notes
987	EMD	NW5	December 1946	3480	Built as GN187	1974	1974	Leased from PTS, to BN 987, to PTS 987, to EPTC 987.
23	EMD	GP30	April 1963	28142	Built as PRR 2234	August 1895	1995	Leased from LRC, to PC 2234, to CR 2234, to LRC 23, to LRCX 23, to NKCRN.

Abbreviations:

B/D	Built date
B/N	Builder's number
Acq.	Year unit acquired
Ret.	Year unit retired
BN	Burlington Northern
CEECO	Coast Engine & Equipment Company
CR	ConRail
EPTC	East Portland Traction Company
GN	Great Northern Railroad
KP	Ketchikan Pulp
LP	Louisiana Pacific-Ketchikan Pulp
NRE	National Railway Equipment
NRHS	National Railway Historical Society
PC	Penn Central
PRR	Pennsylvania Railroad
PTS	Pacific Transportation Services
SOO	Soo Line
SP	Southern Pacific
T&NO	Texas & New Orleans
BALDWIN	Baldwin Locomotive Works, Eddystone, PA
EMD	Electro-Motive Division of General Motors, LaGrange, IL
WHITCOMB	Whitcomb Locomotive Works, Rochelle, IL

Chapter 19

On the Drawing Board

Over the years, many railroads that were announced for the Alaska/Yukon region never got past the planning stage. Some were merely stock promotions. Others were thoroughly planned but fell by the wayside because of a lack of funds. Still others were well planned, seriously considered, and apparently funded but were dropped due to changing needs or economics.

The Russian Connection

Since the early days of development on the Seward Peninsula, various proposals have been put forward to connect Alaska to Asia. As recently as 1991, the Interhemispheric Bering Strait Tunnel and Railroad Group was formed to investigate the feasibility of connecting Alaska and Siberia with a railroad tunnel. Undaunted by the fact that there is no current rail connection from the Seward Peninsula to the "South 48," or that the gauges of North America and the former Soviet Union are not compatible, the group attempted to market its idea. To date, no discernable progress has been made.

In 1906, the American Trans-Siberian Company announced plans in Russia and the United States for a railroad with Alaskan routes that would run from Cape Prince of Wales via one of two routes. One ran east from Kingegan following the shores of Kotzebue Sound, over to the vicinity of Nulato on the north bank of the Yukon, and then up the river to Dawson City. The other traveled from Kingegan south through the Kavizagemut to Nome, along the shore of Norton Sound to a point opposite St. Michael, and from there east across the Yukon. The company, incorporated for $250,000,000, ultimately had plans to tunnel under the Bering Strait from Cape Prince of Wales to East Cape in Siberia. One condition of the construction of the road through Alaska was that the company would receive alternate sections for 8 miles on each side of the line, together with mining concessions. These land and mining grants from the government would be similar in scope to those given to the Union Pacific some 40 years before and would be an incentive for private capital to invest in such a remote area—with only marginal prospects of financial return. Neither the grants nor the railroad ever materialized.

Another of the imaginative, early day railroad proposals involved a line of railroads thousands of miles in length through the vast territory of Siberia and through the uninhabited arctic tundra of the Chukotsk Peninsula. The proposal included the construction of a 40-mile–long submarine tunnel under the Bering Strait and the continuation of the line through Alaska and British Columbia to connect with existing railroads on the North American continent.

A series of companies planned to operate the system. One of these companies was the Grand Trunk Pacific Railroad, which had been incorporated by an act of the Dominion of Canada Parliament in 1903. The system would reach 3,600 miles across Canada from the Atlantic to the Pacific. One branch would extend from Edmonton to Dawson City in the Yukon, and from there across Alaska, where it would involve some of the railroads already built, under construction, or planned in the areas between Dawson City and Nome.

Another potential railroad operator was the Trans-Alaska Siberian Company, a French-Russian-American firm headed by Baron Loug de Lobel, a noted French engineer. The firm, incorporated in New Jersey with a capitalization of $6 million, had obtained concessions from the Russian government that would tie the line in with the Siberian railroad. A 3,000-mile route across the United States, through Alaska, and under the Bering Strait via the Diomede Islands to East Cape was planned. One of the conditions of the project was that alternate sections for 8 miles on either side of the line, together with mining concessions, would be granted to the company. Although various parts of the project were completed at one time or another, the promoters were unable to tie it all together and the plan went by the boards.

The Alaska Short Line Railway and Navigation Company of Washington planned a line from Iliamna Bay to Anvik on the Yukon, a distance of 369.2 miles, and then to the Bering Strait. The proposal was filed in January 1904, and the estimated cost was $44,300 per mile, which included a tunnel through the Coast Range at a 475-foot elevation. The greatest pass height would be 975 feet, providing easy gradients and favorable alignments. It was proposed that this railroad would connect with the Trans-Siberian railroad via the Bering Strait. Capitalization was $15 million, and Colonel J. T. Cormforth headed up the company as president.

The Trans-Alaska Railroad & Navigation Company, headquartered in Washington State, was incorporated with capital of $50 million in 1902 under the laws of the state of Arizona by a group of Colorado capitalists. The Trans-Alaska line was to run from Iliamna Bay on Cook Inlet to Port Clarence on the Bering Strait, where the road would connect with the Trans-Siberian Railroad by the use of immense steel ferries that would carry the trains across the strait. Steamers would connect the Alaska portion of the route with Puget Sound. This railroad was said to have been started by a group of wealthy free-lovers and that colonization was a major part of the overall planning.

A large amount of timber, ties, rails, and camp equipment was loaded at Iliamna Bay, and some offices and headquarter buildings were erected, along with line grading. A tunnel was started through the mountains, and shops and office buildings were constructed at the northern terminus. But the line died an inglorious death because of lack of capital. Some of the construction materials are still visible at Iliamna and Railroad City.

A rival company bearing almost the same name was the Trans-Alaska Company, incorporated in California at $100,000. This company caused considerable trouble in stock-selling programs for the other firm, and it is cited as one of the reasons for the Trans-Alaska Railroad and Navigation Company's failure. The second company also failed within months.

Ties to the South 48

A World War II–era military program for the north resulted in one of the most ambitious Alaska railroad schemes ever proposed. It was in reality two functional divisions with different names, with Fairbanks as the division point. To the east of Fairbanks, it would run to Prince George, where it would connect with the Pacific Great Eastern and the Canadian National, and would be known as the Trans-Canadian Alaska Railroad. The actual length of this section was to be 1,417 miles. West of Fairbanks, the railroad, which would be known as the Western Railroad, would run to the ocean terminal to be established at Teller. It would be 735 miles in length.

The Trans-Canadian Alaska, and Western Railroads were the brainchildren of Frederic A. Delano, a relative of President Franklin D. Roosevelt, and came at a time when the United States was desperate to get materials to Russia, which was battling the Axis on the Eastern Front. Delano was an experienced railroad man, a former president of the Burlington Route, and an official in other companies. The suggestion for these railroads was reportedly made before the planning of the Alcan Highway, the construction of which started on March 17, 1942.

A major stumbling block in the building of the railroad was the shortage of steel in 1942. The War Department, however, was interested in the project, and a week before work on the Alcan started, the department ordered the rail route surveyed. The route was to go via the Rocky Mountain Trench from Prince George to Fairbanks. The survey was to be pushed to completion during the summer of 1942. The plan also called for reconnaissance of the area west of Fairbanks. About $2 million was earmarked for both projects, and Canadian approval for the project was secured.

Among the projects of the western reconnaissance was the location of suitable sites for ocean terminals from Norton Sound to Point Barrow; the practicality of both rail and highway routes; and general features such as topography, climate, soil, forest growth, inhabitants, and existing roads, trails, and waterways. A preliminary report was to be completed by June 1, 1942.

One of the requirements for the ocean terminal was a sheltered, deep-water harbor large enough to accommodate the maximum traffic density anticipated over the military railroad, up to 20 trains weighing 1,000 tons each day, each way. This was the equivalent of about 15 boxcars per train, plus a locomotive and a service car.

Port Clarence, near Teller, was deemed the best protected deep-water harbor on the west coast of Alaska, north of the Aleutians. Golovin Bay on the south shore of the Seward Peninsula, Unalakleet, St. Michael, Nome, Kotzebue, and Deering were also considered. Reconnaissance on routes to all suggested destinations was completed via air and ground. The report submitted in June stated that a railroad or highway was feasible between Fairbanks and Port Clarence. It also stated that such a route would be difficult, as was typical of all Alaska construction, mainly due to inaccessibility of sites, making the supply of materials and construction machinery uncertain.

The shortest, most logical route west of Fairbanks would be through the Yukon River valley. The existing Alaska Railroad would be used from Fairbanks to Dunbar, a distance of 39 miles. In the event a highway seemed suitable, it would run parallel to the railroad at this point. The 300-mile route from Fairbanks to Council was the same as had been selected in a reconnaissance under Major Wilds P. Richardson of the 9th U.S. Infantry in 1906, when he was president of the Alaska Railroad Commission.

The favored Trans-Canadian Alaska Railroad route went from Prince George, along the main line of the Canadian National Railway, to Fort Frances, along the Pelly River valley to the Yukon River, along the White River from its mouth to Ladue River, and then down the Tanana River Valley to Kobe (now Rex) on the Alaska Railroad, some 84 miles south of Fairbanks. Sifton Pass, at an elevation of 3,273 feet, was the highest point on this route. The railroad would be built with 60-pound rails, and it would be standard gauge, with diesel-electric locomotives specified. The actual construction would require 16,937 workers and 400 work days.

The estimated cost of the project was $86,576,000 for the Trans-Canada Alaska Railroad; $60,222,000 for the Western Railroad; $23,187,000 for the port; $11,500,000 for an oil pipeline; and $420,000 for two rail-river terminals. It was given the go-ahead on February 17, 1943, with construction to start on May 15, 1943.

Meanwhile, the tide of war was beginning to change in Europe. Military action to regain the Aleutian Islands was underway, and thousands of American aircraft were being moved to Russia via Canada and Alaska. As a result, the need for the Trans-Canada, Alaska, and Western Railroads and a military port on Alaska's western shore diminished, and the Delano program was filed away—never to be revived.

A railroad from Vancouver, B.C., to Cape Prince of Wales, Alaska, was in the headlines several times between 1891 and 1893, when it was announced that the survey of an easy route found as far north as Juneau, and not exceedingly difficult beyond that point, had been completed. This proposed line would also connect via the Siberian and Russian railroads to Europe. The articles pointed out that the present Trans-Siberian Railroad was to end at Vladivostock and that it would be necessary to extend that line approximately 1,000 miles to connect with the Alaska Railroad. The project never got past the preliminary survey stage.

The Sitka Alaskan, the leading newspaper of the time in the territory of Alaska, carried several stories in the late 1800s about railroads to be constructed to and within the territory. On February 6, 1886, the paper ran a story stating that the Canadian Pacific Railway proposed to extend its routes from British Columbia along the coast of Alaska to Mt. St. Elias, and then across Alaska to the Behring (Bering) Strait, which would be bridged to connect with a Siberian line and continue on to Europe. In April of that year, a story appeared related to a proposal to connect the western states with Alaska through New Westminster, B.C., and then on July 6, 1889, a similar line was proposed from Victoria, B.C.

Another proposal was made by the Alaska-Northwestern Railroad Company, incorporated under the laws of the territory of Arizona with capitalization of $60 million, "to build a single-track, standard-gauge steam passenger and freight railroad from the city of Vancouver, B.C., to Cape Prince of Wales (Tin City), Alaska, a surveyed distance of 2,300 miles between terminals." This firm was headed by Cesilius Swenson of New York.

Connections Within Alaska
A relatively recent proposal for a new rail line in Alaska followed the cold summer of 1975, when severe icy conditions in the Arctic disrupted the shipment of vital oil pipeline construction materials to the North Slope.

Former Alaska Governor Walter J. Hickel renewed efforts to extend the Alaska Railroad to the North Slope, as the Northern Operations of Rail Transportation and Highways Commission (NORTH), chaired by Albert Swalling, had done a few years before. Governor Hickel's 1975 proposal called for an extension of the Alaska Railroad north from Nenana to Deadhorse on the North Slope. A line would also branch west from Alatna to Kobuk, and then to Teller and Nome. Yet another branch would extend east from the Fairbanks area to Whitehorse to connect with a proposed northern extension of the British Columbia Railway. The NORTH Commission originally made a similar proposal in 1967–68 in conjunction with the development of Alaska's North Slope.

The Commission was charged with pushing major development into the Arctic northland and favored the building of an extension of the Alaska Railroad to serve the petroleum- and mineral-rich areas of the north. The proposed program involved extending the (then) federally-owned Alaska Railroad northwest from the Dunbar areas south of Fairbanks to a point where two lines would branch off—one west to Bornite and eventually to Nome and the other north through the Brooks Range and Anaktuvuk Pass to the Prudhoe Bay area. Governor Hickel and the late Senator Bob Bartlett advocated the program. During the winter of 1967–68, a crew had hacked a survey trail into the Kobuk River country. In making the survey, it was recalled that the Army Corps of Engineers had made a similar survey in 1942 for a railroad between Dunbar and the Nome area. It was also noted that this was the fourth time since 1900 that a railroad survey had been made from the Fairbanks area to Nome.

The North Slope of Alaska has since been developed via highway, air service, and ships. It is highly unlikely that the economic rationale for a rail connection will ever be present.

In 1910, the Alaska Midland Railroad proposed to construct a line from Haines to Fairbanks. The railroad was the brainchild of financier John Rosene and listed its chief advantage as not requiring an open-water journey to go from Seattle to Fairbanks. As of November 1910, the survey crew had determined that the railroad was feasible with minimal grades (1-½ percent) and required a high point of only 2,735 feet. The decision by the federal government to support a Seward terminus for the Alaska Interior Railroad dampened efforts to construct the Haines route. By the first World War, the project was dead.

The Alaska and Northwestern Railway Company, incorporated under the laws of West Virginia, planned to build from Portage Cove on Lynn Canal to the international boundary, a distance of 36 miles. This firm filed its proposal in May 1898.

Just after the turn of the century, a Chicago company proposed a railroad from Iliamna on Cook Inlet north to the Kuskokwim River, along its upper course, and across the divide to Nulato at a point where the Koyukuk flows into the Lower Yukon. From Nulato, the line was proposed to continue to Nome.

In 1891, a bill was introduced in the Senate authorizing the construction of a railroad in Alaska. The bill granted the Alaska Coal Mining and Development Company the right to construct a railroad and telegraph line on the most eligible route from Portage Bay to Herendeen Bay on the Bering Sea and to mine coal deposits on the Alaskan Peninsula.

Several railroads were planned for the Nome-Seward Peninsula area, all of which were abandoned before actual construction began. They are listed here:

- The Norton Bay and Yukon Railway and Navigation Company of Washington, which planned to build from Norton Bay to the Yukon River, a distance of 76.5 miles, with extensions. Filings were in October 1898.
- The Bering Sea Council City Railroad was another that was planned but soon fell by the wayside. It was a New Jersey corporation.
- Another was the Nebraska, Kansas, and Gulf Railway Company of Kansas, with plans to build from Nome to Port Clarence and from Nome to Golovin Sound, a total distance of 227.12 miles. Filings were made in July 1901.
- The Yukon River and Bering Strait Railroad Company planned to build from Teller City on Grantly Harbor to Council City, with various branches. Filing was in January 1901.
- The DeSoto Mining Company planned to build a standard-gauge line from Nome to Council City according to Dr. DeSoto, president of the firm. This road, pro-

posed during the summer of 1903, would go by way of Osborne Creek and St. Michael Gulch, from there across country, tapping the Eldorado, Bonanza, and Solomon districts, along with the Casadepogo and the Neukluk.

- The Tin City and Arctic Railroad Company of Washington planned to build from Lost River on the Bering Sea to a point near Shishmaref Inlet, a distance of 20 miles. Filings were in November 1904.
- The Alaska Northern Railroad Company of Maine (not to be confused with the Alaska Northern, which eventually became part of the Alaska Railroad) planned to build northwesterly from Port Clarence, a distance of 68 miles. Filings were in April 1906.
- Another was the Alaska Coast Line Railroad Company of Alaska, planned as a route from Nome along the coast of the Bering Sea to the U.S. Military Reservation at Port Clarence. Filings were in November 1907.

The Unuk River Mining and Smelting Company proposed an electric railroad to be built from Ketchikan to the Unuk River (Burroughs Bay) to tap gold and silver resources in the area. It was never constructed, although a wagon road operation was completed over a similar 42-mile route in 1906.

There were other railroads proposed too, of which little was heard after their filings with the Land Office of the Department of the Interior:

The Alaska-Yukon Railroad and Navigation Company of New Jersey proposed to build from the Unalaklik River on North Sound to the junction of the Kaltag and Yukon Rivers, a distance of 79.19 miles. This proposal was filed in March 1899.

Another proposed line was the Pacific Alaska Transportation and Coal Company of New Jersey, which planned a route from Portage Bay to Herendeen Bay and from Northwest Harbor to the mouth of the Chignik River, with branches to other areas. The filing was in January 1903.

The Setuck Company of Washington proposed to build a railroad from a point near Ocean Cape to a point near Setuck River with two spur lines. The total length of trackage was 12 miles. The filing was in January 1903.

The Alaska Coke and Coal Company of California proposed a 10-mile line from the Yukon River, along Washington Creek to California Creek. The filing was in January 1903.

The Juneau, Douglas, and Treadwell Railroad Company of Washington filed in October 1902 to build from Juneau to Douglas, a distance of 6 miles.

The Alaska Southern Railway Company of Washington filed in February 1907 to build from the city limits of Juneau to the city limits of Douglas via a 7.2-mile route.

The defining characteristic of North America during the latter half of the 19th century and the early decades of the 20th century was expansionism. Hand in hand with expansionism was the development of a rail system to exploit the natural resources and support a (hopefully) burgeoning population base. The Alaska-Yukon region was no different from literally dozens of developing areas that had gone before. The entrepreneurs planned many railroads but constructed few in their fervor to secure wealth in the land of opportunity.

Stock certificate for the Trans-Alaskan Railroad Company, just one of many promotions by organizers of railroads in various parts of the Alaska territory. This one was organized in 1913 under the laws of the state of Arizona to operate from Iliamna Bay near the mouth of Cook Inlet to Railroad City near Holy Cross, a distance of about 350 miles. (Clifford Collection)

Index

Italic page numbers refer to items in photos or information in photo captions.

A

Abercrombie Canyon, Alaska, 174, 179, 182–183, 185, *193*
Acklen, J. A., 12
aerial tramways, *4*, 11
air transportation, 29–32
Akron, Sterling, and Northern Railroad Company, 160
Alaska, Copper River, and Yukon Railroad Company, 161, 162
Alaska and Northwestern Railway Company, 10, 238
Alaska Anthracite Coal and Railway Company, 177
Alaska Bank and Trust Company, 217
Alaska Central Railroad Company, 159–160
Alaska Central Railway
 background, 75–76
 construction headquarters, *75*
 construction of line, 76–79
 finances, 75, 80
 northbound special, *81*
 prospectus title page, *81*
 rail route, 76
 in receivership, 82
 reorganized as Alaska Northern Railway, 82
 Seward as terminus, 76, *76–79*
 snowplow, *78*
 steam locomotives
  early locomotives, *77, 80*
  No. 1, *77, 78, 79*
  roster, 82
Alaska Coal Mining and Development Company, 238
Alaska Coast Copper Company, 166
Alaska Coast Steamship Company, 166
Alaska Coast Transportation Company, 169
Alaska Coke and Coal Company, 177, 239
Alaska Development Company, 166, 177
Alaska Engineering Commission. *See* Alaskan Engineering Commission
Alaska-Gastineau Mining Company Railroad, 224–225, 228
Alaska Gulf and Yukon Railway Company, 162
Alaska Highway, 29, *33*, 33–34, 59, 235
Alaska Home Railroad Company, 159, *164*, 165–169, *167, 168*

Alaska-Juneau Gold Mine Railroad, 224, *224*, 228
Alaskaland, 97, *144*
Alaska Lumber and Pulp Company, 226, 229–230
Alaska Marble Company Tramway, 226
Alaska Midland Railroad, 237–238
Alaska Moving Picture Corporation, *107*
Alaskan and Northwestern Company. *See* Alaskan and Northwestern Territories Trading Company
Alaskan and Northwestern Territories Trading Company, 7
Alaskan Engineering Commission
 as builder of Government Railroad, 93–102
 dissolution of, 102
 initial surveying tasks, 89–90
 members, 89
 narrow-gauge locomotives, 91–92
 narrow-gauge railcar used between Nenana and Fairbanks, *132*
 rehabilitation of Alaska Northern Railroad, 85–86
 steam locomotives
  No. 151, *114*
  No. 802, *116*
  roster, 91–92
 in take over of Tanana Valley Railroad, 98, 145, 151
Alaska Northern Railway
 as Alaska Railroad, 91
 background, 83
 construction of gravel train, *84*
 financial problems, 84–85
 purchase of by U.S. government, 90–91
 reconstruction of, 96, 98
 rehabilitation by Alaskan Engineering Commission, 85–86
 steam locomotive roster, 86
 as successor to Alaska Central, 75
Alaska-Northwestern Railroad Company, 237
Alaska-Pacific Coast Company, 177
Alaska Pacific Express Company, 213
Alaska-Pacific Railroad, 176–177
Alaska-Pacific Railway and Terminal Company, 172, 173–174
Alaska Petroleum and Coal Company, 177
Alaska Petroleum and Gas Company, 177
Alaska Railroad. *See also* Government Railroad
 administration of, 106–107
 after completion, 103–104

Alaska Railroad *(continued)*
 Anchorage machine shop and coach shed fire, 105
 vs. British Yukon Navigation Company, 28
 closing of Matanuska Valley branch, 107
 completion from Seward to Fairbanks, 102
 diesel locomotives, *130, 131, 133, 136*
  diagrams of, *126*
  No. 1000, *127*
  No. 1001, *128*
  No. 1050, *129*
  No. 1526, *131*
  No. 2502, *131*
  roster, 124–125, 127–132, 134–141
 driving of golden spike, 101–102, *102*
 fiftieth anniversary ceremony, *102*
 impact of 1964 earthquake, 108–110, *112, 113*
 impact of trans-Alaska oil pipeline, 111, 169
 impact of World War II, 104
 list of general managers, 106–107
 map of route from Seward to Fairbanks, *133*
 ownership transferred from federal government to state of Alaska, 111
 Panama Canal connection, 95
 postwar rehabilitation of, 104–106
 proposals to sell, 110
 rail bus "Ice Worm," *134*
 railcar No. 215, *114*
 railcar roster, 142–144
 river transportation service, 97
 scenic Loop, elimination of, 105–106, *108, 109*
 services available in 1999, 112
 steam locomotives, *46, 133*
  200 series, *128*
  300 series, *117*
  400 series, *118*
  first, *94*
  last, 107
  No. 1, *116*
  No. 31, *96*
  No. 225, *99*
  No. 285, *96*
  No. 312, *117*
  No. 315, *117*
  No. 502, *118*
  No. 551, *119*
  No. 556, *121, 123*
  No. 557, 107, *121, 122*

Alaska Railroad (continued)
    No. 562, 120
    No. 605, 99
    No. 610, 113
    No. 701, 125
    No. 801, 124
    roster, 115–123
    shops in Anchorage, 110
    switching, 138
    as successor to Alaska Central, 75
    as successor to Alaska Northern Railway, 91
    as successor to Government Railroad, 91, 102
    unsuccessful proposal of, 162
    Whittier Cutoff branch, 104
Alaska Railroad Act, 85, 90
Alaska Railroad Commission, 85, 87–88
Alaska Railroad Corporation, 111
Alaska Railway and Transportation Company, 11
Alaska Road Commission, 214, 220, 221
Alaska Rural Rehabilitation Corporation, 104
Alaska Short Line Railway and Navigation Company, 234
Alaska Southern Railway Company, 239
Alaska Southern Wharf Company, 11
Alaska Steamship Company, 62, 156, 180
Alaska Syndicate
    and Battle of Keystone Canyon, 166, 166–168
    and Copper River & Northwestern, 84–85, 172, 180
    formation of, 164, 180
    impact of, 90
    purchase of Copper River Railroad, 183
    rivalry with Alaska-Pacific workers, 173
Alaska Territorial Act, 85
Alaska-Yukon Railroad and Navigation Company, 239
Alberta Railway and Coal Company, 219, 220
Alcan Highway. See Alaska Highway
Alsek River, Alaska, 156
American and Canadian Transportation Company, 10
American Bridge Company, 100, 101
American Trans-Siberian Company, 233
American Yukon Navigation Company, 97
Anchorage, Alaska. See also Ship Creek, Alaska
    Alaska Railroad steam locomotive No. 556 on display, 121, 123
    first business in, 95
    incorporation of city, 100
    land sale in, 95
Anderson, Robert H., 107
Andrews, C. M., 76
Angelo American Corporation of Canada, 36
Anglo-American Construction Company, 162
animals. See dog teams; draft animals; horse-drawn tramcars; pack animals
Antonelle and Nelson, 165

Anvil Creek, Alaska, 203, 204, 205, 206, 209
Apollo Consolidated Mining Company, 227, 229
Army Corps of Engineers, 104
Atlin, British Columbia gold strike, 24, 57–58
Atlin Consolidated Mining Company Railroad, 223
Atlin Short Line Railway and Navigation Company, 57–58
Atlin Southern Railway Company, 60
aviation, and White Pass & Yukon, 29–32

B

Baird Glacier, Alaska, 192
Baldwin, George F., 162
Ballaine, Frank, 77, 79
Ballaine, John F., 75, 77, 78–79, 81, 84
Ballinger-Pinchot controversy, 175
Bannister, F. D., 161
barges, 23, 35, 37, 38, 97, 108
Bartlett, Bob, 237
Bartlett Glacier, Alaska, 82, 105–106, 108
Bates, Llewellyn N., 63
battery locomotives, 142
Bean, Edward, 5
Beatson copper mines, 180
Bellingham Canning Company, 155
Bell Telephone Company, 212
Bering River coal fields, 159, 171, 172, 173, 175–176, 177, 179, 180, 181, 197
Bering River Railroad Company, 175
Bering Strait, 160, 233–234
Berners Bay Gold Manufacturing Company Railroad, 223, 224
Berry, M. P., 8
Billinghurst, E. E., 5
Bliss, Cornelius N., 7, 8
Bonanza Copper Mines, 180, 181
Bonanza Creek, Canadian Klondyke Mining Company construction camp, 67
Bone, Scott C., 102
Bookwalter, Vernon, 29–30
Boulder-Alaska Copper Company, 165
Brackett, George A.
    charging of tolls on wagon road out of Skagway, 4, 12–13
    as leader of Skagway & Yukon Transportation and Improvement Company, 12
    as wagon-road builder, 3, 4, 12–13
    and White Pass & Yukon Route, 16
Brackett Wagon Road
    advertisement for, 5
    construction of, 3, 4, 12–13
    hardships of travel along, 6
    toll gates along, 4, 12–13
    use of pack animals, 7
Bradshaw, Frank, 161
Brady, John C., 165
Brammall, Roger, 71
bridges
    Brackett Wagon Road, 3, 4, 12, 13
    and Bullen Bridge Company, 12

bridges (continued)
    Copper River, 185–193, 187, 188, 189, 192, 194, 195
    Dead Horse Gulch, 22, 53
    East Fork of Skagway River, 12, 13
    Gilahina River, 193
    Hurricane Gulch, 100, 100–101, 101
    Kuskulana River Gorge, 192, 194, 195
    log bridges on Brackett Wagon Road, 3, 4, 13
    Miles Glacier, 185–192, 187, 188, 189, 192, 202
    Tanana River, 101
    on White Pass & Yukon Route, 34
Brill gas-electric railcars, 152
British-American Transportation Company, 9
British Columbia Development Company, 5
British Columbia Yukon Railway Company, 16
British Yukon Company, 5
British Yukon Navigation Company, 26, 28
British Yukon Railway Company, 16
Brooks, Alfred H., 87, 87
Brownlee, J. H., 58
Bruce, Miner W., 7
Bruner, Dr. M. W., 173
Bryntesen, John, 204
bucket tramways, 11
Buckner, General Simon B., 104
Bullen, C. A., 12
Bullen Bridge Company, 12
Burns's Hoist, 11
Burrall and Baird Limited, 72

C

Caine, Capt. E. C., 76
Cameron, Valdez, 167, 169
Campbell, John, 8
Campbell, John A., 177
Canadian Development Company, 26, 62
Canadian Development Corporation, 58
Canadian government, and Klondike Mines Railway and Stage Company, 63–68
Canadian Klondyke Mining Company, 67, 72
Canadian National Railway, 236
Canadian Pacific Airlines, 29, 32
Canadian Pacific Railway, 236
Cannon Ball Express, 218
Canol pipeline system, 33
Canyon and White Horse Rapids Railway, 61–62, 62
Cape Prince of Wales, Alaska, 233, 236, 237
Carcross (Caribou Crossing), Yukon Territory
    rail connection with Whitehorse, 24
    Torpedo Catcher barge trip to, 22–23
    White Pass & Yukon train at, 55
Carlson, August, 70
Catalla and Carbon Mountain Railroad Company, 174, 177
Chamberlain, Senator, 88
Chatanika, Alaska, 146, 152

Index

Cheechakos, The (film), *107*
Chena, Alaska, 146, *146*, 147
Cheyenne Creek, Alaska, 214
Chiamis, Sam, *102*
Childs Glacier, Alaska, 179
Chilkat and Yukon Railway Company, 10
Chilkat Inlet, Alaska, 9
Chilkat Inlet Railway and Navigation Company, 10
Chilkat Oil Company, 171
Chilkat River, Alaska, 10, 88
Chilkoot Pass, Alaska
   aerial tramways along, *4*
   illustrated, *2*
   packing goods over, 11
   as proposed rail route, 1, 8, 9, 88
   vs. White Pass, 1, 11, 12
Chilkoot Pass and Summit Railroad Company, 9
Chilkoot Pass Transportation Company, 9
Chilkoot Railroad and Transport Company, 11
Chilkoot Railroad and Transportation Company, 9
Chitina, Alaska, 173, 193
Chute, Jerome, *63*, 64
Clear Creek, Alaska, 175
Clifford J. Rogers (ship), 35
Close Brothers firm, 13, 14, 145, 174, 179, 183
coal, 70, 72, 107, 159, 179, 238. *See also* Bering River coal fields
Coal Creek, Alaska, 214
Coal Creek Coal Company, 70, 72, 73
Cohen, Abraham, 8
Columbia and Puget Sound Railroad, 11, *44, 46*
container ships, 35, 37, *38*
container trucks, 35, *35*, 36
container unit trains, *36*, 55
Controller Bay, Alaska, 175, 177
Controller Bay and Navigation Company, 177
Cook Inlet Coal Field Company Railroad, 227, 229
copper, 159, 171, 172, 179. *See also* Copper River & Northwestern Railway Company
Copper River, Alaska, 159, 160, 177, 179, 181. *See also* Abercrombie Canyon, Alaska
Copper River and Yukon Railway Company, 160
Copper River flats, 184–185, *185*, 186
Copper River & Northwestern Railway Company
   abandonment of, 198–199
   in Alaska Railroad Commission report, 88
   bridge construction, 185–193, *187, 188, 189, 192, 194, 195*
   completion of railroad, 197, *198*
   construction of line, 183–193, *184, 185, 186, 187, 188, 189, 190, 193, 194, 195, 196, 197, 197*
   early records, 163
   and Guggenheim-Morgan partnership, 84–85, 172, 180

Copper River & Northwestern Railway Company (continued)
   equipment acquisition from Valdez-Yukon Railroad, 169
   key personnel also involved with White Pass & Yukon, *16*, 25
   move of operations from Valdez to Katalla, 164, 172
   vs. other proposed builders, 159, 172
   rivalry with Alaska-Pacific Railway and Terminal Company, 173–174
   route map, *201*
   steam locomotives
      No. 20, *199*
      No. 23, *202*
      roster, 199–200
   success of, 197–198
   as tourist attraction, 197–198, *202*
Copper River Railroad
   first spike driven, 181
   planning and construction of, 174, 180–182
   sold to Alaska Syndicate, 183
Copper River Valley, 159, 162, 163, 180
Cordova, Alaska, 174, 180, *181, 182*, 183, 197
corduroy roads, 9
Council City, Alaska, 203, *203*, 207, 211, 213, 214
Council City & Solomon River Railroad, 208, 211–216, *213, 214*
Cox, Leonard M., 87, *87*
Crooked Creek and Whiskey Island Railroad, 227
Cunningham, Clarence, 180
Curry, Dave, *64*
Curtis Condor, 31, *31*

D

Davis, Clark, 174
Davis, H. C., 217
Davis, T. A., 217
Dawson, Grand Forks and Stewart River Railway Company of London, 66
Dawson, Yukon Territory
   Klondike short line railways, 69–74
   Minto Park display of railroad and mining equipment, 66, *66*, *70*
   proposed rail route to, 162
   as terminus of Klondike Mines Railway, *63*, 64–65
   transportation to Whitehorse, 28, 29, 30–32
   view of downtown in 1904, *67*
Dawson Electric Light and Power Company, 70, 72, 145
Dead Horse Gulch, *22*, *53*
Dead Horse Trail, *7*, 11
DeLamar, Capt. J. R., 161
Delano, Frederic A., 235
deLargero, F. C., *125, 133*
Denny, Charles L., 76
de Pascal, Tony, 173
Detroit Yukon Mining Company, *48*, 70, 71, 72, 73–74
Dickinson, C. W., 75, *77*, 81
Dickson, Alaska, *211, 212*, 212–213, *216*

Dickson, J. Warren, 211, 212, 213, 215, 217
Ditmeyer, Stephen A., 107
Dixon, Duncan, 166
dog teams, *13*, 148–149, *151, 152*, 219, *220*, 221
Dollywood Park, *50*
Dorcy, William, 107
Douglas, Alaska, 225
Dowdle, John, 80
draft animals, 149, 221. *See also* dog teams; horse-drawn tramcars
Duchess (of Wellington) locomotive, *58*, 59
Duke, Emma, 96
Duke, James, 96
Dyea, Alaska, 8, 9, 11
Dyea-Klondike Transportation Company, 11

E

Eagle City, Alaska, 160, 161, 162
earthquake, 1964, Alaska
   damage to Miles Glacier bridge, *189*, 199
   impact on Alaska Railroad, 108–110, *112, 113*
Eccles, S. W., 197
Edes, William C., 89, 93, 99
Edison-Beech storage battery railcars, 151, 152
Emanuel, Ernest S., 211
Emanuel, J. H. Jr., 211
English, James, *192*
Ernestine Pass, 159
Eska, Alaska, 99–100
Evans Jones Coal Company, 142
excursion trains. *See also* tourist railroads
   Klondike Mines Railway, *64*
   Tanana Valley Railroad, *150*
   White Pass & Yukon, *47*
   Wild Goose Railroad, *209*
explosives, transporting, 148
Eyak, Alaska, 181, *181*. *See also* Cordova, Alaska

F

Fairbanks, Alaska
   completion of Alaska Railroad to Seward, 93–102
   growth of community, 150
   map of Alaska Railroad route from Seward, *133*
   proposed rail links with Russia and Canada, 235–236
   proposed rail link with Seattle, 237–238
   rail extension to airport, 111
   and Tanana Valley Railroad, *145*, 146, 147, 149, 150
Federal Emergency Relief Administration, 104
Federal Industries Ltd., 36
Fisher, Walter, 85, 87
Flannery, David, 5
Foy, Mr., *16*
Fraser Lake, British Columbia, 56
French, Major L. H., 217

Frost, A. C., 81

G

Garside, George W., 9
Gedney, Jerome D., 214
Gilahina River Bridge, Alaska, 193
Gila Monster locomotive, *49*
Godwin, J. W., 75
golden spike ceremonies
    Alaska Railroad from Seward to Fairbanks, 101–102, *102*
    White Pass & Yukon Railway from Skagway to Whitehorse, 24–25
gold rush, impact on transportation, 3–4, 5, 9
Goldstream Creek, Alaska, 147–148
Golofin Bay Railway, *204*, 207–208, 210
Goose City, Alaska, 177
Goose City Railroad, 175
Gorman & Company, 155
Goulding Railroad, 227
Government Railroad
    construction by Alaskan Engineering Commission, 93–102
    Fairbanks division, 96
    first locomotive, *94*
    first spike driven, 93, *93*
    Hurricane Gulch Bridge construction, *100*, 100–101, *101*
    impact of World War I, 98–99
    Northern and Southern Divisions abolished, 100
    river transportation service, 96
    as successor to Alaska Central, 75
    Susitna Route chosen, 93
    transition to Alaska Railroad, 91, 102
    workers on construction project, 93–95
Grand Forks, Yukon Territory, 66
Grand Trunk Pacific Railroad, 234
Graves, Samuel H., *11*, 14, 16, *16*, 179
Guggenheim and Sons, 27, 164, 180
Guggenheim-Morgan partnership, 84, 163, 164, *166*, 166–168, 172, 173, 174, 182–183. See also Alaska Syndicate

H

Haight, J. A., 83
Haines Mission, Alaska, 10
Haines Mission and Boundary Railroad Company, 10
Hamilton, T. A., 177
Hammond, John Hays, 162
Hanging Rocks, Alaska, *28*
Hansen, F. A., 183
Harding, Warren G., 91, 101–102, *102*, *144*
Harris, Rich, 81
Hasey, Ed C., 166, 167, 168
Hastedt, W., 104
Hatcher Pass, Alaska, *107*
Hatfield, Robert, 107
Hawkins, Erastus C., 14, *16*, 25, 64, 174, 182, 183, 189, 191, *192*, 193, 197, *198*
Hawkins, H. L., 175, 179, 183
Hazelette, George C., 163, 175, 180
Healy, John J., 70, 160

Healy & Wilson's Trading Post, 8
Hedican, Dan, *192*
Heiden Canyon, Alaska, 159
Heinze, Herman, 211
Henderson, George, 217
Heney, Michael J.
    as builder of White Pass & Yukon, *16*, 17–18, 25
    and Copper River project, 164, 172, 174, 179, *179*, 180–187, *192*, 193, 196, *198*
    death of, 193–194, 196, 197, *198*
    St. James Hotel meeting, *9*, *13*, 15
    and Valdez-Eagle Railroad, 161
Heney, Patrick A., 174, 183
Hepburn, John, *61*, 62
Herron, Sam, 8
Hickel, Walter J., 237
Hislop, John, *16*
Holm, Monte, 107, *122*
Home Railroad Company. See Alaska Home Railroad
Homestead Act, 13
Hoover, Herbert, 102
Hopper, Dr. William, 212–213
horse-drawn tramcars, *57*, *61*, *62*
Huron, Herbert S., 104
Hurricane Gulch Bridge, *100*, 100–101, *101*
hydraulic mining, 27

I

"Ice Worm" rail bus, *134*
Iditarod Trail, 84
Iles, Alfred B., 161, 162
Iliamna Bay, Alaska, 234, 238
Ingersoll, Charles E., 167
Ingersoll, John M., 87, *87*
Ingram, John W., *102*
Interstate Commerce Commission, 148
Irving (John) Navigation Company, 26, 58
Isthmian Canal Commission, 95, *96*, 99, 116

J

Jelm, F. C., 162
Jemmett, F. C., 83
Johanson, Carl, 70
Johnson, John P., 107
Johnson, Walter S., 107
Jones, Frank H., 107
Jones Coal Company, 142
Joslin, Falcon, 70, 145, 175
Juneau, Alaska, 224, 225
Juneau, Douglas, and Treadwell Railroad Company, 239

K

Kalbaugh, Frank E., 107
Kanak Island, Alaska, 174
Katalla, Alaska. See also Bering River coal fields
    aftermath of regional winter storms, *175*, *176*
    as boomtown, *171*, 171–173, 178
    oil activity, 171, 178

Katalla, Alaska *(continued)*
    as operations headquarters for Copper River & Northwestern, 164, 172
    as part of route surveys, 164, 172, 180
    problems as shipping port, 171, 172–173, 183
    role in Prince William Sound railroad construction, 171–178
Katalla Coal Company Railroad, 175
Katalla Company, 172, *172*, 174, 176, 177
Kayak Island, Alaska, 175
Keep, A. Dwight, 211
Kelly, Charles, 12
Kenai Mountains, Alaska, 83
Kennecott mines, Alaska, 180, *191*
Kesler, E. R., 80
Ketchikan, Alaska, 226, 239
Ketchikan and Northern Terminal Company, 226
Ketchikan Pulp Company, 226, 230
Keystone Canyon
    battle between Guggenheim and Home Railroad workers, *166*, 166–168
    as element in Copper River rail route, 159, 163–164
Keystone Construction Company, 173
Klehane River, Alaska, 10
Klondike City, Yukon Territory, 64, 65, 66
Klondike Kate, *49*
Klondike Mines Railway
    acquisition by Yukon Consolidated Gold Corporation, 68
    advertisement for, *65*
    background, 63
    finances, 67
    first excursion train, *64*
    hauling of cord wood on, *65*
    rail route, 63, 64–66
    steam locomotives
        No. 1, *66*, 66
        No. 2, *45*, *46*, *66*, 66
        No. 3, *65*, *66*, 66
        No. 4, *47*, 66–67
        roster, 68
Klondike River Bridge, *63*
Knowlton, Theodore, 214
Koch, William, 167
Krutzsch, August, 221
Kuhn, Loeb, & Company, 164
Kush-Ta-Ka Southern Railroad Company, 174, 175
Kuskulana River Bridge, Alaska, 192, *194*, *195*
Kuzitrim River, Alaska, 217, 218

L

Lacey, Bill, 13
Lake Atlin, British Columbia, 9
Lake Bennett, Canada
    completion of White Pass & Yukon to, 19, 20–23, *25*
    log church, *51*
    proposed rail route from Skagway Bay, 1, 9
    proposed wagon road from Skagway Bay, 7–8
    use of barges on, 23

Lake Bennett, Canada *(continued)*
  view of container unit trains, *36*
  as White Pass & Yukon terminus, *29*
Lake LaBerge, Yukon Territory, 26
Lake Linderman, Yukon Territory, 9
Lake Tagish, Canada, 9
Lamar, L. Q. C., 5
Landis, Lee H., 106
Lane, Charles D., 204–205, 207, 208
Lane, Franklin K., 89
Lane's Landing, Alaska, 217, 219
Larabee, O. G., 83
LaTouch-Alaska Copper Company, 166
Leoning Keystone Commuter amphibian aircraft, 30, *32*
Libby, McNeill, and Libby, 155
Lindbloom, Erik O., 204
Lindeborg, Jefet, 204, 208, 219, 220
Lloyd, John H., 107
Lobel, Baron Loug de, 234
locomotive rosters
  Alaska Central Railway, 82
  Alaska-Gastineau Mining Company, 228
  Alaska-Juneau Mining Company, 228
  Alaska Lumber and Pulp Company, 229–230
  Alaskan Engineering Commission, 91–92
  Alaska Northern Railway Company, 86
  Alaska Railroad, 115–125, 127–132, 134–141
  Apollo Consolidated Mining Company, 229
  Coal Creek Coal Company, 73
  Cook Inlet Coal Fields Company, 229
  Copper River & Northwestern Railway Company, 199–200
  Council City & Solomon River Railroad, 216
  Detroit Yukon Mining Company, 73–74
  Golofin Bay Railway, 210
  Ketchikan Pulp Company, 230
  Klondike Mines Railway and Stage Company, 68
  Nome-Arctic Railroad, 210
  Northern Light, Power, and Coal Company, 74
  Rush and Brown Copper Mine, 229
  Salmon Creek Dam Railroad, 228
  Seward Peninsula Railroad, 221–222
  Taku Tram, 60
  Tanana Mines Railway, 153–154
  Tanana Valley Railroad, 153–154
  U.S. Army Transportation Corps, 44–46, 48
  White Pass & Yukon Route, 37–41, 43, 44–46, 48, 50, 52, 55
  Wild Goose Railroad, 210
  Yakutat & Southern Railroad, 158
locomotives, battery, 142
locomotives, diesel. *See also* Alaska Railroad; White Pass & Yukon Route
  Alaska Railroad roster, 124–125, 127–132, 134–141
  White Pass & Yukon Route roster, 50, 52, 55

locomotives, diesel *(continued)*
  Yakutat & Southern Railroad, 156, *156*
locomotives, steam. *See also* locomotive rosters; *individual locomotives under names of specific railroads*
  0-4-0T, *116*
  0-4-2T, *226*
  0-4-4T, *214*
  0-6-0, 218–219, *220*
  0-8-0, *138*
  2-6-0, *43, 44, 66, 96, 99, 113, 128*
  2-6-2, *47*
  2-8-0, *118, 119, 120, 121, 123*, 190, *199, 202*
  2-8-2, *49, 50, 51, 96, 125*
  4-4-0, *77, 78, 148*
  4-6-0, *48*
  4-8-2, *124*
  Alaska Railroad roster, 115–123
  saddle-tankers, *48, 69, 71*, 95, *98, 103, 106, 111, 145, 146, 147, 152, 190, 223*
  White Pass & Yukon roster, 37–41, 43, 44–46, 48
London, Jack, 61
London Loan, Mortgage, and Trust Company, 161
loop trestles, *79*, 83–84, 105–106, *108, 109*
Lowe River Valley, Alaska, 159
Lynn Canal, Alaska, 5, 10, 11, 238
Lynn Canal and Short Line Railroad, 11

M

Macaulay, Norman D., 61, 62
Macaulay tramway, *61*, 61–62, *62*
MacKenzie & Mann, 9
Magee, Hugh F., 214
mail service, 26, 31–32
Maine Northwestern Development Company, 219
Manley, John E., 107
Mantasta Pass, Alaska, 161
maps, route
  Alaska Railroad from Seward to Fairbanks, *133*
  Copper River country, *201*
  White Pass & Yukon from Skagway to Whitehorse, *42*
Marshall Pass, Alaska, 159, 160
Martin, Thomas, 221
Martin Islands, Alaska, 173
Mason, Skookum Jim, 1
Matanuska Valley, Alaska, 98, 104, 107, 181
Mathews, E. A., 217
McConachie, Grant, *31*, 32
McCord, Jack, 174
McCune, W. L. M., *192*
McDonald, James F., 162
McGiverin, Harold, 63
McGraw, John H., 75
McKenzie, Alex, 208
McKenzie, D. A., 162
McPherson, J. L., 174
Mears, Frederick J., 89, 93, 99, 102
Miles Canyon, 61

Miles Canyon and Lewes River Tramway, *61*, 62
Miles Glacier, Alaska
  cantilever bridge, 185–192, *187, 188, 189, 192*, 199, *202*
  as element in Copper River rail route, 179
Mill Creek Flume and Manufacturing Company, 219
"Million Dollar" bridge, 185–192, *187, 188, 189, 192*, 199, *202*
Mills, W. R., 8
Monroe, W. N., 208
Monroe, William V., 205
Moore, Ben, 2–3, 5
Moore, Bernard, 8
Moore, Captain William (Billy)
  as Alaskan rail pioneer, 1–8
  as explorer of Skagway River route to Upper Yukon Valley, 1–2
  as fund-raiser for Alaskan and Northwestern Territories Trading Company, 7
  money-raising efforts, 5
  and pack trail from Skagway Bay to Summit Lake, 6, 7
  photograph, *1*
  as settler at Skagway, 2–3
Moore, J. M., 80
Moore Trail, *10*
moose, and railroads, 105
Moose Creek coal mining operations, *111*
Morgan, J. P., 84–85, 164, 180, 211
Morrow, Major J. J., 87, *87*
Moses Lake, Washington, 107, *122*
Mount McKinley Park Hotel, Alaska, 104
Mulvihill, Carl, 59
Munday, Charles F., 174
Murchison, Sam, 179, 183, *192*, 197
Myers, Frank, 8

N

Nash and Dowdle, 80
National Park Service, 104
Nebraska Midland locomotive, *49*
Nenana, Alaska, 96, 97, 151
Nenana River, Alaska, *114*
Nixon, Richard, 110
Noble, John W., 7
Nome, Alaska
  proposed rail routes to, 145–146, 160, 238–239
  as terminus of Wild Goose Railroad, 203, 204, *205*, 206, 207
  use of dog teams, 219, *220*, 221
  view of Seward Peninsula Railroad equipment, *218*
Nome-Arctic Railroad, 208, 210, 217
North American Transportation and Trading Company, *69*, 69–70
Northern Commercial Company, 97
Northern Light, Power, and Coal Company, 72, 74
Northern Pacific Railroad, 12
Northern Transportation Company, 28
North Slope, Alaska, 237

North Star Line. *See* Council City & Solomon River Railroad
Northwestern Commercial Company, 180, 212
Northwestern Development Company, 217, 219
Northwestern Railroad Company, 180. *See also* Copper River & Northwestern Railway Company
Northwest Fisheries, 180
Northwest Mounted Police, 61, *61*
Northwest Steamship Company, 180
Norton Sound, Alaska, 160
Nowell, George, 8
Noyes, Arthur J., 208

O
O'Brien, Johnny, 183, 197
O'Brien, Pat, *192*
O'Brien, Thomas W., 63, 64
Ogilvie, William, 1–2
Ohlson, Otto F., 106
Olds, Edward A., 211
Olsen, Chris, 167, 168
Olympia and Tenino Railway, *148*
O'Neill, A. C., 183, 186
O'Neill, William, 167
Ophir Creek, Alaska, 203, 207, 211
Oregon Railway and Navigation Railroad, 218
Osborne, H. C., 81

P
Pacific Alaska Airways, 32
Pacific Alaska Transportation and Coal Company, 239
Pacific and Yukon Railroad Company, 162
Pacific & Arctic Railway and Navigation Company, 10, *11*, 16
Pacific Coal and Oil Company, 175
Pacific Coast Company, 11
Pacific Northern and Omineca Railway Company, 60
pack animals, 7, 8, *12*
Packard, P. L., 9
pack trails, 5–6, 7, *8*, 11, 12. *See also* wagon roads
Panama Canal, 95. *See also* Isthmian Canal Commission
Parker, C. L., 161
Parsons, W. H., 64
Peabody, Charles E., 12, 62
Peck, Charles W., 76
Penelope Creek, Alaska, 214
Perseverence Mine, 225
Pioneer Hall, Skagway, Alaska, *28*
Pioneer Mining and Ditch Company, 219, *220*
pipelines, 29. *See also* trans-Alaska oil pipeline
Placer River Canyon, Alaska, 81
Portage, Alaska, impact of 1964 earthquake, 109, *112*
Portage Cove, Alaska. *See* Lynn Canal, Alaska
Port Clarence, Alaska, 160, 235
Pratt, William A., 9

Prince of Wales Island, Alaska, 225–226
Prince William Sound, Alaska, 159, 161. *See also* Katalla, Alaska
pupmobiles, 219, *220*
Pyramid Harbor, 10, 88

Q
Quigg, N. W., 177
Quinn, T. C., *168*
Quitsch, William, 167

R
rail bus "Ice Worm," *134*
railcars. *See also* locomotive rosters; locomotives, steam
  Alaskan Engineering Commission car used between Nenana and Fairbanks, *132*
  Alaska Railroad No. 215, *114*
  Alaska Railroad roster, 142–144
  The Denali, *144*
  private, *144*
rail-marine services, 26–29, 57–58, 97, 108. *See also* barges; container ships; steamers; stern-wheelers
railroads. *See also* locomotive rosters; *names of specific railroads*
  Alaskan Engineering Commission construction, 93–102
  construction of Copper River & Northwestern, 183–193, *184*, *185*, *186*, *187*, *188*, *189*, *190*, *193*, *194*, *195*, *196*, *197*, *197*
  construction of White Pass & Yukon, *10*, *14*, *15*, *16*, 16–22, *17*, *18*, *19*, *21*, *22*
  first proposed for Alaska, 8
  first trains on White Pass & Yukon, 17, *20*, *22*, *25*, *26*
  impact of Yukon gold rush on, 9
  proposed routes to Klondike gold fields, 8–10
  report of Alaska Railroad Commission, 88
Railway Act of 1898, 163–164
Reader, Charles M., 221
Red Ball Express, 20
Red Line Transportation Company, 19–20
Reinhardt, Fred, 167, 168
Resurrection Bay, Alaska. *See* Seward, Alaska
Reynolds, Henry Derr, 165, 166, 168, 169
Reynolds-Alaska Coal Company, 166
Reynolds Bank, 165, 169
Richardson, Wilds P., 214, 236
Riggs, Thomas Jr., 89, 93
river navigation. *See* rail-marine service
roadhouses, 27, 62
Robinson, Bill, 18–19, 20, 23, 25
Robinson, W. C., *192*
Rogers, Clifford J., 35
Rogers, M. K., 164, 172, 180
Rogers (ship), 35
Rose, William R., 63
Rosene, John, 163, 217, 237
rosters, locomotive. *See* locomotive rosters

roundhouses, 35, *40*, *41*, 59
route maps
  Alaska Railroad from Seward to Fairbanks, *133*
  Copper River country, *201*
  White Pass & Yukon from Skagway to Whitehorse, *42*
Rowan, Noble, 7
Royal Northwest Mounted Police, 18
Rush and Brown Copper Mine Railroad, 225–226, 229
Russia, proposed rail links with Alaska, 233–235

S
saddle-tankers, *48*, *69*, *71*, *95*, *98*, *103*, *106*, *111*, *145*, *146*, *147*, *152*, *190*, *223*
Salmon Creek Dam Railroad, 225, 228
Samson, David, 12
Scotia Bay, British Columbia, 57, 58
Seattle, Washington, proposed rail link with Fairbanks, 237–238
Seattle Sand and Gravel Company, 183
Setuck Company, 239
Seward, Alaska
  completion of Alaska Railroad to Fairbanks, 102
  impact of 1964 earthquake, 109, *113*
  land sale in, 95–96
  map of Alaska Railroad route to Fairbanks, *133*
  as railroad headquarters, 83, *84*
  as terminus of Alaska Central Railway, *76*, 76–79
Seward City, Alaska, 224
Seward Construction Company, 80
Seward Peninsula Railroad, 214, 217–222
Seybold, James A., 63
Shaw, Frank, 206
Shay locomotive, 72
Shedd, C. B., 78, 80, *81*
Shedd, E. A., 78, 80, *81*
Sheffield, William, 107
Shellcross-Richards Telephone Line, 11
Shelton, Alaska, 217, 218
Shields, A. W. "Archie," 183, *192*
Ship Creek, Alaska, 93, *94*, 95, *95*
Siberia, proposed rail links with Alaska, 233–235
Siemer, Henry, 70
Simpson, H. R. "Rotary Bill," *192*, 193
Sitka, Alaska, 226
Sitka syndicate, 9
Skagway, Alaska
  1897–1898 view of, *2*
  completion of White Pass & Yukon to Whitehorse, 24
  early history, 1, 2, 5
  and first White Pass & Yukon locomotive, *24*
  impact of gold rush on, 5
  improvements to wharf, 5
  map of White Pass & Yukon to Whitehorse, *42*
  pack trail to Summit Lake, 6, 7, 11
  proposed rail route from Dyea, 11

Skagway, Alaska *(continued)*
  proposed rail route to White Pass and beyond, 9, 10, 11
  proposed wagon road to Lake Bennett, 7–8
  St. James Hotel, *9, 13,* 15
  waterfront scenes, *50, 52*
  White Pass & Yukon depot in different eras, *54*
  White Pass & Yukon maintenance terminal, 27
  White Pass & Yukon roundhouse fire, 35, *41,* 59
  White Pass & Yukon tracks and trains on Broadway, *11, 28*
  during World War II, *33*
Skagway Airlines, 30
Skagway Bay, Alaska, first envisioned as gateway to Upper Yukon Valley, 1, 2, 5. *See also* Skagway, Alaska
Skagway-Carcross Highway, 36
Skagway & Yukon Transportation and Improvement Company, 12
Skookum Jim. *See* Mason, Skookum Jim
sledges. *See* sleds, White Pass & Yukon
sleds, White Pass & Yukon, 26, *30*. *See also* dog teams; horse-drawn tramcars
Small, Eugene, 217
Smith, C. J., 175
Smith, Donald J., 107
Smith, Jefferson Randolph (Soapy), 12, *12*
Smith, M. E., 183
Smith, Noel W., 106
Smith, Norman, 12
snowplows, *22, 51, 120, 148,* 193
Solomon, Alaska, 212, *212*
Solomon River, Alaska, 213
Sovereign Bank of Canada, 81, 82, 83
St. James Hotel, Skagway, Alaska, *13,* 15
State Agent and Transfer Syndicate, Inc., 163
steamers, 20, 57–58, 97, *197*. *See also* stern-wheelers
steam locomotive No. 802, Eagle Harbor, Alaska
steam locomotives. *See* locomotives, steam
stern-wheelers
  Alaska Railroad use of, 97
  Klondike refurbished for tourism, 29
  White Pass & Yukon use of, 26, 27–29, *30*
  Yukon on display at Dawson, *33*
Stevens, Mrs. Blamey, *167, 168,* 169
Stikine railroad route, 9
Stimson, F. S., 155
Stimson Lumber Company, 155
Sulphur Springs, Yukon Territory, 66
Summit Lake, White Pass, 19
Sumpter Valley Railroad, Oregon, *51*
Surrey, J. C., 183
Swartz, A. W., *79,* 163
Swineford, A. P., 6

T

Taft, William Howard, 85, 87
Taft Commission. *See* Alaska Railroad Commission
Tagish Lake, 57
Taku Arm (Taku Inlet), *9,* 57
Taku Tram, 57–58, 60
Tanana Construction Company, 77–78, 80, 81
Tanana Mines Railway, 145–147. *See also* Tanana Valley Railroad
  beginning of operation from Chena to Fairbanks, *146, 146,* 147
  construction of line, 146–147
  early locomotives, *145, 146,* 147
  steam locomotives
    No. 51, 147
    No. 52, 147
  roster, 153–154
Tanana River, Alaska, 96, *103,* 160, 180
Tanana River Bridge, 101
Tanana Valley Railroad
  and Edison-Beech storage battery railcars, 151, 152
  excursion train, *150*
  finances, 151
  at height of service, 149–150
  improvements to, 100, 146–147, 149, 151–152
  operations, 147–152
  sample time schedules, *147, 149*
  steam locomotives, *46, 145, 146,* 147, *148, 150, 151, 152, 153*
    No. 151, *103*
  roster, 153–154
  taken over by Alaskan Engineering Commission, 98, 145, 151
Tancrede, Sir Thomas, *9, 13,* 14, 15
Tanner and Clark Lumberyard, 212
teamsters, *4,* 20
Teslin Lake, Canada, 9
Thompson Pass, Alaska, 159
Thomson, Monty, 163
tide tables, 155
Tlingit Indians, 155
tolls, for pack trails, roads and bridges, *4, 6, 7–8, 12–13, 13*
tourist railroads. *See also* excursion trains
  Copper River & Northwestern Railway, 197–198, *202*
  Dollywood Park, *50*
  Sumpter Valley Railroad, Oregon, *51*
  White Pass & Yukon Route as, 37
tramways
  aerial, *4*
  Alaska Marble Company Tramway, *226*
  Atlin Short Line Railway and Navigation Company, 57–58
  Canyon and White Horse Rapids Railway, 61–62, *62*
  horse-drawn, *57, 61, 62*
  Macaulay Tramline, *61,* 61–62, *62*
  Miles Canyon and Lewes River Tramway, *61, 62*
  Taku Tram, 60
Trans-Alaska Company, 235
Trans-Alaskan Railroad Company, *240*
trans-Alaska oil pipeline
  impact on Alaska Railroad, 111, 169

trans-Alaska oil pipeline *(continued)*
  impact on Valdez, Alaska, *160,* 169
Trans-Alaska Railroad Company, 160–161
Trans-Alaska Railroad & Navigation Company, 234–235
Trans-Alaska Siberian Company, 234
Trans-Canadian Alaska Railroad, 235–236
Transportation Act, 159
Treadwell Mine Railroad, 225
trestles. *See also* bridges
  Kuzitrim River, Alaska, 217–218
  loop, *79, 83–84, 105–106, 108, 109*
troop sleepers, *104*
trucks, as locomotives, *158*
truck transportation, 29, 35, *35, 36*
tundra, 204, 205, 206, 211, *213,* 216, 218, *220*
Tunnel Mountain, Alaska, *15,* 16–17, *17, 19*
Turnagain Arm, Alaska, *79, 84, 94, 112*
Turpin, Frank, 107
Tusnuna River, Alaska, 159
Tutshi steamer, *58,* 59

U

United Air Transport, 32
Unuk River Mining and Smelting Company, 239
U.S. Army Corps of Engineers, 104
U.S. Department of the Interior, 89
  and Alaska Northern Railway, 85, 87
  and Alaskan trail applications, 5, 6, 7
U.S. Government Railroad. *See* Government Railroad
U.S. Interstate Commerce Commission, 148

V

Valdez, Alaska
  and Alaska Home Railroad, *164,* 165–169, *167, 168*
  in early 20th century, *160*
  loss of Copper River & Northwestern operations to Katalla, 164, 172
  proposed rail routes from, 159–163
  and trans-Alaska oil pipeline, *160,* 169
Valdez, Copper River, and Tanana Railroad Company, 159, 162, 163
Valdez, Copper River, and Yukon Railroad Company, 162
Valdez, Marshall Pass, and Northern Railroad Company, 162
Valdez and Copper River Railroad, 161
Valdez and Copper River Railway Company, 162
Valdez-Eagle Railroad, 161
Valdez Trail, 180
Valdez-Yukon Railroad Company, 159, *161,* 163, *166,* 169
Van Cleve, J. R., 183
Van Clive, J. R., *192*
Vancouver, British Columbia, proposed links with Alaska and Russia, 236, 237
Vilas, William F., 5

W

wagon roads
  Brackett's road from Skagway to White Pass, 3, *3*, 12–13
  and construction of White Pass & Yukon Route, 10
  proposed through White Pass, 5, 7–8, 12
Wallace, Henry, 102
Wallace, Hugh C., 11
Walla Walla and Columbia River Railroad, 218
Wann, Clyde, 30
Washington and Alaska Steamship Company, 12
Wasson, Ed, 30–31
Weatly, A. H., 83
Welch & Company, 81
Western Alaska Construction Company, 211, *211*
Western Railroad, 235–236
Wheeler, Herbert, 29, 30, 32
Wheeler, Samuel O., 5
White, Babe, 93, *93*
White, Thomas, 1
Whitehead, Cable, 217
Whitehorse, Yukon Territory
  completion of White Pass & Yukon from Skagway, 24
  log depot, *56*
  map of White Pass & Yukon from Skagway, *42*
  rail connection with Carcross, 24
  river transportation to Dawson, 28, 29, 30–32
  White Pass & Yukon highway division headquarters, *37*
  White Pass & Yukon roundhouse fire, 35
  as White Pass & Yukon terminus, *30*, *31*
White Horse Rapids, Yukon Territory, 61
White Pass (railroad). *See also* White Pass & Yukon Route
  first envisioned as entry point to Yukon gold fields, 2
  naming of, 16
White Pass (trail)
  vs. Chilkoot Pass route, 1, 11, 12
  early travel across, 7, *8*, 11, 12
  first gold prospectors to travel, 4
  first trip from Skagway Bay to Lake Bennett, 1–2
  naming of, 1
White Pass & Yukon Corporation, 35, 36
White Pass & Yukon Railway Company, Ltd., 16
White Pass & Yukon Route. *See also* British Yukon Navigation Company
  abandonment of airline business, *31*, 32
  addition of aviation division, 29–32
  addition of river navigation services, 26–29
  addition of wholesale petroleum business, 29
  in Alaska Railroad Commission report, 88
  along Fraser Lake, *56*
  construction of line, *10*, *14*, *15*, 16, 16–22, *17*, *18*, *19*, *21*, *22*

White Pass & Yukon Route *(continued)*
  construction of roadhouses, 27
  container ships, 35, 37, *38*
  container trucks and other cargo units, 35, *35*, *36*
  container unit trains, *36*, 55
  decline after World War II, 35
  defined, 16
  diesel locomotives
    No. 90, *52*, *53*
    roster, 50, 52, 55
  earnings of, 22
  as excursion train, *47*
  financing source, 5
  first locomotive, *24*
  first trains over summit, 17, *20*, 22, *25*, *26*
  highway division headquarters at Whitehorse, *37*
  impact of World War II on, *33*, 33–35
  key construction personnel, *16*
  key personnel also involved with Copper River & Northwestern, *16*, 25
  Klondike stern-wheeler refurbished for tourism, *29*
  last steam locomotive, 35
  locomotive rosters
    diesel/gas, 50, 52, 55
    steam, 37–41, 43, 44–46, 48
    U.S. Army Transportation Corps, 44–46, 48
  map of route from Skagway to Whitehorse, *42*
  number of workers, 25–26
  purchase of Irving Navigation Company, 58
  purchase of Northern Transportation Company, 28
  rail route, 26, *42*
  role of Captain William (Billy) Moore, 1–3, 4–7, 8
  roundhouse fire, 35, *41*, *59*
  Skagway roundhouse facilities, 35, *40*, *41*, *59*
  snowplows, *22*, *51*
  steam locomotives
    last, 35
    No. 2, *24*
    No. 4, *46*, *47*
    No. 5, *45*, *46*
    No. 7, *28*
    No. 51, *44*, *59*
    No. 52, *24*, *41*, *43*, 59
    No. 59, *48*
    No. 69, *49*
    No. 70, *50*
    No. 73, *51*
    No. 81, *51*
    roster, 37–41, 43, 44–46, 48
  successful proposal for U.S. section of railway, 10
  terminus at Lake Bennett, 29
  terminus at Whitehorse, *30*, *31*
  three railroads in, *11*
  as tourist line, 37

White Pass & Yukon Route *(continued)*
  tracks and trains on main street in Skagway, *11*, *28*
  trestles and bridges, *34*
  and truck transportation, 29, 35, *35*, *36*
Whiting, Dr. F. B., *16*, 25, 183, *192*
Whitman, Reginald N., 107
Whittier, Alaska
  Alaska Railroad branch to, 104, *105*, *133*
  rail-marine services, 108
  switching locomotive being unloaded, *138*
Wickersham, James, 88, 147
Wild Goose Mining and Trading Company, 204–205, 206, 207
Wild Goose Railroad, 203–210. *See also* Golofin Bay Railway
  excursion train, *209*
  first train, *207*
  locomotive roster, 210
  steam locomotives, *206*
  terminus at Anvil Creek, *209*
Wilkinson, C. H., 5
Williams, Alfred, 183
Williams, J. D., 83
Williams, James, 70
Willow Creek, Alaska, 163, 180
Wilson, Lt. Colonel William P., 33
Wilson, Woodrow, 89, 90, 93
Wingate, C. E., 183
Work, Hubert, 102
World War I, 98–99
World War II, *33*, 33–35, 104, 235–236
Wrangell Mountains, Alaska, 179

Y

Yakutat, Alaska, 155
Yakutat & Southern Railroad, 155–158
Young, Charles W., 7
Yukon Consolidated Gold Corporation, 68, 71, 72
Yukon Miners Association, 8
Yukon Mining, Trading, and Transportation Company, 9
Yukon Railway Company, 9
Yukon Southern, 32

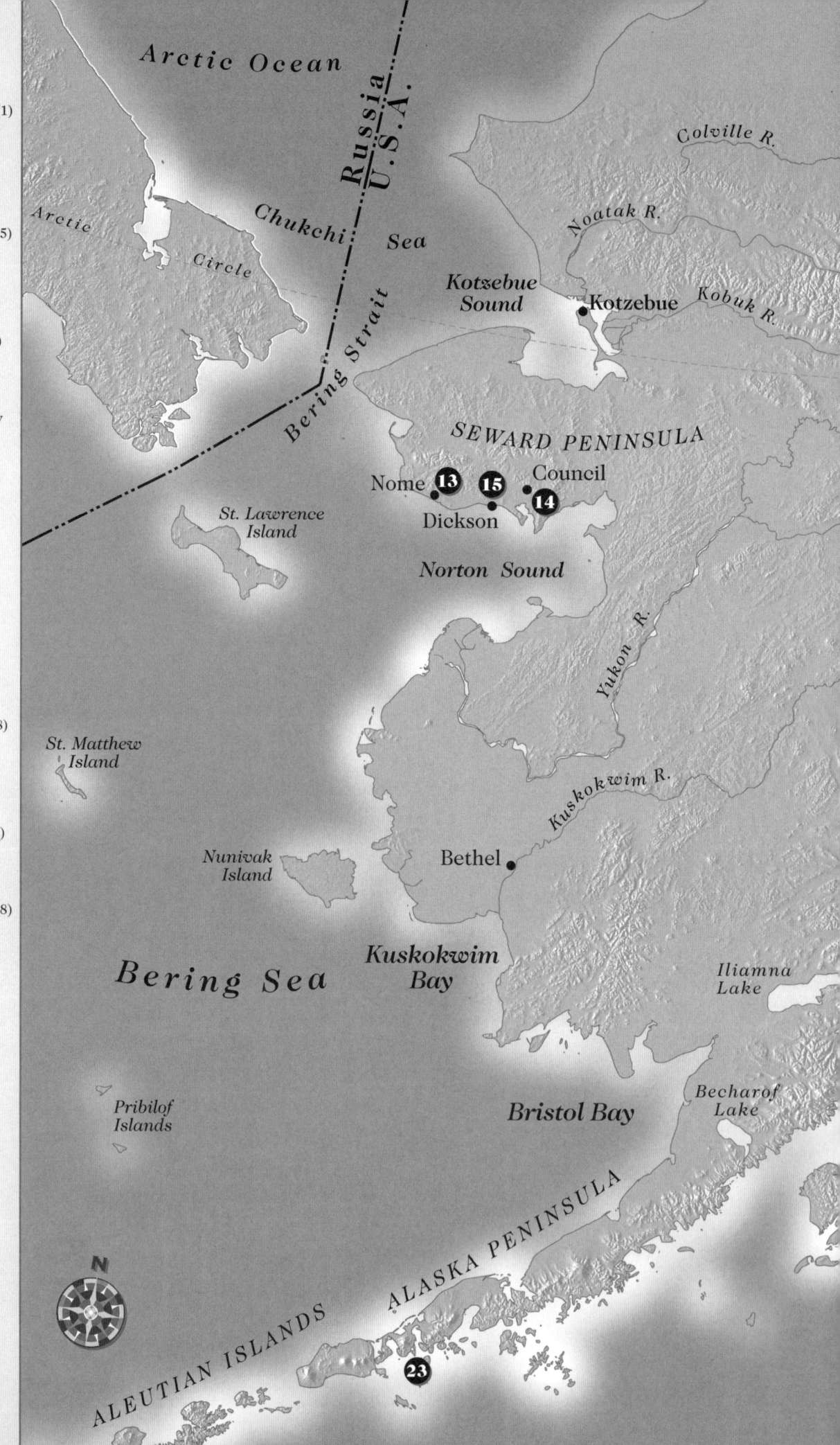

Alaska/Yukon Railroads

1. White Pass & Yukon Route (1)
2. Taku Tram (2)
   Atlin Consolidated Mining Company (18)
3. Whitehorse Tramways (3)
4. Klondike Mines Railway (4)
   Detroit Yukon Mining Company (5)
5. Coal Creek Coal Company (5)
   Northern Light, Power & Coal Company (5)
   North American Transportation and Trading Company (5)
6. Alaska Central Railway (6)
   Alaska Northern Railway (7)
7. The Alaska Commission (8)
   The Alaska Railroad (9)
8. Tanana Mines Railway (10)
   Tanana Valley Railroad (10)
   Crooked Creek and Whiskey Island Railroad (18)
9. Yakutat & Southern Railroad (11)
10. Valdez-Yukon Railroad Company (12)
    Alaska Home Railroad Company (12)
11. Copper River & Northwestern Railroad (13)
    Alaska Anthracite Coal & Railway Company (13)
12. Copper River & Northwestern Railway (14)
13. Wild Goose Railroad (15)
    Seward Peninsula (17)
14. Golofin Bay Railway (15)
15. Council City & Solomon River Railroad (16)
16. Berners Bay Gold Manufacturing Company (18)
17. Alaska-Juneau Gold Mine Railroad (18)
    Alaska-Gastineau Mining Company Railroad (18)
    Salmon Creek Dam Railroad (18)
    Treadwell Mine Railroad (18)
18. Rush and Brown Copper Mine Railroad (18)
19. Alaska Marble Company Tramway (18)
20. Ketchikan Pulp Company (18)
    Ketchikan and Northern Terminal Company (18)
21. Alaska Lumber and Pulp Company (18)
22. Cook Inlet Coal Field Company Railroad (18)
23. Apollo Consolidated Mining Company (18)

(Parenthetical numbers indicate the book chapter.)